City of Segregation

One Hundred Years of Struggle For Housing in Los Angeles

Andrea Gibbons

VERSO

London • New York

First published by Verso 2018
© Andrea Gibbons 2018

1 3 5 7 9 10 8 6 4 2

Verso
UK: 6 Meard Street, London W1F 0EG
US: 20 Jay Street, Suite 1010, Brooklyn, NY 11201
versobooks.com

Verso is the imprint of New Left Books

ISBN-13: 978-1-78663-270-8
ISBN-13: 978-1-78663-499-3 (HBK)
ISBN-13: 978-1-78663-271-5 (UK EBK)
ISBN-13: 978-1-78663-272-2 (US EBK)

British Library Cataloguing in Publication Data
A catalogue record for this book is available from the British Library

Library of Congress Cataloging-in-Publication Data

Names: Gibbons, Andrea, author.
Title: City of segregation : 100 years of struggle for housing in Los Angeles
  / Andrea Gibbons.
Description: Brooklyn : Verso, 2018.
Identifiers: LCCN 2018017690| ISBN 9781786632708 (paperback) | ISBN
  9781786634993 (hardback)
Subjects: LCSH: Discrimination in housing—California—Los Angeles. | African
  Americans—Housing—California—Los Angeles. | Housing
  policy—California—Los Angeles. | Los Angeles (Calif.)—Social
  conditions. | Los Angeles (Calif.)—Race relations. | BISAC: SOCIAL
  SCIENCE / Discrimination & Race Relations. | SOCIAL SCIENCE / Sociology /
  Urban. | SOCIAL SCIENCE / Ethnic Studies / African American Studies.
Classification: LCC HD7288.76.U52 L6734 2018 | DDC 363.509794/94—dc23
LC record available at https://lccn.loc.gov/2018017690

Typeset in Minion Pro by Hewer Text UK Ltd, Edinburgh
Printed by Maple Press, US

To my dad, Patrick Gibbons, and to my friend, Mark Anderson.
I wish both of you were here to share this with me.

A high degree of racial residential segregation is universal in American cities. Whether a city is a metropolitan center or a suburb; whether it is in the North or South; whether the Negro population is large or small—in every case, white and Negro households are highly segregated from each other . . . In fact, Negroes are by far the most residentially segregated urban minority group in recent American history.

—Karl Taeuber and Alma Taeuber, *Negroes In Cities: Residential Segregation and Neighborhood Change*, 1965

Contents

Acknowledgments

Writing this book finally fully brought home to me the truth that our struggle is not for a day or even a lifetime, but was a gift to us from the generations who came before and will be carried on through the generations after. It is beautiful and humbling and an immense responsibility to be part of something so big— above all this book owes everything to those who have dedicated themselves in some way to changing the world, and to the people and organizations whose fierce struggle fills its pages. From Charlotta and Joe Bass to the activists of CORE to the people I have come to know at the LA Community Action Network, who have changed my life and ways of thinking, I have no hesitation in how I answer the question of how to change the world. My question is instead what needs doing to support such work. Becky Dennison in particular helped me organize things, and I owe a huge debt of gratitude to Gary Blasi from UCLA for many of the documents cited here—I can only aspire to the breadth and length of their commitment to justice. So many in LA have helped and supported me both in struggle and in this project, and so to name only a few that I have argued and learned and laughed with: Gilda Haas and Gary Phillips, Beverley Keefe and Jose Zamarippa, Monic Uriarte and her family, Leonardo Vilchis, Steve Diaz, Davin Corona, Tafarai Bayne, Gloria Serrano and Reyna Monterrosa, Lidia Castelo, Gerry Villa, Thelmy Perez, Monic Uriarte and her wonderful family, Maria-Elena Rivas, Norberta Gonzalez, Aracely Rodriguez, Maria Ramos, Agustina Ramirez, Jackie Cornejo, Evelin Montes, "Bobby" Bustillo, Cecilia Brennan, Revel Sims and Carolina Sarmiento, Sister Diane, Nancy Ibrahim, the gorgeous Osorio Lambs, and many others.

I'm afraid I love lists, and a very large number of people. That my words did not run away with me altogether is due to my wonderful editor Rosie Warren, and to all of the people at Verso. Publishers are a key thread within the radical movement to change the world and I am more grateful than I can say that Verso has taken this on. For the most thoughtful and helpful of all reader's reports, Jordan Camp.

This book started out as a PhD at the London School of Economics, and I owe a huge debt of thanks to my supervisors Sharad Chari and Gareth Jones whose support and constant questions and stacks of required reading improved my work tremendously. So many others helped me get through the hard years in

London: Helen Shaw and Sean Geoghegan, Ruth Cashman, Ali Crabtree, Rosanne Rabinowitz, China Miéville, and Celine Kuklowsky. Who got me through LSE and academia? Murray Low, Jenny Mbaye, Antonis Vradis, Jayaraj Sundaresen, Taneesha Mohan, Tucker Jordan, Meredith Whitten, Ulises Moreno, Bob Caterall, Michael Edwards, Barbara Lipietz, Jane Wills, and Anna Richter.

I owe tremendous thanks as well to the many others from the city and the BIDs who shared their knowledge and allowed me to interview them, as well as to the various archivists and librarians who helped me so much with the historical research: Michelle Welsing from the Southern California Library, Brooke Black from the Huntington Library, Lee Grady of the Wisconsin Historical Society, Michael George of the Torrance Public Library, and Gabriel Botsford for his help accessing the archives at the California State University Northridge.

And to come back to center, I owe so much to all of my family (including Julie St John, whom we have drafted as one of us) and to my partner Mark Bould. None of this would have been possible without you.

Introduction

For all its hype and sprawling uniqueness, Los Angeles shares one thing in common with all other large US cities—its segregation. LA's segregation only grew deeper after the victories of a vibrant civil rights movement, and it has survived with great vigor despite decades of struggle against housing discrimination. It is no exaggeration to say that segregation continues to be a matter of life and death for both individuals and communities. It is assuredly nothing natural; it has been built in LA just as it has been built in cities across the US, year by year and decade upon decade, with immeasurable impact on equality, well-being and life itself. Shocking inequalities in wealth—much of it grounded in the homes people own—continue to haunt Angelenos: Mexicans have a median wealth of $3,500, African Americans of $4,000, and whites of $355,000.[1]

While Milton Friedman's arguments that segregation comes down to individual choice continue to hold sway among some, the research at the foundation of this book is part of a long tradition of rigorous urban studies documenting the combination of regulation, discrimination, structural inequality, and violence that expose such claims as false. Douglas S. Massey, coauthor of one of the most influential studies of segregation in US cities of the 1990s, wrote in 2016 that though segregation might have changed, it remains "the linchpin of racial stratification."[2] Writing specifically on LA, Philip Ethington and fellow researchers at the University of Southern California graphically described a city in which whites had moved to the suburban periphery, African Americans remained most isolated in the interior areas, and Asians and Hispanics were increasingly isolated from whites as well as from each other; the researchers concluded that whites alone have "the freedom to settle wherever their wealth enables them to purchase a home" and use that freedom to isolate themselves from others in exclusive suburbs around LA's peripheries. This isolation has been maintained through continuing and pervasive discrimination.[3] An earlier mapping of LA from 1940 through 1994 showed that home values matched this pattern, with communities of color consistently locked into a center where property values rose slowly, failed to rise, or even fell.[4] Thus—in addition to the brutal disinvestment endured as a legacy of absentee landlords and redlining—even homeowners in LA's central neighborhoods were constantly losing economic ground.[5]

LA is not alone in any of this. Academic studies have consistently shown segregation to be both ubiquitous and systemic. In 1965, Karl and Alma Taeuber found "a high degree of racial residential segregation to be universal in American cities."[6]

Later studies by Massey and Denton showed that segregation levels across the nation increased after the civil rights gains of the 1960s, despite those victories allowing growing numbers of African Americans to move out of hyper-segregated areas.[7] South and Crowder note that not only do wealthier African Americans tend to live in suburbs closer to the inner city, where the population is generally at least 50 percent Black and poverty is much higher than in typical white suburbs, but that they are far more likely to move back to the inner city than whites.[8] Most African Americans, however, never leave those central, resource-starved spaces. The consequence, as Patrick Sharkey writes, is that

> racial inequalities that exist in one generation typically linger on to the next . . . Since the 1970s, more than half of black families have lived in the poorest quarter of neighborhoods *in consecutive generations*, compared to just 7% of white families.[9]

This is due to the ways in which "various forms of inequality are organized or clustered in space, and neighborhoods are often the *site* of inequality."[10]

While Ethington's team found that African Americans in LA have remained as highly segregated as almost anywhere else, LA has always been distinguished by high levels of Latino and Asian immigration, and thus never developed the kind of Black–white binary typical of Central and East Coast cities such as Detroit or Baltimore.[11] Now, as all US cities grow increasingly diverse, LA is an increasingly meaningful place to study in order to explore how ideology, economics, politics, and space have come together to create this kind of segregation, to think about how these dynamics continue in new forms into the present, and above all to think about how we might do better.

LA is a relatively new city, one whose developers and residents were allowed to invent as they wished once the automobile freed them from the need for the high-density settlement required by older forms of transportation. As a city it demands struggle with its vastness, its grids, its divisions, and the glamour of Hollywood stars set alongside the ghetto reputation of South Central that Hollywood has been so instrumental in creating. This absurdity of form, this checkerboard of desperate poverty and immense wealth forming an unsustainable sprawl of multiplying cities and jurisdictions as seen in Map 1, seems to emerge from logic completely alien to that of urban planning. This book helps demonstrate that they are in fact intrinsic to it. Map 1 shows not only the vastness of LA and its larger metropolitan area, but also the fragmentation of municipal authorities and the overlapping of city and county authorities, where whole areas remain entirely under county authority, as they were never incorporated (seen in lighter grey).

This fragmentation of municipal responsibility maps onto the political and economic fragmentation of LA, causing immense challenges for achieving any kind of regional cooperation or equity. The drivers for such sprawling fragmentation, the ways in which it has consistently worked to support the wealth of all-white neighborhoods, and the widespread support for it from residents and planners alike, demand a hard look at how race and capital have intertwined.

And, of course, it is not only its segregation that makes LA a meaningful city to examine. In celebration of what he called the all-new "edge cities," journalist Joel Garreau wrote: "Americans are creating the biggest change in a hundred years in how we build cities. Every single American city that is growing, is growing in the fashion of Los Angeles, with multiple urban cores."[12] This is just one of a number of superlative claims made for LA as emblematic of the "new" and "postmodern" city.[13] The enormous popular success of Mike Davis' *City of Quartz* has been built upon to posit LA as a city of the future—one of diversifying sprawl and decentralization, a phenomenon itself inspiring a wealth of literature.[14] Some have argued the existence of an entire "LA School," theorizing a postmodern understanding of the city as "heteropolis," or fractal city. Theorists like Edward Soja, Michael Dear, and Steven Flusty have also acknowledged LA's intense polarizations along lines of class and race,[15] but work on its spatiality is often far removed from its long history of discrimination and struggle.

There is much about LA that is unique and noteworthy, not least this well-documented place as a (frighteningly unsustainable) model for future growth, particularly for other Western cities—but that is not the focus of this book. Rather, of interest in what follows is what connects LA to almost all US cities *despite* any differences and potentialities—the broad patterns of capital flows and (de)industrialization, and a shared history of white discrimination and violence to preserve white privilege through keeping nonwhites, and above all African Americans, "in their place."[16] In this, *City of Segregation* stands within a well-established tradition, following a number of studies on other cities, including Cayton and Drake's *Black Metropolis* (1946) and Hirsch's *Making the Second Ghetto* (1983) on Chicago; Clark's *Dark Ghetto* (1965) about Harlem; Gordon's *Mapping Decline* (2008) on St. Louis; Self's *American Babylon* (2003) on Oakland; Sugrue's *The Origins of the Urban Crisis* (1996) on Detroit; Du Bois's *The Philadelphia Negro* (1899); and Meyer's book that sums up the general findings very neatly: *As Long As They Don't Move Next Door* (2000).

It is curious, given this wealth of material on segregation emerging from critical studies of race, sociology, and history, that for the most part these racialized geographies of poverty, power, and privilege remain absent from studies of capital and the development of the city. So much foundational theory critical to urban studies has emerged from the work of David Harvey, Neil Smith, and Mike Davis—this book would have been unthinkable without the strides they made in understanding the connections between capital, ideology, and space.

While they begin to grapple with how class and race might intersect, though, they never fully engage with the ways in which the drive to preserve white supremacy has impacted the urban form. This oversight is a consequence of taking capital alone as their starting point. Though they acknowledge segregation and racism as important factors in the city's development, both remain secondary to capital's demands and flows. From such a starting point it is very hard to see why someone's race should have anything to do with the value of their money. *City of Segregation*, however, follows in the footsteps of Cedric Robinson to argue that capital has always been structured by race.[17] This is particularly visible in the ways in which the unique nature of land as a commodity makes homes both investments tied to the market, but also something that shapes the everyday lives and the futures of those living within them. Ruth Gilmore describes racism as "a practice of abstraction, a death-dealing displacement of difference within hierarchies."[18] Alongside many other critical race scholars, she demonstrates a world in which race is socially constructed, yet at the same time works to define the neighborhoods that we grow up in, the opportunities opened to us, and our chances at a full and long life. These destructive hierarchies articulate with and illuminate the geographies of privilege and destruction so visible in US cities.[19]

In thinking about racism and distinguishing discrimination against peoples of color in the US from that against European immigrants (Slavs, Italians, Irish, etc.), I am indebted to Albert Memmi's work. He writes,

> racism is not simply of the order of reason; its real meaning does not reside in its apparent coherence. It is a discourse, at once both functional and naïve, that is called forth and maintained, in its essence and its goals, by something other than itself . . . Whatever its little detours may be, ultimately, the goal of racism is dominance. [20]

Given the particular history of American racial ideology, second- and third-generation European immigrants have been able to assimilate and become "white" in ways that others have not.[21] This has only worked to further entrench the importance of constructions of race in the United States, along with a commonsense understanding of upward mobility among many whites that serves to obscure this importance.

Inspired in part by the eloquent work of Barbara Fields, this book is a turn to LA's history, an attempt to understand the ways that the complex and often contradictory ideologies of race and the concrete formations of place have been articulated into hierarchies over time.[22]

LA's segregation, however central, has also always been complicated by the presence of racial hierarchies. This is particularly true in thinking about supporting liberatory movements to transform our cities, as the establishment of racial hierarchies under a white hegemony—and the possibility of building counter-hegemonic solidarity across racial boundaries—has long been present. White racism itself, while creating conflict over limited resources, has also created some of the impetus for multiracial organizing as peoples of color have traditionally shared neighborhoods where they have confronted similar white racism and their own racialization on what Leland Saito describes as "common ground."[23] Scott Kurashige, for example, looks at how African American and Japanese communities emerged from a shared early history of segregation and struggle, which ensures a strong spatial sensibility in his account of LA's history.[24] He masterfully describes the material and ideological triangulations between Black, Japanese, and white Americans as they sometimes came together and sometimes played one off against the others for material gains.

I build on these works and others, including Tomás Almaguer's *Racial Fault Lines*, a key text both for understanding LA and for theorizing beyond the racial binary of Black and white, in which Almaguer argues that California's early diversity—where populations of Chinese, Japanese, Filipino, and Mexican migrants lived alongside Native, Mexican/Spanish, and African Americans— demands understandings of race dynamics through a conception of racial hierarchies. The flexibility of these hierarchies and the promise held out to each ethnic group that they might be able to supersede others in privilege and power allowed whites to take over land and control immigrant labor populations while maintaining their position at the top of the pyramid.[25]

Solidarity across race, ethnicity, and immigration status have all been consistently undermined by the varying degrees to which different communities of color have been able to rise within a hierarchy at others' expense, defining group access to jobs, land, legal rights, housing, and other basic structures of opportunity within a system preserving European-American domination. The focus of this book is on African Americans' experiences, as the group most consistently (but not always) relegated to the very bottom of this hierarchy through domination and force, and their struggle to escape the boundaries placed around them. Clearly, African American struggle has always taken place and been shaped within these hierarchies. Their complexity is explored where they have arisen in the discourses of the African American community, or where they have been illuminated within the struggles I examine. This also holds true of understanding the role that gender discrimination has played in housing markets and struggle— clearly, the close connection between women and the home along with white masculine fears around the sanctity of white womanhood have been part of the dynamics underlying segregation's strength and power. While the book's primary focus is on race within the movements it studies, the intersection of race with gender (as well as class) is a constant thread throughout the book.

But it is the segregation of African Americans that remains the deepest, the most visible, and the most entrenched over time.[26] As Camille Zubrinsky Charles writes of the results of her intensive study of attitudes on housing in Los Angeles:

active, present-day racial prejudice and concerns among racial minorities about white hostility play important roles in driving neighborhood racial preferences . . . [with] whites, the group at the top of the status hierarchy and, arguably, the group with the most to lose. Maintaining their status advantages and privilege requires a certain amount of social distance from nonwhites—particularly blacks and *Latinos*, the groups at the bottom of the racial queue—since more than token integration would signal an unwelcome change in status relations. Indeed, this racial hierarchy—in which whites occupy the top position and blacks the bottom—is so pervasive that immigrant adaptation includes the internalization and even exaggeration of it among *Latinos* and Asians, as seen in the pattern of preferences for both groups.[27]

Charles's findings highlight another possible reason that segregation has not been understood by many as a central issue in urban formation: "While whites thought of themselves as easy to get along with, no other group agreed with that self-assessment . . . whites still seemed to hold negative racial attitudes."[28]

Land is in fact a place where economics and ideologies come together, and where an intensely racist past lives on forcefully into our present. This book attempts to develop a rigorous explanation of the city and its form, deepening our understanding of how the relationship between understandings of race and the value of land have been established over time. While real estate markets have generally been treated as simply economic phenomena, I argue that we must shift this view. Land is a commodity like any other, bought and sold on the market, with its price subject to market fluctuations. It is an important source of investment and profit. Yet at the same time, it is lived on, used.[29] The land we live on and the properties we inhabit structure our experience, shape our lives (and deaths), open up opportunities or close them down. Our home's value as a *home* is as important, in this sense, as its value when we come to sell it on the open market. Restated in economic terms, the use value of land as central to the social reproduction of power and opportunity is always linked to its exchange value as an investment. For homeowners who hope for the best future possible for their children, this use value is as important, often more important, than its exchange value—though clearly the ways in which people understand use values in terms of the "best" neighborhood for raising their children is inseperable from exchange value.

From the very beginning of California's occupation by Anglo settlers, whites worked to control access to the best land, and land's legitimate ownership and development were established on white occupation. Following this early period of conquest, the history of real estate demonstrates that racialized real estate evaluation—where one person's money is not actually as good as another's—has long been the rule in the US, rather than the exception.

This is visible in the obvious sense: lands that were more fertile and farthest from noxious uses were reserved for the conquerors—and the conquest of this land from Mexico and Native Americans, alongside the justification of holding men as property, was intertwined with openly racist ideologies in its support.[30] Over time these simple logics of white supremacy became intrinsic to the very logics of property development itself. Homogeneity and the protection of resources was the prize. A horror of miscegenation entered into the language of the planning and real estate professions even as segregation reinforced a fear of the consequence of sharing space with others, both in terms of the purity of the white race and its ongoing power to dominate others.

This connection between race and land value makes sense of pollution patterns, underpins sprawl and segregation, and helps explain ever greater fears, the privatization of space and city functions, the gating of communities and steady increases in security and demands for police. Seen from this historical trajectory, neoliberal ideology becomes only one of the drivers of these pivotal movements of modern times, a flexible, free-market(ish) theory that helped facilitate an older and uglier drive for white supremacy, which it has helped to reshape.[31] Above all, the articulation of race and land value helps explain the vast inequities of race and class not just in quality of life, but also in opportunity and the possibility of life itself. This is the nature of the urban canker that racism has caused, that damages everyone.

It is small wonder that the past few years have seen US cities once more rocked by unrest and uprising. For many, the question has not been why this was suddenly happening, but why it had not happened sooner or more often. From the point of view of the residents of inner-city neighborhoods, the deep inequalities that accompany highly visible segregation mark a status quo that is obviously unjust and cause for both hurt and fury.[32]

How can segregation still exist in this terrifying and malignant form even after so many civil rights struggles and victories? When resources finally return to neighborhoods, which are falling apart through absentee-owner neglect and the abandonment by municipal services and investment, why do they come as a wave of gentrification that seems to inexorably and unjustly force out the community that has long suffered under these inequalities? Why does discrimination seem to remain central to real estate markets, marked by the massive displacement of people of color wherever wealth and development return to central neighborhoods? And perhaps most importantly: how do we build consensus that we must do better?

These questions become less urgent the farther you move from inner city to suburb, given that segregation's damage to communities with wealth and amenities is much more subtle. Yet its damage is ever present. The fact remains that there are hard truths to face about US cities: among them, that racism has been central to the way that they have formed and grown, and remains central to all of the problems they now confront. People living in many (though increasingly not all) US suburbs have better access to good schools, jobs, grocery stores and quality food, banks, health care, gyms, and parks. They can access networks of friends, family, neighbors, and schools that lead to better, higher-paying jobs and open up other opportunities. They suffer less from pollution, live in owner-occupied neighborhoods—thus escaping the prevalence of absentee owners maximizing short-term profits by letting properties run down into slums, impacting negatively on the whole of the neighborhood even as they collect rents from insecure apartments damaging to their tenants' physical and mental health. Homes steadily appreciating in value in such neighborhoods, become valuable assets, and give access to loans and further investments that can be passed down to children.

Inner-city neighborhoods and a growing number of inner suburbs have long reflected the absence of all that white neighborhoods often take for granted. One key aspect of the poverty trap is a continuing differential in median income by race. These wage differences have been widely argued as a combination of racism and economic restructuring, spatial mismatch between suburban jobs and inner city residents, low education levels, the criminalization of African American youth, and poor job preparation.[33] They also, of course, reflect the continuing wage inequalities between men and women, and studies show women of color to be at a continued, deeper disadvantage than white women.[34] Allen J. Scott has studied the connections between industry and urban form extensively, describing the movement of unionized factories farther and farther into suburban areas (and thus away from communities of color) up through and after the Second World War, followed by the replacement of those jobs during the 1970s and '80s with service jobs and post-Fordist manufacturing. This process of economic restructuring, with its wave of factory closures, massive layoffs and unemployment, hit nonwhite communities first and it hit them hardest.[35]

In LA, high concentrations of dangerous environmental conditions and toxic chemicals concentrated in poor communities and communities of color have been documented by multiple studies, along with a lack of green spaces;[36] a lack in both quantity and quality of educational provision;[37] a lack of hospitals, clinics, and access to health care;[38] a lack of access to healthy food;[39] and a lack of banks and other services.[40]

South Central LA, birthplace of the Crips and the Bloods, has become famous in popular culture, fiercely and contestedly stereotyped to become "one of the entertainment industry's favorite and most frequently portrayed spatial characters" in movies such as *Boyz N the Hood* (1991), *Menace II Society* (1993) and *Straight Outta Compton* (2015), among others.[41] The reality is both more and less than the hype. Contributing to South Central's devastated landscape were the skyrocketing numbers of people forced onto the streets through the 1980s due to the combination of economic restructuring and massive cuts in welfare, and the mass shutdown of both outpatient health clinics and mental health clinics in the early 1980s.[42] This confluence explains why homelessness is also highest in South LA, as well as why such a high percentage of those who find themselves homeless are African American.[43] These seemingly intractable issues—above all, the absence of meaningful work and an influx of drugs, particularly the crack epidemic of the 1980s—resulted in South Central becoming best known for the crime and violence arising from this desperate poverty.[44]

Yet no government program has really tried, much less succeeded, in eradicating these well-documented and long-studied conditions. Instead, older programs of "urban renewal" entered popular common sense as "Negro removal," and later forms of development have only succeeded in further breaking up and devastating communities by displacing them into new situations exactly the same or worse than the old ones, without the benefit of their established support networks. It is a testament to the spirit of survival and the multiple sacrifices parents and communities have made that many have not just survived but excelled against great odds. Perhaps no one has better dramatized this struggle and those deadly odds than Ta-Nehisi Coates in *The Beautiful Struggle*, but there is also a vibrant tradition of community building and organizing to be found in LA, which offers some hope for the city as a whole.

The aim of my research is to better understand segregation, why it should continue despite these many decades of powerful struggle, and how our generation can be the one to end it. It is hard to imagine a single factor that does more to shape our lives and our potentials than the neighborhoods and cities in which we live. And we likewise shape them. In order to change them for the better, we have to understand the past, and how its legacy lives on in concrete and brick as well as in the contours of the lives and dreams held within these homes. Their physical form reflects both the ideals and failures of our society just as the injustices cemented into place inflict a kind of violence on their residents. But the historical relationship between injustice, violence, and geography remains absent in discussions and media coverage about the "inner city," particularly news emerging from the "ghetto" or any of the major uprisings. Not much has changed in the discourses of criminality and fear between the reporting on Watts and other urban uprisings across the United States in the 1960s, LA of 1992, and the recent coverage of Baltimore and Ferguson.[45]

The inner city and the suburb may appear to be divided by a gulf, but the neighborhoods are closely, intimately linked in terms of allocations of subsidies, resources, and amenities. The abandonment of central areas and the stripping of their resources by government and business not only caused the suffering of their residents. It is also intimately connected to the simultaneous boom of the suburbs and the rising wealth and assets of many white Americans of all classes. White residential flight and the movement of capital were deeply intertwined, as this book will go on to explore. As we shall see, both white residents and developers moved out of the city, doing their best to raise the drawbridge behind them.

This is a part of the heritage still almost invisible to the beneficiaries of centuries of discriminatory policy and budgeting decisions. These histories of racism and segregation have shaped urban geographies to insulate and isolate many whites from the realities faced by residents of poorer segregated communities, whose exploitation and abandonment have been central to a suburban prosperity driven by development and government investment. The opportunities of suburban living have become taken for granted and treated as normal in press and television, while residence in these same suburban neighborhoods insulates families from any kind of challenge to these commonsense feelings of entitlement. This is a key aspect of what I join others in referring to as white privilege. Segregation insulates whites from the knowledge of the ghetto and any disturbing views into poverty, as well as from their own complicity in its continued existence through their support of the status quo. Building on Laura Pulido's powerful insights in this field, this book examines many of the ways that white spaces maintain white privilege. She writes that "[b]ecause most white people do not see themselves as having malicious intentions, and because racism is associated with malicious intent, whites can exonerate themselves of all racist tendencies, all the while ignoring their investment in white privilege."[46] A segregated geography makes the likelihood of unsettling questions being raised by those in the suburbs vanishingly low.

The discourses rationalizing this status quo, both the discrimination and the violence that traditionally maintained white neighborhoods as white, have formed the building blocks for today's hate-filled and accusatory refusals to engage with some of the uglier aspects of our past. In the face of the stubbornness of such resistance, it is crucial to remember that for most of American history, white supremacy has been openly, vigorously, and violently defended. Civil rights struggles have ensured that while white supremacist attitudes continue to be openly voiced by some, the mainstream at least gives lip service to equality and the universal provision of certain civil rights. Despite this, most have refused to be "inconvenienced in order to achieve full equality."[47]

Understanding how these various threads come together to form our cities cannot be done without holding a number of factors in focus and examining how each articulates with the others and how they work as a whole. Four such threads run through this book: (1) an examination of ideologies—the beliefs held as common sense by different groups, particularly around how the concept of race and the ideals of home, community, and nation have been constructed; (2) an examination of economics—the role that understandings of property value, the desire for profit, and the needs of national and international capital have played in shaping property markets and real estate development; (3) an examination of politics—the laws, rules, and regulations that shape how we think, that limit what we can and cannot do, and that prescribe the use of force through police action, as well as the process for changing these societal parameters when they are unjust or unworkable; and (4) an examination of space—the ways in which all of these things shape the city, but also the way that existing buildings and neighborhoods, with all of their history and character, in turn shape our identities, our politics, our future, and our commonsense ideas.

Understanding how these interlinked and complex factors come together to form the city cannot be done in the abstract. To do so would obscure complexities as they are and as they have been lived, and in doing so inflict a kind of violence on those who suffer. Once we hold these complex details in our hands and respect them, we can shake them until the patterns emerge, engage theory and see the bigger picture that helps explain the universality of racial segregation in US cities.

A final key to the foundations on which this book is built—understanding how we can end death-dealing differences and create cities that promote life—can hardly be done without centering our inquiry within the long history of struggles for social and racial justice that have always reached toward the same goal. Grounding the text within the spaces of those experiencing and battling the deadly aspects of segregation honours their knowledge of every brick in segregation's walls, awareness gained by fists bloody with pounding against them. Yet my hope is that this book also demonstrates that the fate of all races are connected to each other just as the fate of the suburbs intertwines with that of the inner cities—ultimately the extreme spatial injustices we have created affect all Americans negatively. The ability of the privileged to close their eyes or barricade themselves away will not change that. Over 100 years ago, Du Bois wrote of "two worlds within and without the Veil," the barrier of segregation that protects whites from the struggle and suffering of Blacks.[48] The problem of the color line remains the problem of our new century—without ignoring the opportunities that new and exciting cultural hybridities bring, and what Vijay Prashad describes as "a ferocious engagement with the political world of culture, a painful embrace of the skin and all its contradictions," which is the hope offered in a new world of polyculturalism.[49]

So what does this historical trajectory of the struggle against segregation actually look like in LA? Map 2 illustrates the lasting significance of segregation in the present by mapping out the concentrations of the African American population from 1890 to 2010. Through my research I have developed an extensive (though by no means complete) database of addresses where racial incidents have occurred that were centered on property disputes; I have titled these "contested spaces." Each circle represents a family who faced down racist attempts to keep them out of white neighborhoods, ranging from lawsuits to threats, from burning crosses to bomb attacks. Each dark line represents what I call a "racial faultline," or recognized boundary between white and Black neighborhoods as these have changed over time. These are the streets that whites attempted to hold with violence.[50] This series of maps shows in simplified form the violence and discrimination that helps explain why African Americans have remained highly concentrated in LA, and next to or still living inside many of the same areas for which they have fought historically. While this kind of shared experience can undoubtedly serve as a source of community strength, a number of people struggling for integration have noted the tragedy that the fight to escape the ghetto drove people south and west, and thus simply expanded the ghetto's walls. The highest concentration of African Americans in the latest census, and emblematic of how incarceration has increasingly been used to control the African American population, lies just north of downtown in a major prison complex.

This historically defined concentration of African Americans is both rooted in, and a driver of, the ways in which LA has developed over time. These often-devastated landscapes and communities stand as constant reminders of a long and violent past. They require a critical view, a recasting of accepted histories to understand, and hopefully take power over, how they shape our present and our future.[51] This is vital work in a country attempting to deny the existence of racism, even as segregation lives on and the gaps between whites and peoples of color continue to grow.[52]

To make this case, and to really understand how LA geography has developed over time, structured by (and in turn helping to structure) ideologies of race and land value, I have centered it in the struggle against segregation—three particular moments, explored in the book's three main sections, when civil rights victories forced real shifts in racist policies and geographies, yet failed in their quest to end the constant drive toward privileged and homogenous white neighborhoods. My hope is that these stories will provide both inspiration and caution in our struggle today, and help us to identify what it really is we are fighting, what this means in our present moment, and where hope might lie for a better future.

The first section opens with the movement against de jure segregation maintained by race-restrictive covenants inserted into property deeds and both promoted and maintained by homeowners, homeowner associations, developers, local real estate associations and governments at the city, state, and national level. Emerging from the racial logics forged through a brutal westward expansion, the struggle to implement and maintain these restrictions became the foundations of both segregation and the spatialities of white racism and white privilege as they exist today. Won through conquest in 1848, the early vision of California as the high point of Anglo-Saxon civilization developed spatially as a white aversion to living or sharing space with peoples of color. The immediate result was the genocidal treatment of California's indigenous populations.[53] Near the turn of the nineteenth century, the desire for segregation was then converted into policy through the country's first attempt at racial zoning. When the courts struck that down, segregation became inscribed through property deeds in the form of racially restrictive covenants. Ensuring the widest possible coverage and enforcement of these covenants required the cooperation not just of property developers, realtors, and lawyers, but also of homeowners themselves, organized into associations. This in itself helped create a tightly knit professional infrastructure as well as a strong understanding of community, of "us" versus "them," based around the protection of residential spaces exclusively for whites using both legal instruments and violence. This was further consolidated and legitimated through the 1930s, as the federal government essentially founded and subsidized the mortgage market in response to the Great Depression. It incorporated wholesale the ideals of homogenous white suburban space as the highest and best value for land, as the private real estate industry dictated federal appraisal guidelines and the heavy subsidizing of a white mortgage market and racially covenanted single-family homes. Thus, white supremacist ideologies, legal contracts, federal regulations and policies, grassroots white violence, and the legal and professional understanding of real estate values articulated to make hegemonic the creation and preservation of white space and privilege through segregation.

In defiance of all of these forces, immense population pressures led to ongoing uncoordinated individual attempts to escape the overcrowding and poor conditions of the ghetto. These efforts slowly expanded the ghetto's borders, street by street to the west and south in the face of both lawsuits and violence, but without achieving integration. White communities came to define themselves through the struggle to defend both physical spatial boundaries—making certain streets such as Alameda and Slauson infamous among African Americans as the racial faultlines that could not be crossed—and ideological boundaries. Open violence, institutional discrimination, and white supremacist rhetoric clearly delineated peoples of color as outside of white definitions of citizenship. Gramsci describes hegemony as constructed through both coercion and consent. The history of Black struggle demonstrates that racism constructed consent along a racialized rather than class-based sense of community among whites, while for communities of color the balance was tipped to a much greater extent toward coercion, which helped create a different sense of community forged in hardship and oppression.

The book begins with this early history of land and constructions of community based on white supremacy as illustrated through stories of resistance against it. This resistance, along with its strategies and discourses as they developed over time, are examined through the archives of a remarkable source—the *California Eagle*, owned and edited by Black newswoman Charlotta Bass between 1912 and 1951. She faced and overcame all of the challenges offered due to both her race and gender, and she played a central role in the evolving campaigns to end racial covenants as they developed in both analysis and strategy over the course of forty years. The first three chapters trace the increasing strength, size, momentum, and radicalization of these campaigns up until their victory with the Supreme Court overturning the legality of enforcing racial covenants in *Shelley v. Kraemer* in 1948 and the legality of suing owners for damages over the breaking of such covenants in *Barrows v. Jackson* in 1951.[54]

The 1960s followed hard on this period, which had already begun to challenge white supremacist ideologies and the legal and political supports for segregation. Bringing serious, almost revolutionary, challenge to white control over power and space, African Americans and other peoples of color built on these earlier struggles to demand full equality and integration. The second section explores the campaigns by the Congress of Racial Equality (CORE) to integrate the outer suburbs, while also working to help pass California's first fair housing legislation. While CORE is most famous as one of the big three civil rights organizations alongside the National Association for the Advancement of Colored People (NAACP) and the Southern Christian Leadership Conference (SCLC), a position gained by its sponsorship of the freedom rides and freedom summers in the Deep South, it had chapters across the US. Almost unknown and previously unstudied, the LA chapter's campaign against housing segregation managed to mobilize marches of thousands of people and major Hollywood figures such as Marlon Brando in its attempts to force a suburban developer to integrate his developments. The organization's archives, containing many of the papers and letters of key CORE activists in LA as well as ongoing coverage in the *California Eagle* and other African American newspapers, allowed for deeper insight into both their understanding of the mechanics of building movements, as well as their wider strategy for social transformation through nonviolent direct action. Like many other campaigns in this turbulent decade, CORE's efforts initially went from success to success and swelled in numbers beyond their wildest hopes, yet ultimately they were defeated by the coordinated efforts of the city government of Torrance, its residents, and its largest developer. In a highly personal campaign that expanded to include the project's investors, CORE's activities would result in a strategy meeting that brought together all of Southern California's major developers.

Developers deployed the lessons learned in CORE's defeat as they channeled capital into the widespread building of amenity-rich privatized communities with well-protected tax bases, insulating their residents from even the sight of the growing poverty and desperation within the communities of color they had cut themselves off from. Segregation thus increased after the 1960s, even while philosophically—if grudgingly—whites came to recognize people of color as their equals. They still continued to maintain white supremacist definitions of true community as white only, ideology now grounded in physical neighborhoods fiercely defended and privileged tract developments. Ideologically, there was a shift from open racism to rhetorics of freedom, property rights, and individual responsibility that cast the blame for poverty back upon ghetto residents.

The final section outlines how this continued connection between race and land value, a suburban and racialized understanding of privileged space, and a new discourse of rights and responsibilities have shaped new development in downtown Los Angeles. With the limits of suburban development reached, widespread suburban opposition to infill development, and a decaying infrastructure ready for exploitation in the city center, an explosion of downtown development has occurred, beginning in the mid-1990s. When this has failed to displace the poor and the homeless, faced with their resistance and success in preserving residential hotels, business interests represented by the Central City Association (CCA) and Central City East Association (CCEA) have carried out increasingly extreme campaigns to cleanse them from the city center. To do so, they have mobilized a number of different strategies and discourses. Initially the Business Improvement Districts (BIDs) provided the ability to privatize and secure downtown's public spaces, moving unwanted occupants. When resistance made this ineffective in achieving displacement, they worked with city and county governments to increase punitive municipal control over these same spaces and further criminalize their residents, while also carrying out public health and hygiene interventions. The restless search for anything that would work to create the highest property values possible, erased of its poverty and color, has to date been successfully resisted by the Los Angeles Community Action Network (LA CAN) and their allies, who continue to put forward a discourse of human rights both to the physical and social community of downtown.

These not only represent the most comparable collective movements against segregation in LA in terms of strength and achievement, they also provide a map of the changing political and ideological struggles that have articulated with the two major movements of real estate capital in our time—its suburbanization and its return to the central city.

PART I

The Long Road to 1948

Ending De Jure Segregation

Chapter 1

As Worthy As You

The Struggles of Black Homeowners Through the 1920s

The early history of "California" as a US territory consisted of decades of openly expressed white supremacy; this is the foundation of the state's expanding geography after the area's annexation through war with Mexico. Although the most violent US racism is almost always associated with the Deep South, California was founded on a policy of Native-American genocide to be a white, Anglo-Saxon state. At the time of US conquest, the indigenous population was around 72,000. By 1880 it had fallen to 15,000.[1] Initially known as *Californios,* to separate them from the darker-skinned "Mexicans" laboring for them, the great Spanish landowners were initially respected as white. But this did not save the majority of them from losing most of their land. Despite the guarantees of the Treaty of Guadalupe Hidalgo, which incorporated California and much of the Southwest into the United States in 1848, Carey McWilliams estimates that the *Californios* were forced to sell at least 40 percent of their land just to pay the costs required to be in compliance with the Land Act of 1851.[2]

Over the next few decades, holdings of thousands of acres were forfeited for lack of cash to pay taxes. The steady despoiling of Mexican/*Californio*-owned land proceeded alongside a white supremacist and pro-Confederate stance during the Civil War, and bills were pushed in the state legislature to ban African Americans from the state entirely. A small Chinese population had been imported as menial labor and allowed to work on sufferance. Barred from citizenship, and with their immigration halted by the national government at the height of rhetoric around the "yellow peril," they were targeted by white Angelenos, who lynched nineteen people in a single night in 1871 in one of the nation's worst race riot known at the time.[3] California would prove to be a dangerous place for anyone who wasn't white.

The institutionalization of racial criteria in the appraisal of properties for federal government subsidies and mortgage finance through the 1930s has already been well documented.[4] This process enshrined race as perhaps *the* primary factor in official evaluations of land's exchange value, but the ways in which this national institutionalization took place in Los Angeles demonstrates the development of key political and economic aspects of the equation between land value and whiteness.

This is only part of the story, however. African Americans fought to break down institutional and legal barriers as they fought to live in their chosen homes. This book begins by charting some of the contours of this struggle, drawing on the point of view of Charlotta Bass, editor of the *California Eagle*. She was a driving force in the early movement to end segregation, and much of the material in these pages comes from her autobiography and editorials. Her newspaper served as a vehicle to instigate as well as document many of the campaigns aimed at breaking the power of white supremacy; the ongoing work to topple racial covenants was not the only resistance necessary. Still, for Charlotta Bass and the *Eagle's* staff, it remained a central site of movement and struggle.

Until 1948, the preservation of white space rested primarily on de jure segregation enforced through racial covenants written into property deeds, white hegemony enshrined in both custom and law with little need of consent from those whom the forces of the state constrained. African Americans and other groups forced the ghetto walls back in two ways: through an unorganized but constant pressure by individuals buying and occupying property against great odds, and through local attempts to organize wider campaigns against covenants. While individuals worked to challenge white boundaries from the beginning, the first organized attempts to do so occurred in the late 1920s. It paralleled the homeowner associations of discriminatory whites, but fell apart in the face of continued hostility and defeat in the courts. It was then left to largely individual efforts again until the context of World War II's fight against fascism; the backdrop of growing militancy renewed local organizing, which combined with a national legal campaign to successfully outlaw racial covenants and force major policy changes onto the federal government around the use of race in appraisals.

Those campaigning believed that this victory would end segregation in LA. If segregation had been maintained simply through institutional and legal methods, this might have been the case. Of course, it was not.

This chapter begins in the early twentieth century and illuminates the ways in which the value of property became firmly linked to the race of its occupants. It moves into the 1940s and '50s, when the legal and—to some extent—moral victory against racial covenants forced a rearticulation of strategies and rationalizations for the maintenance of a hegemonic white and privileged spatiality during the decline of Jim Crow. While violence in defense of white neighborhoods was nothing new, its increase following efforts by Blacks to move into previously covenanted areas underlined that they had failed to win any kind of support among whites for integration. Even as bombs exploded and homes burned, segregationists' rhetoric turned toward increasingly "race-neutral" arguments that emphasized segregation as simply a natural outcome of economics and market forces. This language obscures the reality of the choices made about where and how the "Black Belt" would expand, realized by a combination of individual judges deciding cases, organized realtor groups and individuals dealing in real estate, banks and other lenders, the Federal Housing Administration, organized homeowner groups, and individual homeowners.[5]

While the movement in part spearheaded by Charlotta Bass initially had little impact on national housing and mortgage policies, the voice of the *California Eagle* did have national reach. Loren Miller, who began writing for the paper in 1930 and would come to own it in 1951, was NAACP chief counsel in the Supreme Court case that overturned racial covenants across the country.[6] At a local level, collective struggle was fundamental in shaping both white and Black strategies in acquiring and defending homes, and their attitudes toward the meanings of home, citizenship, and community. The results of this contest inscribed a pattern of segregation into the urban fabric that persists today. White responses went on to feed capital's development of the suburbs and an increasing privatization of space, and mapping these responses geographically delineates the white privileges at risk—privileges once taken for granted. These are the rights and privileges African Americans fought to enjoy, sometimes alongside and sometimes at the cost of other peoples of color in the city.

Charlotta Bass, born Charlotta Spears in Sumter, South Carolina, arrived in LA in 1910 at the age of twenty-nine or thirty. She had traveled there from Rhode Island on advice from her doctor, although as a cure for what illness remains unknown.[7] In fact, very little is known about her life before she arrived—her autobiography *Forty Years: Memoirs from the Pages of a Newspaper* is almost exactly what it calls itself: the autobiography of the *Eagle* and its central role in Black struggle in LA. Her private life remains very much her own in its pages, but elsewhere she writes (speaking of herself in the third person) with a lingering sense of surprise about the chance that helped put her at the center of Black struggle:

> the paper miraculously passed into the hands of a militant young woman, a new arrival to Los Angeles, Charlotta Spears, who together with her husband, Joseph Bass, waged a ceaseless battle for all the principles laid down by the Eagle for a period of forty years. Twenty of those years, following the death of Joseph Bass in 1934, this lone woman, Charlotta Bass, carried the responsibility of waging the militant fight for freedom and equality through the publication of the Eagle, until ill health forced her to retire.[8]

Big Joe Bass, as he was known, had come to work with Charlotta Spears as an editor in 1913. They were soon married and worked closely together in what seems to have been a remarkable partnership throughout which she remained sole owner and lead editor of the paper as a whole. She would continue to document and campaign throughout her life against both the legal challenges and physical violence faced by African Americans, and increasingly over the years the violence against other communities of color crossing the geographic boundaries set by whites. Upon her retirement she became the first Black woman to run for national office in 1952, on the Progressive Party ticket, as candidate for vice president.[9]

As a woman, Charlotta Bass continues in many ways to elude us. Her public voice was heard strong and true through her many articles and regular editorials, but she maintained a strict distance between her public persona and both her past and private life.[10] These chapters have to glean what they can from her public face, her general prioritization and focus on race over other struggles such as gender, and the various coalitions and organizations she formed while working and strategizing within the changing political conjunctures of a pivotal forty years in US history. Within these parameters, however, much can be uncovered about how her understanding grew alongside a more collective understanding of what the Black community in LA faced, and the key strategies they employed in transforming their city to a place where all could flourish. A rich tradition of community discussion and debate already existed upon Charlotta Bass's arrival in LA, in institutions such as the LA Forum—established in 1903 as an organization to promote discussion and debate on key issues of the times—along with a rich tradition of women's clubs that filled the *Eagle's* back pages throughout Bass's tenure.[11] She would build on this and embody what Melina Abdullah and Regina Freer describe as a tradition of "womanist" leadership that grew up organically in LA, marked by "group-centered leadership, and the use of traditional and non-traditional methods."[12] Such a practical tradition is demonstrated clearly in these pages—a drive to achieve concrete changes through collective action, and within that a willingness to draw from multiple sources and employ multiple strategies to do what was needed.

It is no surprise, then, that Charlotta Bass begins her book reframing the history of LA and highlighting the importance of Black women in that history. She opens with the original founding of LA in 1781 by "forty-four individuals . . . there were only two Caucasians among the founders, but there were *sixteen Indians and twenty-six Negroes*."[13] She details their history, describes the ways in which textbooks, history books, and journalists reproduced this story with representations of the founders as white, and their refusal to bow to the romanticized myths of the European *Californios*. She writes that, particularly in education, still "to date white supremacy rules supreme on this subject."[14] Six streets in downtown LA were named after these founders: Lara, Navarro, Mesa, Camero, Quintero, and Moreno. Not one of these streets fully remains; there is only a fraction of Lara Street in East LA as a last asphalt whisper of how much has been erased. The newspaper's earliest articles, and Bass's description of them, drive the feeling that LA's Black history always needed to be written and actively recovered, as an ongoing act of resistance from passive silences as well as active silencing.[15]

Charlotta Bass's description of the city's incorporation in 1850, and its tremendous jump in population with the arrival of the railroad, focuses on the key roles played by Black settlers in the early city, as documented by her predecessor, John J. Neimore. Principal among these was another Black woman, Biddy Mason, born into slavery in 1818 in Georgia. She escaped first to Missouri and then to California. She invested wisely in real estate and owned a number of properties in downtown Los Angeles: Bass lists them, a tally of the property owned by a Black woman along Third and Spring, Second and Broadway, and Eighth and Hill. Mason used her wealth to establish the first day nursery for orphans.[16] She died in 1881; five generations of her descendents had already grown up in the Black community by Bass's time.

Mason was sixty-one when Neimore founded *The Owl* in 1879—the paper that would become *The Advocate,* and then *The Eagle.* It would be renamed the *California Eagle* in 1913 by Charlotta Bass, a year after she took it over at Neimore's request.[17] Bass describes her predecessor's vision for the paper as a publication that would "stand as a watchtower, pointing the way for freedom and progress for his people, the Negroes of Los Angeles and of the State of California."[18] This is the tradition that she carried on in her own forty years of owning, editing, and writing for the newspaper, all of which substantiates her claim that "The history of Los Angeles and the Negro people's role in its making is inseparable from the establishment and growth of THE CALIFORNIA EAGLE."[19]

Anchoring the *Eagle*'s story in this early history frames its news within a much longer history of Black struggle. Bass never forgets this, even once things were a little better for Blacks in Los Angeles—particularly when compared to the rest of the country—despite the racism they had always faced.[20] She never forgets that the sweeping tide of Jim Crow started in reaction to Reconstruction, but really came into its own around the turn of the century.[21] She is quick to remind us that it was nothing natural, much less something to be endured rather than resisted. Yet her arrival in LA coincided with a resurgence of racism rather than a new emergence—she had arrived in a city where many whites held an unquestioned ideology of white supremacy. This had already begun to be articulated geographically, through legal mechanisms to ensure white-only spaces. California pioneered protective zoning, although its attempt to thus limit Chinese residence was struck down by state courts in 1892.[22] Unable to enforce racial restrictions on their land through zoning, property owners turned to private agreements—the desire for segregated white space being stronger than a court ruling. Prominent race attorney Willis O. Tyler believed the first covenant was from 1900; it restricted property against "sales or transfers to Negroes or Mongolians or persons of Asiatic blood."[23] Restrictions became increasingly common between 1905 and 1910—years before the larger migrations of World War I brought population pressures and growing racial tensions.[24]

Bass writes of how J.B. Loving, described as LA's "leading Negro realtor," had already described the shifting battle over space as early as a 1904 article in *The Liberator.* He writes, "The Negroes of this city have prudently refused to segregate themselves into any locality, but have scattered and purchased homes in sections occupied by wealthy, cultured white people, thus not only securing the best fire, water, and police protection, but also the more important benefits that accrue from refined and cultured surroundings."[25] The article goes on to describe growing segregation and property restrictions in Bass's summary "as a menace to the Negroes' health, culture, safety and economic advancement."[26] The geographies of privilege and oppression could hardly be better outlined, though even then a clear concentration of the Black community existed in downtown LA as well as in Watts and Pacoima.[27] Thus dawned the century in which the greatest problem was that of the color line, and the establishment and protection of "whiteness" was already a growing international concern in the United States as well as across Britain's former colonies.[28]

This is the historical context for the battle taking place in the first half of the twentieth century over the right to own and to occupy land, and it is foundational to understanding the changing articulations between racial ideology, policy, and the urban form, as well as the forging of links between race, property, and value. As McWilliams writes in 1946, "the brutal treatment of Indians in Southern California in large part explains the persistence of an ugly racial arrogance in the mores of the region of which, alas, more than a vestige remains."[29] In his study of white-collar culture in early LA, Clark Davis notes the pervasive and firm belief in Anglo-Saxon superiority, both in terms of hiring policies as well as the vision for the city itself. He quotes an LA Chamber of Commerce article titled "The Los Angeles of Tomorrow," which encapsulates their vision: "For centuries, the Anglo-Saxon race has been marching westward. It is now on the shores of the Pacific. It can go no farther. The apex of this movement is Los Angeles County."[30]

Such fealty to a white ideal of LA was also observed by Loren Miller, noted NAACP attorney, who wrote, "we were well on our way toward the creation of little islands of super-paradise in that Paradise of the Pacific; communities in which none could dwell but blond-haired, blue-eyed Aryans, certified 99.44 % pure for at least seven generations . . . addicts of Little Orphan Annie and life-time subscribers to, perhaps, *The Cross and The Flag*."[31] Lawsuits show that several influential early subdividers were using restrictive covenants, though it is impossible to tell how many without an exhaustive review of individual deeds.[32] By a 1914 issue of the *Eagle*, a Black real estate man's advertisement states that on his arrival in Glendale there was only one other African American who owned property there. Initially informed that all properties were already covered by restrictive covenants, he proceeded to scour the deeds for homes that those of his own race could buy, and went on to list the handful that he had been able to uncover.[33]

Efforts to widely implement the use of racially restrictive covenants for the preservation of white space grew as part of the early efforts to professionalize the real estate industry. The first formal association of white real estate men came as early as 1905, with the California State Realty Federation.[34] Marc Weiss has shown the leading role that these men would play in innovation and the standardization of real estate practices nationally, in both private and public spheres.[35] A number of California real estate men both sat on the board and held office in the National Association of Real Estate Brokers (NAREB), founded in 1909. Restrictive covenants were promoted at the opening convention, as well as in the 1910 National Conference on City Planning.[36] NAREB was, of course, restricted to whites, and from its beginnings equated patriotism with expanding land ownership among all classes of whites. The preamble to the 1924 code of ethics connects definitions of land's "highest use" to both patriotic duty and the growth of civilization:

Under all is the land. Upon its wise utilization and widely allocated ownership depend the survival and growth of free institutions and of our civilization. The Realtor is the instrumentality through which the land resource of the nation reaches its highest use and through which land ownership attains its widest distribution. He is a creator of homes, a builder of cities, a developer of industries and productive farms. Such functions impose obligations beyond those of ordinary commerce; they impose grave social responsibility and a patriotic duty to which the Realtor should dedicate himself, and for which he should be diligent in preparing himself. The Realtor, therefore, is zealous to maintain and to improve the standards of his calling and shares with his fellow-Realtors a common responsibility for its integrity and honor.[37]

This moral emphasis on the realtor's social responsibilities continues down through the years, exemplifying the way that a business structured to maximize land exchange values mobilized a rhetoric, whether cynically or not, connecting this to the highest of social values.

Early documents show that the defense of white communities was intrinsic to this morality, with white occupation and use of land being established as this "highest value." The defense of whiteness as a patriotic duty thus became mobilized spatially; rigidly segregated spaces became co-constitutive with understandings of community and an ignorance of those outside of that community. This articulation of race and class prejudice with the social value of space led to a heavy emphasis among practitioners, policy-makers, and academics on the ideal of creating neighborhoods homogenous by class and race as they sought to provide a sound foundation for a scientific and professional approach to real estate. NAREB's 1924 code of ethics states: "A Realtor should never be instrumental in introducing into a neighborhood a character of property or occupancy, members of any race or nationality, or any individuals whose presence will clearly be detrimental to property values in that neighborhood."[38] This article continued unchanged until 1950, two years after the Supreme Court struck down restrictive covenants.[39] Through this standardization of real estate practices, these prejudices formed the basis of exchange value. NAREB founded the American Institute of Real Estate Appraisers, building a framework for property appraisals that found "destruction of value" to occur where a neighborhood's white homogeneity was lost.[40] Thus, the value of homogenous whiteness was enshrined not just among realtors and appraisers, but also among lenders.[41] NAREB also established a new Home Builders and Subdividers Division in 1923, and began consulting with planners to further promote responsible development through the adoption of deed restrictions and the creation of homeowner associations able to maintain them.[42]

At state level, the California State Realty Federation consolidated and renamed itself the California Real Estate Association (CREA) in 1917.[43] The very first issue of its new bulletin pushed the transformation of anti-Chinese prejudice into law, prohibiting Asian immigrant ownership of land, and underlining forcefully to its members the connection between being an American citizen and the right to property:

> The organization is now reincorporated under the name of "California Real Estate Association" . . . It's for the protection and advancement of the property interests of California. At the last District Conference of Directors, held at Los Angeles, recommendations regarding the proposed amendments to the Constitution, to be voted on at the November election, were made as follows: No. 1 Alien Land Law—Vote "Yes" . . . The ownership of our soil must not pass to an alien race.[44]

A 1927 CREA survey sent to all member boards gives a snapshot of industry practices and racial geographies. The headlines revealed that the "color question" was a big issue in Southern California. Below is a selection of quotes from various locations in the greater Los Angeles metropolitan area:

> The Los Angeles Realty Board recommends that Realtors should not sell property to other than Caucasian in territories occupied by them. Deed and Covenant Restrictions probably are the only way that the matter can be controlled; and Realty Boards should be interested. This is the general opinion of all boards in the state.

> Practically all subdivisions are provided with restrictions to protect them from future depreciation as far as possible through encroachment of a foreign race . . . Attention is called to the fact that court records show that most of the crime in this country is committed by members of these races.

> Pasadena has a large number of negroes who are recently trying to move into desirable sections of the city. Through subdivision restrictions and owners agreements it is attempting to hold them in check.

> Santa Monica reports that it is "fortunate with deed-restricted property."

> The only people of foreign races in Beverly Hills are servants.

> At Bell, the color problem is governed by a "Gentlemen's Agreement" not to sell to objectional [sic] people.[45]

Glendale made explicit that only whites were considered citizens and Americans in their report: "Glendale, too, considers itself an all-American city." CREA's analysis further distinguished between races, stating that:

> Mexicans do not wish to force themselves into better districts and when improvements are made they usually leave for a poorer district. They do not try to force

themselves where they are not wanted; but negroes, it is held, seem anxious to get . . . into a white district to command a big price to leave.[46]

It is not simply the remaining quiescent within approved ghettoes that white realtors desired, but also voluntary removal from land if it should become desirable for development to benefit white "Americans." Cities further inland, such as Monrovia, made explicit suggestions around creating a segregated area for people of color, while Riverside highlighted the important work that homeowner associations provided assisting realtors to "control the foreign population."[47]

AFRICAN AMERICAN EXPANSION—1926

For communities of color, desperately overcrowded into ghettoes containing both the poor and emerging middle classes, the goal became simply to break down the walls being erected against them. For Charlotta Bass, as editor of the *California Eagle,* as well as the editors of a second Black-owned paper in LA, the *Sentinel* (founded in 1933), real estate transactions were a race matter worthy of front-page headlines. Any development or home purchase outside of the "Black district" represented a race victory. The unspoken subtext of these stories is both the physical hardship caused by the restriction of the entire race to the worst housing, but also an implicit understanding that these walls also separated African Americans symbolically from the community created through shared social and public spaces. Any escape became worthy of celebration.

An early example of the ways in which whites fought to maintain the walls around their community is the case of Mary Johnson, who in 1914 bought a house on an all-white street:

When Mrs. Johnson had left the premises for a few hours one day they entered her home, and when she returned she found her furniture, bedding, kitchen utensils, and other belongings spread out on the front lawn. A crudely hand-painted sign across the nailed-up door read: Nigger if you value your hide don't let night catch you here again.[48]

Johnson called the *Eagle.* This was one of the first real calls to arms that Charlotta Bass received, and she responded in grand style. She did not rely on the authorities to respond, instead mobilizing 100 women to go to the house, where they found the windows and doors nailed so tightly shut they couldn't get in. They camped out on the lawn and stood guard over Mary Johnson's possessions. The sheriff delayed, but under pressure he arrived by midnight. With his help the house was opened, the belongings moved inside, and Mrs. Johnson remained in her home.[49] Like the celebration of the work of Black real estate men in buying or developing properties as a victory for the race, this powerful response on the part of women to defend a home once bought demonstrates an implicit understanding of how this kind of violent construction and maintenance of a white-only community could only be successfully confronted collectively by African Americans.

The white rhetoric describing reactions to these efforts to escape over-crowded slums verges on the hysterical, even reaching the courts, where it is assumed such language is kept to a minimum. In an early racial covenant case, *Letteau v. Ellis*, Superior Court Judge Parker summarizes the process of neigh-borhood change that was then taking place (the italics are my own):

> when the tract was originally laid out, the territory embraced therein and the adja-cent territory was sparsely settled and close to the then city limits, and occupied by Caucasians only ... that in 1909 persons of Negro descent commenced buying, owning, controlling and occupying land all around the tract ... *that Negroes do now, and for over ten years last past, have been used to congregate, walk, drive, pass and appear at all hours of the day and night, openly, publicly, continuously, notori-ously, constantly and extremely noticeable* ... that as results thereof, nearly all persons not of Negroes descent have moved out of said tract and locality and have been replaced by Negroes; that most of the real estate in said tract and locality is now offered for sale and occupancy to Negroes, who are the only ones easily avail-able; that said tract and locality are included within the "Negro District" and ... *that public authorities and the public generally have taken cognizance of and have submitted to this enlargement of the said Negro district.*[50]

It is clear that "Negroes" in public spaces "at all hours of the day and night" cannot be borne by whites, that whites object to Black visibility itself. It is equally clear not only that this expansion is against the wishes of the authorities and the public, but that such a sentence can only have been written by someone for whom members of the Negro race could neither be members of the power structure seen as the "authorities," nor even members of the commonly under-stood "public" itself.

Letteau v. Ellis is only one of a number of key court cases fought over de jure segregation, as early attempts to move out of the recognized "Negro district" confronted legal challenges alongside the kind of violence inflicted on Mary Johnson. The *Eagle* celebrated an initial race victory in 1919, when *Title Guarantee and Trust Co v. Garrott* established that restrictive covenants could not restrict the right to "sell or transfer" property, hoping the legal battle at least was won.[51] Yet whites only fought harder to maintain the legal supports for segregated and privileged space, rewriting their racial restrictions to focus on occupancy rather than ownership.

This new strategy was upheld only a few months after Garrott's case in *Los Angeles Investment Co v. Gary*, when the California Supreme Court ruled in favor of a large and influential developer that people of color had the right to buy property, but not reside in it where restrictive covenants were in force.[52] This defeat was followed by another lawsuit brought by the Janss Investment

Corporation in 1922 against a white man named Walden accused of breaking the restrictive covenant on his property by reselling it to an African American.[53] By 1925, when the case was decided in favor of Janss Investment, the company had already subdivided, and undoubtedly largely covenanted, 100,000 acres in the greater Los Angeles and Orange County areas.[54] Subdividers and developers themselves, or their heirs, brought forward these initial lawsuits to protect the value of their product by proving they could ensure their real estate's promised exclusivity. Map 3 plots these early incidents, both court cases and incidents of violence, in relation to 1948's Black community boundaries, showing how whites were disciplining outlying African American families into ever-hardening ghetto boundaries, preserving privileged and segregated spaces that whites would fight to maintain for decades.

Thus, individual African Americans were forced to expand on a safer block-by-block basis outward from the already consolidated African American neighborhoods as they sought adequate housing, searching out properties where either the restrictions had expired or where they hoped they would no longer be enforced. Some covenant cases, though not all, could be won on technical issues with the covenant itself.[55] The 1932 case of *Letteau v. Ellis* quoted extensively above, however, established a new defense that held at its heart the duality of race's impact on the use and exchange value of properties. The decision was in favor of the Black defendants, as "neither said lot nor said tract is any longer suitable for use with restrictions against occupancy by persons of Negro descent." In the view of an "impartial" court, the lot had been ruined for any higher, white use. To protect what little exchange value was left for those white property owners invested in such areas and unable to sell their property to other whites as required by covenant, the court allowed racial restrictions to lapse.

This represented a bittersweet legal victory, with the court ungallantly bowing to a hard-won reality. It underlines the common sense of white hegemony at the time: a process actually driven by racism is described as a "natural" white reaction to the visible, audible presence of Black people. Returning to hegemony as a specific conjuncture of the political, economic, and ideological, this passage emphasizes the need to include the articulation of the spatial.[56] It is in defense of white space—and white desire for Black invisibility—that ideology, policy, and land value are here being articulated and defined.[57] The boundaries of community and the understanding of the "public" that the courts exist to defend become terribly clear, both politically and geographically, when Black presence alone makes neighborhoods unsuitable for white use. Black resistance to covenants had forced the acknowledgment that the most perfect of covenants could not always protect an investment, and that more was needed to fully protect the exclusivity of new housing development.

Race restrictions existed to preserve the value of property. Where the presence of peoples of color had diminished the use value of property to a great enough extent in the eyes of the white public, the court was forced to rule that such restrictions were unfairly punitive to sellers in the realm of exchange value. A legal expert supportive of the struggle to end restrictive covenants notes that more than one such court decision was handed down in areas across the country where restrictions were prevalent and Black communities were expanding. He writes:

> Because of infiltration of members of the unwanted race into the restricted area or into areas closely adjacent to it a judicial discretion has been exercised to relieve the parties to the agreement of a bad bargain, where enforcement would curtail the market for the restricted property without protecting the benefited property from a shrinkage in value that has already occurred. The discriminatory covenantors are relieved from a white elephant.[58]

Even a sympathetic lawyer still uses language like "infiltration" and "unwanted race." This passage exposes the contradictions of a liberal, free-market ideology emerging from and rationalizing a market operating by the rules of a white supremacy demanding segregation. The sanctity of contracts forms a cornerstone of US law, yet here this sanctity is trumped by the logic that equates market value with the racial makeup of the neighborhood, the courts yielding a small area to the ghetto with the goal of preserving white space and privilege on a larger scale. African Americans put pressure on these contradictions without being able to fully destabilize them, but by paying exorbitant prices in areas in which whites had become so desperate to leave that they were selling to speculators at a loss, the racial boundaries were steadily pushed back along with the limits of contract law.[59]

Covenants, court cases, and realtor regulations might have codified white supremacy through laws and civil society, but daily enforcement keeping communities of color in their place was also a very grassroots affair. Many families faced threats and violence from new neighbors. The Ku Klux Klan flared up in communities throughout LA and Orange counties in the 1920s as part of a national revival.[60] Kenneth Jackson describes the impetus for its growth:

> Immediately after World War I, the impression was common among white people, both North and South, that a "new Negro," anxious for social and economic equality, was coming home from France. The widespread uneasiness was reflected in savage race riots in Chicago and Tulsa and in a rapid rise in the number of lynchings in 1919.[61]

The horror of decades of lynching—what journalist and anti-lynching campaigner Ida B. Wells called "this awful hurling of men into eternity"—was covered extensively in African American papers like the *California Eagle*. The failure of long-running national campaigns for anti-lynching laws proved the political power of white supremacists nationally.[62] While lynching of the kind described by Wells and others were primarily confined to the South, the same was not true of the KKK. Jackson estimates that between 1915 and 1944 there were about 18,000

Klan members in LA and Long Beach, and numerous incidents are recorded in the *California Eagle* as well as the *Los Angeles Times*. In 1922, police recovered Klan membership lists that revealed about 10 percent of public officials and policemen in California to be Klan members. In LA alone, the 1,500 retrieved names included the chief of police and the sheriff. The city had three chapters, and the Klan was active in many suburbs, including Santa Monica, Huntington Park, Glendale, San Pedro, Santa Ana, South Gate, Torrance, and Anaheim.[63]

Many of these areas were also centers of industry and oil production at the time, attracting Southern whites who worked the rigs, some of whom brought Klan affiliations with them.[64] This was not the whole story, however; nor was membership concentrated amongst stereotypically poor whites. Cocoltchos writes of a typical member of the Anaheim branch:

> Contrary to any notion that the typical Klansman was left behind in the race for economic success, he possessed almost the same exact amount of real and personal property as the average non-Klansman in Anaheim. The high proportion of property-owning Klansmen also reflects their relative prosperity and substantial stake in the community.[65]

The Klan has been described as an outlet for violent white supremacist thinking and action, a secret society providing meaning and belonging along with business and social contacts, and an income generator of immense proportions through its fees. Based on Cocoltchos's findings and the distribution of Klan activity and industry as seen in Map 4, it can also be argued it was used to protect the wealth of natural resources and jobs for Anglo-Saxon males.[66] Building on the reputation of lynching and open violence of the South while organizing itself as a business that sought economic and political control of territory, the California Klan insinuated itself and its openly white supremacist ideologies into more than a semblance of legitimacy. Some of its members pursued elected office to take control of the government briefly in Anaheim in 1924, while their associates held high-ranking positions in other city governments and bureaucracies.[67]

Given this context, the launch of what seems to be the Black community's first concerted and strategic effort to break down the residential prejudices underlying race restrictive covenants in the mid-1920s is essentially conciliatory, seeking not to trouble hegemony but to prove the community's worth in upholding it and thus that it deserved inclusion. Charlotta Bass played a key role in this effort. As documented in the pages of the *Eagle*, it consisted primarily of an effort to professionalize Black real estate structures along the same lines as whites', while out-boosting the city's white boosters and out-homeownering its white homeowners to prove their class position and desirability as neighbors and to win acceptance in the greater Los Angeles community.

Self-defining as a movement of homeowners certainly raised issues of class and privilege within the Black community itself, an issue not fully grappled with for decades. Augustus Hawkins notes how a common Southern background and an inability to socialize in most public places meant that social activity generally took place through informal clubs among better-off members of the African American community hosting barbecues in their backyards or drinks in their homes, an "activity that brought them together and made them somewhat clannish."[68] This is one of the central places from which Hawkins obtained the support he needed to become the first African American elected to Congress in California, in 1935, and probably where most of the conversation leading to the effort of forming homeowner associations took place. It entailed an acceptance of white standards, challenging only the labeling of African Americans as detracting from property values rather than the "science" of real estate and its valuation itself. Thus, its primary goal seems to have been proving through example that African Americans could increase property values through their hard work, both on their own homes and in the community. Their efforts embodied a view of exchange values closely tied to use values, the concrete and measurable qualities of well-maintained homes and gardens, along with active homeowner associations involved in neighborhood improvements.

With African Americans excluded from both CREA and NAREB (NAREB went so far as to copyright the term "realtor" for their members only), the *Eagle* announced with pride the formation of a Black professional real estate group in 1922.[69] Two years later, the entrance of two Black realty men into night school at the University of Southern California merited a front-page story.[70] In December's front-page news, a group calling themselves the California Realty Board put forward a call for increased Black immigration to LA. Their counsel, Hugh McBeth, another key figure in the legal battles over covenants, stated to the *Eagle* that its purpose was:

> to broadcast to colored Americans everywhere, the opportunities, the welcome, the hope and cheer, which free California, its hills and valleys, its industries and commerce, its fruits and alwayshine, offer to the American Negro.[71]

Like the White California Boosters' Club, the California Realty Board declared itself to be working to attract new settlers, but was forced to add that it was also working with the California Legal Society to protect newcomers' rights. McBeth wrote that this was necessary because:

> just as colored people have migrated chiefly from Texas, Louisiana and Oklahoma seeking freedom from oppression and congenial surroundings, so whites from these states have come in large number and no sooner do they arrive than they try to make their presence felt.[72]

It is telling that the narrative shifts from a traditional boosting discourse to something of a plea for balance between the Black community and the white Southerners arriving in LA, if only for protection.

Charlotta Bass formally announced the launch of the West Side Homeowners Protective and Improvement Association through the *Eagle*'s headlines on March 24, 1923. What follows is essentially a show of strength and an attempt to measure the value of its residents through their property:

> The West Side district is without question the largest colored residential district west of the Mississippi river, comprising 483 property owners who own and control $1,683,000 worth of valuable residential property. About 20 square blocks are completed, covered with modern California bungalows costing on an average of $4000 each.[73]

While the lawsuits over restrictive covenants highlighted contradictions in contract law, this initial campaign threw into high relief the contradictions between white supremacy and aspirational mythologies and capitalist definitions of success. It claimed respect and white acceptance based on material success and the achievement of assets, reminiscent of Booker T. Washington's strictures and strategies:

> I believe it is the duty of the Negro . . . to deport himself modestly in regard to political claims, depending upon the slow but sure influences that proceed from the possession of property, intelligence, and high character for the full recognition of his political rights.[74]

As a campaign of homeowners, the West Side Homeowners Association broke racial ranks to seek solidarity along class lines, and under a theoretically color-blind capitalism, it should have worked. Campaign rhetoric repeatedly emphasizes the "possession of property, intelligence, and high character," and the injustice of white society in not recognizing those who have worked hard to establish themselves as worthy of it. One article, for example, describes a covenant lawsuit against approximately fifteen families, stating: "The action is considered the boldest attempt of its kind yet instituted in California for reason of the exceedingly high character of those of our race group who own property in that vicinity."[75] They had begun the battle to convince white neighbors of the value of both Black character and Black property.

In February 1926, the *Eagle* published an article with the headline "Are You Sleeping?" It claimed the existence of eighty-one "White Home Improvement and Home Protective Associations" in LA:

> The white Home Protective League is raising their funds for this fight from the white property owners thru their Neighborhood Improvement Associations, because they know that this is the most effective way to wage a home protection fight and because of the undisputable fact that the property owner is the one most vitally interested in such a fight. This same fact is true of our own people. Any question involving property rights will be of most vital interest to the property owner and the property owners' associations.[76]

By April 1926, eight different Black homeowner associations were announcing their meetings in response, all of them working together through the newly formed Progressive Federation of Improvement and Protective Associations. While full numbers participating are not given, each of the eight associations had at least a president, vice president, treasurer, and secretary along with a general membership, and the Federation as a whole had various committees, each with their own chairs. As an example, the East Adams Association had seven officers, all but two of them women. It had committees on publicity, housing, investigation, finance, and membership, and listed a total of sixty-seven active members by name, twenty-nine of them women, thirty-eight of them men.[77] This may have been an effort restricted to homeowners, but it still represented a very bottom-up collective effort grown outside the confines of national organizations like the NAACP (though with a large amount of overlap) that also had committees looking at business, industries, and segregation on trains. Charlotta and Joe Bass were active in the movement as both homeowners and activists, and the *Eagle* served as the mouthpiece of their efforts to combat the racism emerging from the real estate profession, white supremacist groups, local homeowner groups, and local white-owned newspapers.

One major effort lay in attempts to reclaim and redefine definitions of "American," and to establish a basis both for a moral appeal to white consciences as fellow Americans and an economic appeal as worthy homeowners:

> An organized effort to restrict the use and occupation of land in Los Angeles County to persons of a particular race, and prohibiting the use and occupation of such land by persons of Afro-American descent, is gaining support from a few of the one hundred per cent type of American citizens, the type who believe that the color of a person's skin is the standard by which his rights and privileges should be determined.
>
> In order to successfully exterminate this un-American idea of segregation, we must get together. Clean up our Homes, beautify our front and back yard, make our surroundings and environment equal in cleanliness and beauty to the homes of any other group in the city and county: and then we will be in a position to appeal to the Christian conscience of the American people who believe as the immortal Lincoln believed—in justice and charity towards all men regardless of race, creed, or color.[78]

The Federation formed a propaganda committee whose first goal was to mail 1,000 letters to prominent white individuals and organizations in the city on "the injustice and un-Americanism of Residential Segregation, and the hardship of the increasing difficulty of colored men and women to find employment, in Los Angeles."[79] It also planned to raise money to insert a weekly notice highlighting an accomplishment of the race, in order, in the words of committee president George Beavers, Jr.:

to KEEP the GOOD things, the WORTHY things, the WORTHWHILE things that our race is doing, before the public, in short to educate the white man to the fact that all Negroes, are not the "Sambos," thieves, and villains, that they are represented as being in the papers, on the stage and in fiction at the present time.

Again, it is hard to ignore the nature of such appeals to fellowship based on class, the clear desire here among the homeowners to separate themselves from those of their race who might fit such stereotypes.

In addition to the propaganda committee, a Home Beautification and Improvement Committee was hard at work getting ready for June, the "Home Beautification Month," and the Business and Industries Committee was preparing for "Negro Trade Week," calling for a week of community patronage of Black businesses only. In their organizing, there seemed a perpetual sense that they were somehow implicated in the racism directed at them, having been somehow backward in their civic duties:

> A committee was appointed to arrange the program for the groundbreaking of the school tunnel. Doubtless it will surprise the white population of the West Jefferson district, to discover that the colored citizens are taking the lead in the arrangement of this civic matter. They are not used to colored people being citizens.[80]

Their goal was to prove themselves worthy of both citizenship and integration into the white homeowning community.

Part of each association's role was also to monitor the actions of their counterparts, which is what has preserved some record of white homeowner efforts and their very different set of goals. Map 5 shows the ways that the Black community extended southward from a small area based in downtown LA, moving both by necessity given the development of downtown, and by choice to escape slum housing.[81] The extent of territories claimed by the Black associations (in grey) is shown as tracked in the pages of the *Eagle*. These, optimistically perhaps, expand far beyond the realities of dense Black settlement through the 1920s as described by the National Register of Historic Places, corroborated by research carried out by J. Max Bond.[82] While the *Eagle* does not give locations for all 81 white homeowner associations, it does record those most active in maintaining racial boundaries. These can be seen massed along faultlines recognized by the African American community, while to the west, the overlap represents the tangle of claims emerging from the wealthier residents of both races, for the most part resolved through lawsuits. The incidents of violence and legal action show how efforts were made to both check African Americans toward the South as well as discipline outlying families back within confined boundaries. Mapping also makes clear how this strongly class-based homeowner initiative did not involve LA's other Black communities such as Watts, which was poorer and distant from both Central Avenue, where the *Eagle* was based, and the more affluent west side community that was home to the Basses.

The battle between these two groups of property owners played out publicly and was thus preserved in the newspapers between 1925 and 1926—on the side of the Black property owners, Charlotta Bass's *California Eagle*, and on the side of the white property owners, the *South Park Bulletin* and the *West Jefferson Press*. Bass considered it important to quote the white papers at length before responding to them, thus creating a kind of challenge and dialogue impossible to achieve in any other fashion. She noted the "ignorant whites" who believed everything they read, and wrote, "we as a race, can no longer afford to ignore the 'South Park Bulletin' and other vile sheets, doing the same ignoble work of stirring up, and keeping at fever pitch, race hatreds and intolerance."[83] Limited as the campaign may have been to winning acceptance for wealthy Black homeowners in white communities, it nevertheless was understood by Bass as a direct ideological challenge to white supremacy. It represents a very practical approach to an immediate challenge—but not one that restricted other forms of resistance. This use of multiple collective strategies exemplifies Abdullah and Freer's description of Bass's activism as "womanist" organizing. While helping to organize the Federation of Homeowners, Bass also served throughout the 1920s as an active member of both the NAACP, under Du Bois, and was briefly part of the Universal Negro Improvement Association (UNIA) under Marcus Garvey—two towering figures of Black resistance who were strategically and often personally at odds with one another.[84]

It is no surprise then, that the Basses would meet any white supremacist challenge squarely. A key editorial from April of 1926 begins with a statement of the problem they confronted in the words of white supremacists themselves—the *Eagle* would attempt to document, as well as understand and challenge, the bases of white fear and prejudice. The first quote is courtesy of the *West Jefferson Press*:

> The Southern states, being under the same constitutional laws as any other state in the Union, insist upon segregation of Negroes, regardless of their so-called "equal rights," because in those states each white man co-operates with his own color, and, demands white supremacy, socially, politically and otherwise. If the southern [sic] states can enforce segregation so can the Northern states, providing there is proper cooperation.[85]

In response to the propaganda efforts and editorials in the *Eagle*, the *West Jefferson Press* continued its attack. The *Eagle* printed large portions of a June 25, 1926, editorial that claimed the "Preservation of the White Race Must Be Maintained," and described the "illusions of a primitive race whose lack of experience among the higher realms of an intelligent thing world has led them to believe themselves equal." It goes on to state, "The Creator had a positive reason for dividing humanity into the various races."

In addition to this line of biological superiority, it also counteracts the economic arguments being made by Black homeowners. "It has been stated with much bombast," the editorial continues, "that Negroes in Los Angeles own more than five million dollars of property." It calls this insignificant, and describes the one to two thousand dollars of value per lot lost when bought by an African American—the dollar amount for white racism. It then calls on true American citizens to take on the spirit of Paul Revere to create laws and enforce zoning to maintain segregation.[86] In response, Charlotta Bass identifies this as part of a growing nationwide sentiment toward segregation, and the need for unity to resist it.

Bass would record several more such attacks over the following months. The *Eagle*'s editorial of December 10 gives a number of examples, such as this from the Fremont Improvement Association:

> The integrity of our homes is endangered. We must preserve the schools and district for our own race. The safe guarding of all property against the encroachment of the Negro and Mongolian races into the district is our most urgent work. Your co-operation and membership in the Association is necessary—it is your Association—you owe it to yourself and the community in which you are a vital part to join and give all possible assistance in keeping your district WHITE.[87]

Here the conflation of racial purity and economic advantage is seen in the safe-guarding of property alongside the preservation of resources like Fremont's High School for whites. The same editorial quotes the president of the Community Welfare Association:

> Why is it that so many blacks want to be called Caucasians? Why are they so relentless in their efforts to associate and be "equal" to the whites? It is envy, it is pride, it is ignorance.
>
>   Envy is responsible for their organized attempts to break into our white communities.[88]

The *Eagle* editorial responds quite tartly, secure in its moral high ground: "we have the spectacle of men and women who doubtless to a great extent are more pitiful in their delemia [sic] of petty prejudice than was ever the most abject son of a slave."[89]

The Basses added an extra dig where perhaps they believed it would hurt most: stating that the white associations' trouble was caused by a lack of funds to buy out the neighborhood. They write: "their only capital or stock in trade is prejudice and this is the sort of propaganda they are sending forth."[90] There is little subtlety in the implication of greater wealth and greater personal worth among their fellow Black homeowners. While this campaign may have been couched in longstanding strategies of wealth acquisition and moral uplift along the lines of Booker T. Washington, Bass's rhetoric and courage broke through its limits to raise wider demands for respect and change.

Given the increasing power of the KKK and the rise in physical violence against Blacks, these were brave words indeed, but not unprecedented ones. Only the year before, on April 24, 1925, the *Eagle* published an open letter on its front page that had supposedly been signed by G.E. Price, "Imperial Representative" of the KKK in California. The letter purportedly sought to sway the upcoming election. It contained precise voting instructions to members in Watts, along with some "analysis" of key political and social figures, suggestions of how to frame one or two with bottles of booze and bring them up before named KKK judges, and instructions to return or destroy the letter and under no circumstances allow it to fall into anyone else's hands under pain of expulsion. The penultimate paragraph states: "The white people in Watts are tired of being run by people who are not 100% Americans." Following publication of the letter in full, a lawsuit brought for libel against the *Eagle* by a handful of those named in the letter made its front-page news on May 8. The following week, Charlotta and Joe Bass headed down to Watts and spoke in front of a standing room-only crowd. The *Eagle* states:

> We journeyed to Watts on last Tuesday night where we spoke to the multitude. We did not fail to pay our compliments to the Ku Klux Klan. Our subject was "Americanism" and we proved our case to the complete satisfaction of all present that no people can excel the colored Americans for 100 per cent Americanism.

The *Eagle* never relinquished the battle of Blacks to be seen as fully American by whites; it fought for this over decades. Imperial Representative G.E. Price himself swore out a warrant for their arrest the next day. On June 5, the Basses used the *Eagle*'s front page to print the text of the KKK complaint, thereby once again printing a full copy of the initial letter—a grand gesture of defiance. They announced victory in the courts on June 26.

Meanwhile, a 150-strong KKK mob had terrorized a Black family in Graham Station, the most notable incident in a more widespread campaign of harassment against African Americans in the community that continued long after the lawsuit. Charlotta Bass wrote:

> But THE EAGLE fought on. And the Ku Klux Klan fought against it in every way, by every device possible. A telephone committee went into effect and from early morning until far in the night calls such as: "Is this that nigger newspaper? Is this that nigger woman who owns that dirty rag called THE EAGLE?"[91]

One night while Charlotta Bass was working alone in their offices, "eight of the hooded boys" appeared at her door and attempted to get in. After a frozen moment she rushed to the desk, pulled the gun from its drawer, and with that scared them away.[92] While in her memoirs she downplays the incident and confesses that she did not know how to use the gun, such bravery still positions her within a long tradition of pragmatic Black self-defense in the face of white violence.[93] They refused to be silenced, and the *Eagle* would continue to work to shape the electoral debate through editorials, as well report the organizing of the federation of homeowner associations, and call mass meetings in both 1925 and 1926 to discuss the problems of racial covenants, KKK intimidation, and the rise of the white supremacist Home Protective League with their goal of complete segregation.[94]

All of it, however—the community meetings, the homeowner associations, the propaganda committees, the hard work to carry out community improvements, and the best legal counsel available—proved to be insufficient to keep aspiring middle-class African Americans in their homes. In June of 1926, the *Eagle* declared the following:

> On Sunday, June 20th, the entire race throughout the city is requested to observe a real day of FASTING and PRAYER for real divine intervention in the case of the twelve families in the Crestmore district, which have been ordered from their homes. This case is so serious, because it is stated by the whites back of the attempt to drive these families from their homes, that the Crestmore District is only the beginning and that as soon as the Negroes, are out of there they expect to clean them out of every desirable neighborhood in the city . . . On Sunday every minister in Los Angeles of our race will speak from his desk on this subject, urging his people to give their support financially to the fund which the Federation is attempting to raise in order to be able to give help to the twelve families that without assistance will find themselves out of doors.[95]

This was a big loss indeed.[96] The possibility of being turned into the street at any time, with prayer as a desperate and ineffective last resort, must have had a very dampening effect on civic pride and organizing for community improvements.

The director of the white Crestmore Improvement Association had no hesitation in rubbing salt into the wounds caused by the eviction of the twelve families:

> We are not trying to crush or humiliate the black race, which is much younger than our own; we are only following a law of nature which has ben [sic] obeyed, respected, and fought for ever since time began—the right of living among our own KIND. The Negro, in his attempt for the uplifting of his own race, is dragging the Caucasian race down to his own level, which is Wholly [sic] a selfish and unnatural effort at self advancement and we are thoroughly justified in protecting our families and our homes against this injustice.[97]

The director was attempting to mobilize a desire for racial homogeneity as a law of nature, along with individual rights to fight for such homogeneity; both were fundamental to real estate ethics as well as white homeowner struggles. Whites in South LA, organizing by neighborhood to restrict their properties, saw themselves as engaged in a war. An announcement from the president of the Citizens and Taxpayers Protective League, Inc. of the West Jefferson district made this very clear:

> At this time the battle between members of the Caucasian race and the Ethiopians residing in the district waged subtly but nevertheless furiously. Strange marks and crosses appeared on the doors and on sidewalks in front of residences occupied by whites. Both races were guilty of making threats to the other in a desperate effort to make the neighbourhood a one race community.[98]

It had briefly—from 1925 to 1926—been a battle between organized groups. But the Black homeowner association movement seemed to fall apart within a few months of the major legal defeat in the Crestmore neighborhood, leaving a fragmented opposition once more.[99] During this entire period, only one story of white solidarity with Black neighbors made the *Eagle*'s pages—and this does not seem to be for lack of desire on the editors' part, as for them it is front-page news. The *Eagle* headline for August 6, 1926, said of Harry Grund: "White Friend of Negro Defends With Gun: Jailed but Unrelenting!" He was defending his Black neighbor Mentis Carrere, who had refused to sell his home in the face of threats from the Southwest Chamber of Commerce, led by Deputy Sheriff F.C. Finkle. There is tantalizingly little information to be found in the *Eagle*, but it reported that Grund had to fire his gun, believing his friend's safety was at risk. No one was hurt. Even while celebrating this example of interracial solidarity, the need for armed defense must have been something of a blow to the hopes for class solidarity embodied by the strategies of the federation of Black homeowner associations.

Still, the *Eagle* continued to track individual court cases in its pages and support homeowners fighting to stay in their homes. In 1931, it reported the restrictive covenant case of Mr. Gray, half Native American and half Scottish, being evicted along with his wife. It quotes him as saying, "I'd like to know which half of me they're going to eject, the white or the Indian."[100] A 1938 covenant case challenged racial definitions, as Mrs. Hattie Burns argued she "had less than 50 percent Negro blood in her veins, and shouldn't the preponderance of 'white' blood classify her as white?"[101] Race has always been complex and contradictory, and the courts were becoming theaters for discussion and argument around many of these complexities.

The Great Depression, as all economic downturns, hit communities of color hardest and survival became the highest priority.[102] While the *Eagle* continued to give voice to the many individual struggles over racial boundaries, no collective action to end segregation would be seen again until the dawn of World War II.

Chapter 2

Victory Abroad and at Home

The Second Campaign Against Race-Restrictive Covenants

The *Eagle* of the mid-1920s documented the radical upsurge in the KKK as well as farther-reaching local neighborhood organizing around white supremacy. Over the same period, the campaign of Black homeowners to prove their worth through neighborhood boostering and proof of their achievement of the American dream of wealth and success went down in defeat, as had their challenge of a racist refusal to recognize that they were Americans at all. The movements both in support of and against segregation would prove to be foundational for what was to come in the next two decades.

The eviction of the families from Crestmore showed the organizers of the Progressive Federation of Improvement and Protective Associations that they were Black first, and middle-class homeowners and professionals second— never again would the *Eagle* put such effort into mirroring white forms of organization or attempting to prove the race's worth along class lines. The newspaper's editors would enter the 1930s with a growing radicalism forged in their struggles against white supremacist movements, looking to build solidarity within the Black community and across class lines. Charlotta Bass would continue down an increasingly radicalized path after the death of her husband, Joseph, in 1934; her grief continued to permeate her editorials through the years that followed. Her activism in labor struggles and growing exposure to the great resistance movements of the 1930s would come to shape a new, very different kind of campaign to end racial covenants.

For whites, on the other hand, the movements of the 1920s helped shape and solidify a broad ideological commitment to white supremacy across the city, the state, and the nation. The successful legal and political battles alongside vibrant grassroots organizing to preserve race restrictions built new conceptions of community while grounding white supremacy firmly in the maintenance of homogenous, privileged white space where white families could only flourish in the absence of people of color. This would become the ideological center around which a new, professionalized economics of land and property would soon be constructed.

INSTITUTIONAL ORGANIZING: THE EQUATION
OF RACE WITH EXCHANGE VALUE

The economic crisis of the 1930s made possible a national restructuring of real estate practices and government policies, creating the opportunity and political will to federally fund and implement a new era of real estate economics that would come to define the shape of Los Angeles (and cities across the US) today. The efforts of the federal government to respond to economic crisis led to both the transformation of real estate financing and the institutionalization of segregation, driven by private-sector members and academic affiliates of NAREB.[1] Urban planner Charles Abrams describes the new era of corporate welfare that emerged, along with the repercussions of open federal support of segregation:

> In the transition from a private to a welfare economy, private housing operations were now being implemented by public power, public credit, and public subsidy . . . From 1935 to 1950, in fact, prejudice and public power were already well advanced toward an alliance which was challenging the fundamental values of the American system.[2]

Civil rights attorney Loren Miller counted the federal government's promotion of segregation as one of the most important and fundamental forces to be fought by the Black community.[3]

It is this period running up to World War II, particularly through the Great Depression, that saw the full and officially sanctioned equation of racial occupancy with exchange value by real estate professionals, academics, and government agencies alike. This formalized and legitimated the racist beliefs espoused by white newssheets, helping to transcribe brutal racist ideologies into the legalistic language of academia and policy-making. As much in the service of preserving the sanctity of white space for social reproduction as creating a foundation for real estate profit, the articulation of a science of property valuation, legitimating government policies, and white supremacist ideals made very visible the forging of the "unity between economic, political, and ideological objectives such that it can place 'all the questions around which the struggle rages on a "universal" not a corporative level, thereby creating a hegemony of a fundamental social group over a series of subordinate groups.'"[4] Clearly, spatial objectives belong in this list, articulated in service of a hegemonic white supremacy where race, not class, defined the fundamental group, and in which white space was established as a key stake. As Lefebvre notes: "Space is at once result and cause, product and producer; it is also a stake, the locus of projects and actions."[5]

The federal government's first attempt to deal with the immensity of the Great Depression's crisis in foreclosures and loan defaults was the Home Owners' Loan Corporation (HOLC). It formed in 1933 to purchase delinquent loans from a variety of lenders and refinance them with new long-term and low-interest loans.[6] As Freund persuasively argues in *Colored Property*, HOLC fundamentally changed the housing market in three ways: "it demonstrated the potential of the long-term, low-interest mortgage not only to shore up but also to expand the market for privately owned homes"; it "set a crucial precedent for further state involvement in the private credit system, suggesting that a federal regulatory and financial presence might create and sustain expanded consumer spending"; and it "set in motion both a new means of achieving the racial segregation of neighbourhoods and a new rationale for defending it."[7]

Philip Kniskern, the head of the American Institute of Real Estate Appraisers (founded by NAREB, which he would also go on to head), designed the appraisal guidelines HOLC used in refinancing loans.[8] These enshrined the link between race and property value at the federal level, creating a series of color-coded maps showing four different levels of lender security in insuring home loans. At the bottom were the red areas. "They are characterized by detrimental influences in a pronounced degree, undesirable population or infiltration of it," it stated in the codes. As if to emphasize it is more about the occupants than the condition of the housing, it continues: "The areas are broader than the so-called slum districts," adding scope for discretion on their exact boundaries.[9]

"Yellow areas are characterized by age, obsolescence, and change of style," the codes continue, "expiring restrictions or lack of them; infiltration of a lower grade population." Housing conditions and location are included here, but there is still a focus on population: "'Jerry' built areas are included, as well as neighborhoods lacking homogeneity." Above these are ranked the blue areas: "They are like a 1935 automobile still good, but not what the people are buying today who can afford a new one." This clarifies another of the code's underlying assumptions—that the housing market is based upon regularly upgrading to the latest model rather than any sense of a home for a lifetime, much less for future generations. Unstated but assumed is that there is complete (white) homogeneity, a condition unlikely to change. At the top? The green areas, the "hot spots," "the new well planned sections of the city." Here the codes state unequivocally, "They are homogeneous; in demand as residential locations in 'good time' or 'bad'; hence on the upgrade."[10]

The two clearest indicators of value under this system are the race of the inhabitants and the newness of the development. More telling are the actual forms for rating each district, which give the race and class of the population, with special boxes for the percentages of "foreign" and "Negro" before the condition of the built environment. From this time forward, lenders would officially and systematically use HOLC maps and definitions to decide lending policies in the practice known as redlining. Banks not only refused to lend to individuals living or building within red areas, but insisted on the insertion of racial covenants into all deeds. Clauses advocating racial restrictions were even automatically inserted where financing was obtained for homes in Black developments.[11]

Freund argues persuasively that federal policy's influence went even deeper than this, however, transforming who was allowed to buy homes, and where. He writes that "the HOLC initiated the creation of a new kind of discriminatory marketplace, one that functioned very differently and that achieved and justified discrimination in a wholly new manner."[12] In this way it created a housing market that channeled real estate wealth almost exclusively to whites. I would argue that the clear racial criteria used in appraisals makes it harder to maintain, as Freund does, that it provided "a state-sanctioned platform for housing experts to argue that racial discrimination was simply a by-product of impersonal economic processes."[13] It did set the foundation for future arguments, however, by ensuring that home appraisals became the exclusive realm of experts using formal criteria rather than informal and personal stipulations carried out between a home buyer based upon their own needs and the local bank's guidelines. Rather, the HOLC implemented a racist national standard of exchange value to be created and applied by private-sector professionals; it also described and delineated racial boundaries in ways that continued to decimate communities long after its demise.

The Federal Housing Authority (FHA) formed in 1934 as part of the National Housing Act. In contrast to the HOLC, which purchased and refinanced existing mortgages, the FHA insured new mortgages, thus "fostering new lending activity, creating a national market for mortgages, and, by doing so, expanding the market for home finance."[14] To create its own underwriting criteria it hired Frederick Babcock, an appraiser long associated with NAREB.[15] The April 1936 edition of its underwriting manual promoted the use of both zoning and racial restrictive covenants to protect neighborhoods from "Adverse Influences." It states:

> The Valuator should investigate areas surrounding the location to determine whether or not incompatible racial and social groups are present, to the end that an intelligent prediction may be made regarding the possibility or probability of the location being invaded by such groups. If a neighborhood is to retain stability it is necessary that properties shall continue to be occupied by the same social and racial classes. A change in social or racial occupancy generally leads to instability and a reduction in values. The protection offered against adverse changes should be found adequate before a high rating is given to this feature. Once the character of a neighborhood has been established it is usually impossible to induce a higher social class than those already in the neighborhood to purchase and occupy properties in its various locations.[16]

Unlike the HOLC, which did in fact refinance loans in all four of its color-coded areas, FHA agents only insured transactions in HOLC's blue or green areas.[17] By providing lenders with risk-free investments, it opened a floodgate of new credit to white first-time homebuyers. At the same time, it categorically denied people of color the same opportunities, defining them as a "permanent, calculable risk to stable property values."[18] HOLC maps were never meant for public use, yet they were accessible to lenders, appraisers, and government officials, and most real estate professionals would most likely have known their contents. This could explain why so many realtors were in the forefront of efforts to organize protective associations, blanket neighbourhoods with covenants, initiate lawsuits, and protect their own neighborhoods' homogeneity at all costs.

By 1939, Charlotta Bass was writing in her regular column that "the breach between white and black Americans was widening as the years go by, and this is not as it should be."[19] She linked this breach to white mobilizations for spatial segregation of the races, and went on to quote extensively from the *Pasadena Independent*, dated October 14:

> Opening gun in a city-wide campaign to end racial conflict in Pasadena was fired yesterday when the board of directors of the Chamber of Commerce endorsed 100 per cent the race Restriction program of the Pasadena Improvement Association.

The article notes that Pasadena's Chamber of Commerce will raise funds for the Improvement Association's efforts to blanket the city anew with restrictions, joining the majority of communities in the western San Gabriel Valley who have taken similar actions. Signaling the pervasiveness of the drive to blanket the LA region with restrictive covenants even through the depths of the Depression, this rhetoric indicates a call for civic action and a new partnership between business and homeowners for the protection of property and white privilege fully in line with the federal government's own recommendations. The article ends by stating that, after all, "the association feels that definite restrictions in neighborhoods is the only 'sensible solution' of the problem."[20]

This more civic-minded and civilizing discourse of peace and harmony through segregation was growing alongside the FHA's economic discourse of "adverse influences," while older and more openly racist praxis also persisted. Only a few months later, the Klan marched through downtown Los Angeles.[21] In February of the following year a bonfire and symbolic lynching was carried out at Fremont High School—the first of several such incidents there.[22] The handbills shown on the following page were passed out.

It brings together all the elements of white fear: loss of status (being known as a "boogie" school), loss of neighborhood and way of life (they have "won ground," underlining the view of a war between the races over land, and that there exists a common assumption that a few Black families will lead to more arriving until they have taken over completely), and of course social mixing of the races inevitably leading to miscegenation. The everyday experience of this animosity as something to constantly navigate spatially, and fearfully, by African Americans is illustrated by a conversation on musician Johnny Otis's radio program:

> Dootsie Williams: We jumped over the white enclaves to get to our homes if we were in Watts and were coming from the downtown area. Drove right through them, actually.
>
> Johnny Otis: Yeah, and fast, too, sometimes. [laughs]

A FREMONT POSTER

NO Niggers

TEACHERS & ADULTS THAT STILL HAVE BABY BRAINS

SAY IT'S THE BAD NATZI'S & COMMUNISTS TELLING US TO

DISLIKE THE NIGGER, BUT IT ISN'T WE KNOW WHAT WE WANT

AND WE DONT WANT FREMONT TO BE CALLED A"BOOGIE" SCHOOL

LIKE WASHINGTON.

ITS TOO LATE NOW, THE NIGGERS KNOW THEY HAVE
WON GROUND AND THEY'LL BE FLOCKING TO THIS SECTION****
THEY HAVE ALREADY MOVED IN ON (Lower part of) 61st
STREET AND THEY'LL SNEAK IN ON 70th, 71st, 76th, and
then 79th UNTILL AVALON BLVD WILL BE A SECOND
CENTRAL AVE.

THEN JUST LET A WHITE GIRL WALK SO MUCH
AS WALK DOWN THE STREET AT NIGHT OR EVEN AT
DUSK******* HAVE YOU EVER SEEN A GIRL AFTER SHE
HAD BEEN RAPED BY A NIGGER??? WELL SHE WOULD
BE BETTER OFF DEAD................

LET'S JUST STOP AND THINK FOR A MOMENT
WIFE??   DAUGHTER???   OR   *MOTHER*

Handbills passed out at Fremont High School Race Riot

D.W.: With that streetcar that would go from way up from LA City College and run all the way down to Manchester and Central Avenue. Then, you had to get off and walk . . . And you were walking through the white district until you came to 95th Street.

Buddy Collette: I used to have dreams about that, about walking through no-man's-land, and late at night too.

D.W.: Social conditions were terrible at that time.[23]

The role of white-inflicted violence in maintaining racial lines is all too apparent in this almost offhand conversation between friends on nightmares about traversing white neighborhoods, described in the same words as the death-dealing space between entrenched armies.

The extent of such white-inflicted violence is indicated by the organizing of several African American gangs through the 1940s to defend Black youth from incursions by white gangs originating in Huntington Park, South Gate, Bell, Inglewood, Gardena, and the Westside.[24] White gangs, such as the Spook Hunters in Southeast LA, formed around explicitly white supremacist objectives, made clear by their use of the racial epithet "Spook," as by the distorted black face with its neck in a noose that they wore as an emblem on the back of their jackets.[25] Not only did they use violence to discipline any Black youth on the wrong side of the ghetto's racial boundaries—from Alameda to Slauson to Main—but also crossed Alameda into the ghetto itself to attack Black youths.[26] In addition to the lynching in effigy and the hate leaflets distributed around Fremont High School, racial gang wars took place at Manual Arts, Adams, and Canoga Park high schools. This corresponded with a rise in KKK activity twenty years after its last growth spurt in the 1920s.[27]

This illustrates the interplay between local and national levels in the formation of hegemonic segregation in the United States: the grassroots racist fears and violence in defense of space and resources for a community defined by whiteness, articulated with policies emerging from real estate professionals, and the government's own views as formalized by the HOLC. In rating this particular area, the HOLC notes successful white resistance to "infiltration," but also resignation that ultimately it will fail, indicating that the future will almost certainly see it dropping its classification two grades and essentially stripping working-class white residents of privilege granted them by their skin color and their location:

The area is predominantly a workingman's district . . . There is a threat of subversive racial infiltration (Negroes largely) in the southeast portion of area. An attempt was made to break the area down but it is in a transition period at present, and it was not feasible. However, it is believed that in the course of time it will be necessary that this be done and will result in a number of areas grading from "low blue" to 4th grade.[28]

These bald appraisals and racial judgments controlling access to insurance cover, loans and investment ensured that white communities in places such as South Central would fight like hell to hold the boundaries, and if that failed, flee to newly built areas still graded green and blue. Real estate men worked along the edge of this dialectic between use and exchange values, selling a home to be cherished but whose equity would be protected:

> And this is the atmosphere that the broker and salesman must absorb. It is the air he must breathe. He is not selling bricks and mortar or shingles and siding, but "Home." He is not a salesman taking orders, but a missionary, a pioneer with a vision . . . leading on to new fields and frontiers.[29]

This evokes Lefebvre's argument about the commodification and development of social space. He writes, "planning becomes an exchange value. The project of developers presents itself as opportunity and place of privilege: the place of happiness in a daily life miraculously and marvellously transformed . . . Here is the context, the setting, the means of your happiness."[30] The logic of white supremacy dictated that this context be a white one, thus homes, as the "place of privilege: the place of happiness," needed to be preserved as much as homes as investments, and defenses against their "infiltration" were necessary:

> The National Association of Home Builders urged forming "homes associations" with "enforcement functions, developing prestige for the builder." The homeowner was assured of "enhancing and protecting his investment, enforcing protective covenants, promoting community activities, insuring stable and attractive neighborhoods."[31]

The weight of white consensus, institutional controls and government support seemed to be tightening the white noose around Black districts.

THE FINAL PUSH: POST-WORLD WAR II STRUGGLE

Instead, as we shall see, the upheaval of World War II would bring the final push that finally succeeded in ending de jure residential segregation. The legal and national struggle coordinated by the NAACP was supported by multiple local grassroots efforts across the country, such as that of the Home Protective Association (HPA) in Los Angeles, which helped support and publicize individual cases and build the political will necessary to achieve radical change. Like the homeowner associations of the 1920s, and led by some of the same people alongside Charlotta Bass, the HPA was primarily a movement of homeowners. Yet it drew from the experiences of its members politicized through the increasingly radical and broad-based organizing work that had developed through the 1930s and early '40s; they joined the fight against covenants to a much broader discourse of rights and more expansive notions of citizenship than the narrow class solidarity of the homeowner associations in 1926. In doing so, they staked their counter-hegemonic ideological claims to the right to own land and to a position of respect within an American community still imagined as belonging only to whites. Strategically they would attack restrictive covenants, the principal legal underpinning of segregation, and thereby bring down the government regulations promoting their use.

One of the key organizations setting the stage for the final struggle against restrictive covenants was the National Negro Congress (NNC). Founded in 1936 at a convention of "more than five thousand men and women-secretaries and social workers, labour leaders and preachers, politicians and doctors," the NNC was formed partially in response to a perceived weakness of the NAACP, and attempted to bring the various strands of Black struggle together, from the Communist Party to organized labor (long resistant to integration) and traditional Black organizations.[32] In the words of A. Philip Randolph, elected its president:

> Its intention was to "mobilize and rally power" in the community around "a militant program" all black Americans could endorse. The "all" included the 99 percent of the "Negro peoples" who "win their bread by selling their labor power.[33]

Although it fell apart in 1940 under the pressures of red-baiting—indeed, for decades it was mischaracterized by multiple sources as a communist front organization—the NNC was a broad-based national organization that for the first time had managed to build bridges between Black activists and labor, as well as challenge the strategic primacy of older civil rights organizations such as the NAACP and Urban League.[34]

By 1939, the LA chapter had started a campaign to improve slum housing conditions that, along with the campaigns around jobs and particularly domestic work, attempted to galvanize the masses of African Americans trapped in the "Black Belt."[35] Charlotta Bass had long been skeptical of communism, even as she had conscientiously covered many of the communist campaigns in the pages of the *Eagle*. Yet the national strength and popular appeal of the NNC ensured her minimal involvement, even as she remained critical of what she called its "rabble-rousing policies" in one of her weekly columns.[36]

With the NNC in disarray, facing intense internal rivalries and external pressure from reactionary anti-communist groups along with the press, Charlotta Bass and Reverend Clayton Russell came to feel the need for a similar mass-based, local organization able to bring together the various progressive organizations and unions in the city. They founded the LA Negro Victory Committee (NVC) in 1941.[37] Kurashige notes that the NVC's focus on the position of Black workers in the war effort, and efforts to elicit struggle from a broader class position, gave it the ability to mobilize far larger demonstrations than had previously been seen in LA.[38] In a key campaign led by Bass that organized the community against job discrimination, she and hundreds of other women flooded the government's employment office, forcing them to lift the ban against Black women in the war industries. Above all in such campaigns, the NVC pushed a variant of the "Double V" slogan first coined by the Black newspaper the *Pittsburgh Courier*—victory over racism at home and abroad.[39] The record of the NVC in the *Eagle* shall be treated in some detail, as Bass ensured covenants always remained part of the struggle, even as she hammered on the contradictions of a war abroad against the fascism of the Nazis while white supremacy and Jim Crow continued unchallenged at home.

The war changed the face of Los Angeles, bringing a new wave of internal migrants to the area seeking work in the wartime industries (although people of color would face uphill battles to be hired, even into the lowest positions). Between 1940 and 1944, the African American population increased from 75,000 to 134,000—78.2 percent—while by January 1, 1945, the Los Angeles Housing Authority had approximately 100,000 unfilled housing applications pending.[40] Although the *Eagle* did not join the drumbeat against the Japanese, its pages were silent through their removal to concentration camps. African Americans moved into the houses they left behind, yet even the rechristening of Little Tokyo as Bronzeville did not provide enough housing for the thousands seeking a home.[41]

Relief for the poor and working class from the desperate overcrowding and slum conditions became a priority for the NVC, and they focused their energies on ending racial quotas in the new public housing being constructed.[42] In laying out a plan around which to organize community action, the goals could not be more distinct from the Black homeowner association campaigns of the mid-1920s to lay claims to integration based on the worth of their property:

- Emergency construction of additional Federal Housing projects on the Eastside.
- Conversion of all large buildings on the Eastside as small apartment units or dormitories.
- Immediate occupancy by Negroes and other minority groups of houses vacant by the score across the "Main Street" ghetto borderline.
- Removal of all housing project "Quota systems" and removal of property race restrictions from all Los Angeles property.[43]

This was sent to the city housing authority, the mayor, and the Board of Supervisors. Radical in most ways apart from its geography, it most likely reflects Black fears of a hostile white community in confining its first three demands to housing in areas within and alongside race boundaries. The fight to end all racial covenants remained a key but small component of this broad-based struggle for housing. Bass convened a roundtable of the NNC, the NAACP, the NVC, the *Eagle*, and the *Sentinel* on the subjects of housing conditions and workplace discrimination. Soon after, the *Eagle* began to reappropriate war terminology, connecting Black struggle to that being fought in Europe: "Big guns of Eastside mass pressure will be directed against Housing restrictions which bottle up Negro workers into an area which is the center of slum housing and bum sanitation . . . Such a move is declared to be vital war necessity."[44]

Over the lifetime of the NVC, the job and public housing campaigns would introduce ever more confrontational tactics, and in the end they won very real concessions. Based at the People's Independent Church of Christ headed by the charismatic Clayton Russell, their mobilization tactics would prefigure the better-known civil rights movements. A member described their operations:

> You had the outline of an organization and the framework, but the actual operation of the organization was done by four people. And it would be our job to outline the strategy for a given campaign and take it before the people. This is because the organization as a whole cannot be the administrator. You have to create the program for the people to follow. So you have to say, "this is what we're going to do" and then go out and sell it to the people and then make it a reality. So, for example, we would call a mass meeting for a Monday because we had a base, and we could send the people home from church on Sunday morning and they could pass the word and have a lot of people at Independent for a night mass meeting.[45]

In 1943, within two years of its founding and two years into the US's war against fascism abroad, the NVC, the NACCP, and organized labor "stormed the City Council chambers" to demand the approval of the new public housing project in Watts without race restrictions, and an investigation of the white groups working to prevent it. As Bass remembers:

> In the midst of the heated discussion some twenty or more Negro youths entered the City Council chambers, marched up front, surrounded the City Council members, marched back again up and down the aisles. They were very orderly. There was no shouting, no haranguing. But there was something about them that made everyone understand they meant business. They carried banners with such slogans as: "Fight Hitler, Not Each Other"; "The Four Freedoms, Not Race Restrictions"; "Homes For All War Workers"; "Let's Restrict Restrictions"; "Freedom For All"; and the like.
>
> These marchers were members of the NAACP Youth Council, and they staged their parade under the leadership of John Kinloch, their president. This was the first time the City Hall was ever picketed from within. It marked the beginning of a long battle for that particular area.[46]

This was on the heels of a 500-strong meeting the previous night and followed the call of NVC leader Reverend Russell, prompting Bass to write an article in the same issue of the *Eagle* with the headline "Mass Meet—People's Weapon." It is clearly in response to ongoing argument over tactics. It had been three years since she had leveled her own critiques at the NNC's mass mobilizations. Her experience campaigning as part of the NVC had clearly moved her further to the left:

> I have heard some protests against the practice of "calling mass meetings." It is alleged in certain cantankerous quarters that nothing is done through the vulgarly public process of the mass meeting. It is further complained that the same people always speak and always say the same things.
>
> I suppose the continued insistence upon every democratic right can become monotonous to those really uninterested in their attainment.[47]

The campaign, led by the NVC and NAACP, succeeded in forcing the Los Angeles Housing Authority to apologize for the limited housing and to liberalize (though not entirely dismantle) their racial quota system. Mass meetings, pickets, and confrontation proved to be effective in certain situations.

For the first time, the *Eagle* began regularly reporting on how covenants—and police brutality—affected other communities of color, to build solidarity with them.[48] This perhaps reflects a growing broad understanding of white supremacy's nature as Bass and others continued to pound on the parallels between Nazi white supremacism and that of Los Angeles homeowners:

> Negroes must make it hot for all those fascist minded forces which would bottle up American citizens into an over-congested slum area just to placate a Hitlerite theory of race superiority.
>
> Pointing out that the health of war workers is seriously endangered by the housing restrictions which render fully 95 per cent of Los Angeles "verboten" to Negroes.[49]

In a later issue, Bass writes:

> On the one hand, there is the Ku Klux Klan, the National Rifle Association, and the scores of race property restriction organizations.
>
> On the other hand, there is the labor movement, both CIO and AFL, the Negro people, the Jewish and Mexican minorities. These forces compose the basic win-the-war element of our city. These are the workers who build the ships, guns, planes of victory. These are the legions of patriots who will fight for the reality of the Four Freedoms, and understand within their own lives, the menace of fascism.
>
> In the middle, there is a bulk of Americans dangerously open to the fascist incitement of the racists.[50]

From among the Black community, the war brought a great surge of support for organizations fighting for civil rights. Nationally, the NAACP went from 50,000 members in 1940 to 500,000 members in 1945.[51] As much as the NAACP, NNC, NVC, and the *Eagle* attempted to frame issues of jobs and housing in terms of the anti-fascist war effort, however, they foundered against a shared bedrock of belief in the white community about white Americanism and peace through segregation.

A 1943 letter from the South Los Angeles Homeowner's Association, for a mass meeting to be held in the American Legion Hall, again emphasizes peace through segregation:

> Protect Your Home—Emergency Action Necessary. Protect Your Home Against the Encroachment of Non-Caucasian People. The Area Between 98th and 104th Street and Avalon and Clovis Aves. Has Been Designated by the National Housing Administration as a Non-Restricted Area with 465 United to be Erected Immediately.
> Attend This Meeting and Help the War Effort by Keeping Peace at Home.

The *Eagle* had uncovered the association's leadership, which included a real estate broker and called on the city council to investigate the group for libel, sedition, and the sowing of race hatred when it could endanger the war effort.[52] Such letters and leaflets underline the explicitly spatial form that racial struggle took along the clearly demarcated boundaries of streets, neighborhoods, and cities—white communities defining themselves by the racial faultlines separating them from all others.

The Great Depression had not slowed the push to insert or renew race restrictions across the city, nor did the war. In 1941 major efforts to renew covenants across the disputed West Jefferson district took place.[53] In March 1942, the *Maywood-Bell Southeast Herald* published the leading headline "Keep Maywood White." Bass quotes extensively from their editorial, which exemplifies the lived experience of property value's dual nature—their exchange value as investment and their use value in social reproduction:

> Within the next few weeks one section of the community will be definitely threatened with the moving in of undesirables since race restrictions run out in this section . . . After they are in, it will take the moving of heaven and earth to remove them.
> If you are interested in saving your investment, if you are interested in preserving that for which you have labored many years; if you are interested in keeping Maywood Caucasian and the type of community that you can be proud of raising your children in, then you will get on the band wagon.[54]

Again it was the local chamber of commerce spearheading the initiative.

Another letter from the University Center Cultural Committee—a curious title for a neighborhood group so focused on property values—shows the ways that the professional language of "infiltration," "absorption," race, and property values found in the HOLC maps has been picked up and reused:

> The colored population of Los Angeles is increasing by leaps and bounds, an illustration of which increase can be found at Jefferson Street and [4-B] Grand Avenue

at any hour of any day . . . The above area is extremely vulnerable to infiltration and absorption as an additional colored residential district. Unless the property owners immediately take steps to prevent it such an absorption can occur and it can be depended that property and income values will immediately drop 50 to 75 per cent . . . A group of your neighbors have agreed to re-restrict and attempt to protect their property values providing you will do likewise.[55]

In November, a meeting occurred in Culver City under the banner "God Bless America with Life, Liberty and Justice for All" with the purpose of "restricting Negroes from living in Culver City, and using the air raid wardens of that city to distribute petitions to the people in the areas where the tract restrictions had expired or were about to expire."[56] African Americans were clearly not included in the declaration "for All." Another "anti-Negro" mass meeting was held in Watts the next week, hosted by the boilermakers' union.[57]

Legal actions continued through the war—a mimeographed white home-owner association letter to its members highlights the white position in opposition to all others: "The property on the North West corner of 21st and La Sale owned by the Burtons, who have betrayed their neighbors by selling to Chinese, is now being occupied by the new owners."[58] It is a calling out, a reminder of the race covenants and their importance to property values, and a notice of legal action. A memo from Loren Miller from the mid-1940s shows forty-three pending covenant cases from Los Angeles, involving ninety-three properties.[59] Sometime after this list was drawn up, the white West Adams Improvement Association filed a suit against a number of Black families for violating covenants—and it included some of the wealthiest and most famous African Americans in the nation. Hattie McDaniel had already won an Oscar for her role as the mammy in *Gone With the Wind* (1939) when neighbors filed the lawsuit to force her, fellow African American actresses Ethel Waters and Louise Beavers, and a number of other Hollywood figures and professionals out of their homes.[60] In December, a crowd of almost 500 met at the call of the NAACP to raise money and decide on other means of support for a family who had just lost their home after losing another race restriction battle in court.[61] The *Eagle* reports from notes taken from the white Property Owners Protective Association's meeting:

Chairman Dye appealed Friday evening for a fund of $2500.00 to keep Negroes out of "white areas." One member, Mrs. Lucille Haber, told how she had sent all the way to Washington, DC, to establish information that two women living at 5879 Crocker St. were Negroes; [s]he could not tell for sure by the color of their skin. Three Negro families in Belvedere Gardens were evicted, another member reported. Law suits are being filed against all former owners of property south of Slauson Ave., between Central and Hooper Aves., who have sold to Negroes. Some of the property involved was first sold to Negroes more than fifteen years ago.[62]

The hysteria at the prospect of "invasion" is very clear; the note also highlights the difficulties of trying to establish race given that it is a cultural construction rather than biological fact. Drawing from the *Eagle*'s reporting, and far from complete, Map 6 shows how whites were organizing to protect the boundaries of their communities in Central and South LA.

THE HPA

Signaling the feeling that the NVC was insufficient to confront restrictive covenants, a joint meeting was held in the *Eagle*'s building between Black activists, labor unions and welfare organizations in August of 1944.[63] This was the beginning of the Home Protective Association (HPA/HOPA), an organization that would meet regularly on Fridays in the *Eagle* offices until the Supreme Court struck down restrictive covenants under widespread pressure just under four years later.[64] It signals in some ways a considered return to the organizing of homeowners who comprised its base, while still remaining committed to, and in active solidarity with, a broader struggle.

Bass served as the president; the secretary and treasurer were both women, as were four of the five members of the executive committee. They decided to focus on one particular case, that of Anna and Henry Laws. The couple had built their own home on a lot they had owned for nine years. Two realtors with no direct interest in the property had brought them to court, able to show that in 1923 the Bank of Italy had included race restrictions in the tract's original plans.[65] The Laws had bought the land believing it to be restriction free, but were willing to fight.[66] At the time the HPA was formed, the Laws were living in their car under a court order to vacate their home. The NAACP had been involved to some extent in their case but had advised them to move. Bass quotes a portion of the unnamed lawyer's letter (though it was almost certainly from Thomas L. Griffiths, head of the local NAACP branch) to the Laws:

> I have been seriously considering just whether or not it wouldn't be for the best interest of all of us, that you endeavor to locate elsewhere . . . I am suggesting, therefore, that you avoid contempt proceedings, and move instead . . . You may desire to dispose of your property, and if so, Mr. Boyer or Mr. Freers could be of some assistance in finding you buyers.[67]

This letter was remarkable considering that Mr. Boyer and Mr. Freers were the realtors who had brought the suit against the Laws in the first place. But Bass and others believed that they could fight this case all the way to the Supreme Court and win.[68]

In terms of strategy, the committee was politically connected enough to draw one of LA's council members to an early meeting to discuss the role that city council could play in the fight to end racial restrictions. The *Eagle* announced his answer in a front-page headline: "NO POWER."[69] After this setback, they seem to have returned to a less overtly political plan of action, gathering community support in preparation for the progress of the Laws case through the courts:

> The committee voted to refer the case to the churches, the NAACP, which took action on the case on a previous occasion, and the Urban League. The committee will raise funds to assist in the expense of carrying this and other cases to the highest courts.[70]

Yet it quickly moved to other forms of protest, and Bass remembers the committee from its beginnings as "a group especially militant, Negro and white, organized under the name of The Home Protective Association."[71]

With the promise of support from the HPA, the Laws family moved back into their home even knowing that it would be considered contempt of court and they would almost certainly go to jail.[72] Another round of appeals commenced. Other homeowners suffering harassment and legal action found support from the HPA, and their weekly meetings were advertised on the front page of the *Eagle*. More covenant cases continued to be lost than won, but lawyers had begun moving beyond legal arguments to call witnesses on overcrowding and conditions in the Black Belt, such as Allen C. Woodard III, a local real estate broker who testified that all properties not covered by restrictive covenants in the area were already inhabited by Black families.[73]

In November 1944, the HPA and NVC co-sponsored a rally with the theme "Restrictive Covenants Are Sabotage."[74] Speakers included attorneys, radio personalities, and a member of the California Assembly, and present were Congress of Industrial Organization (CIO) reps and Loren Miller, who would go on to argue the test cases before the US Supreme Court for the NAACP. In December 1944, the HPA laid out its fight on two fronts. The first was educational:

> The people must be taught through education that this country is a democracy, a real democracy.
>
> To promote this educational propaganda the HOPA plans to hold meetings in every section of the city—in halls, auditoriums, churches, school buildings, homes—everywhere a meeting can be held. We propose to have speakers, white and black, from every minority group give heart-to-heart talks on the absurdity of fostering this horrible Fascism at home, while hypocritically supporting our boys fighting Fascism in Europe and Japan.[75]

The second front was in the courts and, in an interesting aside, "The HOPA does not advocate violence of any kind. We shall vigorously oppose anything of the kind. But we do plan to unite all the legal forces of the city, of the state, and of the country, if necessary, on our side."[76]

A conference in February 1945 revealed the number of affiliated organizations that felt housing was a primary issue: sponsors included the HPA along with the National Lawyers Guild, Council for Civic Unity, Catholic Interracial Council, NAACP, Urban League, Los Angeles Industrial Union Council-CIO, American Civil Liberties Union, and the American Veterans Committee, among others.[77] The panels focused on legal, legislative, political, and educational strategies whose findings fell into two basic categories—that of support for concrete policies and bills that ended de jure segregation through covenants and appraisals and created new laws to outlaw discrimination, and the creation of more housing to relieve the desperate problem of overcrowding, such as the following recommendations:

- That the National Housing Authority immediately program 40,000 public housing units and 14,000 private homes, all of which shall be made available to all races.
- That FHA policies and procedures be clearly formulated so that the agency will cease:
  - the extension of racial restrictive covenants in new areas;
  - basing the guaranteeing of loans on the use of such covenants;
  - referring to race in any form in the Underwriting Manual as relates to considering applicants for FHA mortgage loans.
- Educating the people to the shocking discrimination, and unfair rationing of homes [that exist] for a group of our population.[78]

In the hope that some whites might desire integration, some effort was also put into winning support within an entire tract for voluntarily opting out of their racial covenants. Another group of recommendations sought to both deconstruct and problematize the idea of race itself, while also educating whites on the bases of their own prejudices:

- That, as a means of confronting the fallacy of race ideology, in litigation, the question of race of each party be put to the test.
- The second aspect is that of helping the people of the community build a broad base of facts and ethical principles which will serve to govern their relationships to individuals and groups. We must throw out the myths of racial superiority. The facts of anthropology and biology regarding race need to become the active possession of everyone in the Los Angeles community. It is a long-time educational program which should be implemented immediately.
- We cannot afford, nor do we really want, to continue to act on emotional, unexamined prejudices. Los Angeles does not need to repeat the patterns of older cities. Los Angeles can eliminate undemocratic and unfair residential segregation now.[79]

The group acknowledges here the differences in LA's form and the less intensely violent, deeply rooted segregation found in older cities like Detroit or Boston—LA continued to be seen in many ways as a relatively privileged place for Black people.[80] At the same time they acknowledged the ultimate similarities in the housing issues that Black communities faced, many of them based in racism and a crude biological determinism.

In line with the growing alliance-building that was taking place, the collective that formed the HPA began to take seriously the need to reach out to other minority groups who also suffered under covenants. Charlotta Bass had already begun this process two years earlier, in 1943, visibly working with the Mexican and Mexican-American communities in support of the youth indiscriminately arrested and charged with murder in the infamous Sleepy Lagoon case, as well as those facing state brutality in the so-called "zoot suit" riots. Regina Freer has noted that this support of brown youth in the face of police brutality and state racism shows Bass to be "one of the city's earliest advocates of a black-brown coalition."[81] On January 1, 1945, the HPA published a resolution in the *Eagle* regarding the return of Japanese citizens interned during the war. Acknowledging that Japanese homes had primarily been occupied by African Americans during their absence, the HPA firmly supported their absolute right of return and called upon all levels of government to provide adequate housing both for those returning and those who would be evicted and unable to find new homes. They also actively invited Mexican, Chinese, and all other minority groups to join them in another mass meeting to be held on the housing question.[82] The *Eagle* also increasingly began covering covenant cases filed against Native Americans, Filipinos, and Koreans.[83]

An electoral strategy was also being brought to bear—Bass decided to run for the city council seat of District 7 to bring visibility to their issues. She proceeded to make restrictions one of the principal topics of her campaign, pledging to end Jim Crow housing.[84] The other planks reflected what were viewed as the most pressing issues of the time:

1. Fight for postwar security;
2. A building program for homes for all who need them, regardless of race, creed, or colour;
3. Adequate health and recreational facilities;
4. Adequate wages, and the right of labor to organize and bargain collectively;
5. Reduce water, power, and light rates to the consumer;
6. Clean the streets;
7. A rehabilitation program for veterans.[85]

Her campaign was promoted in Black churches, clubs, social and political organizations, theaters, and gala fundraisers. Bass won enough votes in the initial contest to force incumbent Carl C. Rasmussen into a run-off, but she lost her final bid for the council seat.

Conditions for African Americans and other minorities continued to worsen.[86] NAACP President Griffith listed them in yet another mass meeting:

> racial and religious bigotry is increasing at an alarming rate . . . Racial tensions are mounting, thousands of Negroes are being laid off without regard to seniority of war needs, returning Negro war veterans are being discriminated against, police brutality is increasing, many Negro families are being evicted from their homes because of restrictive covenants.[87]

The struggle was coming to a boil on all fronts as mass meetings and conferences took place. In July 1945, the NAACP called a conference in Chicago; over the course of two days, thirty-three experts on restrictive covenants hammered out the road map for the NAACP's legal strategy to bring down racial covenants. At the local level, the Council for Civic Unity had formed in Los Angeles as a preventative response to the race riots in Detroit in 1943, and it began convening meetings of experts and organizations to strategize around rent hikes and the issue of housing covenants.[88]

The "Mobilization for Democracy" committee formed in July 1945 to protest the LA visit of fascist Gerald L.K. Smith—it would bring together the NAACP, the Hollywood Independent Citizens Committee of the Arts, Sciences and Professions, the National Citizens' Political Action Committee, the Abraham Lincoln Brigade, and others against what they called "native fascism."[89] In August the Mobilization held a conference, the goal of which, the *Eagle* stated, was to "sweep LA clean of fascist propaganda and organizations." According to the *Eagle*, over a thousand organizations attended the conference, held at City College, and set out a program to oppose housing discrimination and to support the new Fair Employment Practice Committee, won through pressure on the federal government.[90] Jobs were also on the agenda—African Americans were being laid off in massive numbers. By August 1945, 4,000 African Americans had reportedly been let go from central war work. The Eagle later reported:

> According to the Urban League survey, North American reported 16,789 white and 1349 colored workers were employed there at its highest peak in 1943. Personnel directors cite that 10,883 whites and 1307 Negroes have been laid off to date. Only 87 Negroes are employed at present, mostly semi-skilled classifications.[91]

Despite protestors' demands for city action and their packing of city hall, the city failed to implement any kind of action around discrimination.[92] The HPA held regular "mass meetings" and packed the courtroom for each appearance of the Laws family. Near the end of 1945, the *Eagle* notes that the city itself labeled the housing crisis "a disaster." Tensions almost reached the level of riot when police officers killed a Black soldier who had just returned from the front.[93]

Meanwhile, the Laws' case was also reaching the end of the appeals process. On November 30, 1945, the judge ruled that the Laws would have to vacate their home or go to jail. The work of the HPA in building a labor–community alliance in their support bore fruit in an impressive show of solidarity: the CIO staged a "mammoth parade" of up to 1,000 people who marched from their offices to the Laws' home, stopping at the judge's quarters and the county jail on the way. The HPA also held pickets in front of the offices of the two real estate agents suing the Laws.[94] In the end, though, Henry Laws and his daughter Pauletta, both workers in the defense industry, were arrested for contempt. Pauletta's brother and husband were serving in the armed forces, and came home after the war to find their family still imprisoned.[95] Upon Henry and Pauletta's release, they continued the struggle to live in their home. Their willingness to be jailed and the mass marches in their support, marshaled by the HPA working together with labor, prefigured the mass movement of the 1950s and '60s more than anything that had come before.

The wealthiest members of the Black community lived on Sugar Hill, and when actresses such as Hattie McDaniel, Louise Beavers, and Ethel Waters were brought to trial for violating restrictive covenants in December of 1945, 250 people packed the courtroom to support them.[96] They won their case, but the white homeowners' group immediately appealed. In their defense brief to the State Supreme Court, attorney Loren Miller appealed to the recently ratified United Nations Charter of Human Rights. Their claim that the UN treaty guaranteed them freedom from discrimination made the *New York Times*, though the handful of paragraphs were surely fewer than any other story covering a major law case involving an Oscar winner.[97]

Whites continued organizing. The San Fernando Valley Council on Race Relations revealed that groups had begun soliciting signatures on restrictive covenants in a coordinated effort to blanket the entire San Fernando Valley with restrictions.[98] Meetings were called by homeowner associations in Lynwood, Ocean Park, and Huntington Park to start drives for the re-covenanting of properties, though the Lynwood and Ocean Park meetings at least were disrupted by activists and veterans who "made it clear that they had not fought to destroy fascism abroad only to have it camping on their doorsteps at home."[99] A clipping from the *Southwest Wave* preserved by Loren Miller shows how groups like the Property Owners' Protective Association were trying to expand the protections of their property even beyond covenants:

> With individual property owners now forced to institute expensive lawsuits to enforce property restrictions, proponents are seeking a more effective way of enforcing restrictions, possibly through governmental channels.[100]

Others were already not leaving it to "expensive lawsuits"; a case of arson claimed a home and the lives of a family of four in Fontana, and numerous cross burnings and hate crimes took place.[101] A handful of letters from homeowners to Governor Earl Warren, all saved as a representative sample, reveal the widespread feeling of a community under attack. Several discuss it as a war; one family asks Warren to please stop the invasion of Negroes as "the Mexican situation is bad enough, but to add negroes!!! Please don't let California be ruined."[102] This echoes the anger of those who feel they have been trapped in areas where all whites have fled in the face of the Black "invasion," all of them mentioning the lowering of property values associated with the visibility and stereotyped behaviour of African Americans.

Nonetheless, African Americans continued to organize. The housing committee of a renewed National Negro Congress began meeting in the Eagle offices jointly with the HPA in August 1946, and together they once more organized protection for homeowners in the face of mobs as Bass had done in 1914.[103] Given the extent of such popular hatred, it shouldn't be a surprise that many of the employees and elected officials of the City and County of LA would channel their hostility into city policies and politics. Yet, it still comes as a surprise that their racism should be so virulent as to cause the city to lose federal funding. Working with an ally in the City Housing Commission, the HPA discovered that the city of LA had lost 40 percent of the federal appropriation for slum clearance by declaring that LA had no slums. In the words of their source: "They refused to let us make a survey of the city's districts . . . They said there were only dirty N— [sic], Mexicans, Chinks, and Japs in those poor districts and they ought to be made to get along the best they could."[104] Once again we see clearly the power of racism to trump economic common sense, creating a new understanding of the city's responsibility as being solely to its white residents. The *Eagle* article continued that only 1 percent of the privately built housing was available for African Americans, and that real estate people "said that they wanted to make everything as unpleasant for Negroes in LA as possible so they would go back to Louisiana and Georgia."[105]

Strategic research carried out by reporters and HPA members brought additional insight into the mechanisms, and profitability, of renewing restrictive covenants in bulk across entire areas. In 1947, a Compton city council member had come up with a scheme to use unemployed vets to solicit restrictive covenants. They were to ask each white homeowner for a $10 fee to set up the covenants; part of the money was to go to the building of a war memorial, and the vet himself was to receive $1 from each transaction. When popular pressure forced the withdrawal of this scheme, the vets were referred to M.C. Friel and Associates for work, an outfit whose unsuspecting secretary gave a great deal of interesting information to the *Eagle* reporter who called her. She stated that Friel and Associates was based in Hayward, but had been brought to Compton by the Junior and Senior Chambers of Commerce—and that they were working in several other towns. She revealed that the FHA had promised that a new housing development in the area would be restricted to whites only if the rest of the area could be "sewed up tight" with blanket restrictions starting at 126th Street—"that's where we hold the line. We're not going to let them (non-Caucasians) get beyond that point."[106] Large portions of the surrounding areas were to be covered. The *Eagle*'s editors clearly didn't believe the FHA's official denial. The city of Compton was not alone in its efforts to maintain restrictions—Pasadena was also sued in October 1947 for inserting racially restrictive covenants into the deeds of properties acquired through tax defaults.[107]

The *Eagle* uncovered another set of connections between homeowner associations, the real estate industry, and finance in analyzing another restriction drive:

> Actively directing the drive as secretary of the Southwestern Wilshire Protective Association is real estate man Charles R. Shattuck, a brother of Edward S. Shattuck, vice chairman of the Republican State Central Committee. President of the racist outfit is W.W. Powell, Vice president of the Title Insurance & Trust Co. advertised as the "largest and oldest trust company pony in Southern California—assets $31,000,000."
>
> It has been estimated that this title company handles 90 percent of all restrictive covenant procedures in Los Angeles.[108]

The homes of both Shattuck—who would go on to lead CREA and play a prominent role on the Los Angeles Real Estate Board—and Powell can be seen in Map 6. Both are very close to the flurry of lawsuits in the Crestmore tract and Sugar Hill. A report directly from the meeting showed that white property owners were continuing to call on a discourse of white patriotism in their defense of white neighborhoods:

> Shattuck urged his listeners on Wednesday night to fight these non-Caucasian residents, as a civic duty. "I could sell out," said he, with a fine show of patriotic martyrdom, "and buy a home somewhere else. That would be easy to do. But I wouldn't be doing my duty as a patriotic citizen if I did that."[109]

On a national level—spurred no doubt by the many member branches such as that in Los Angeles fighting tooth and nail against such covenants and the pressure of papers like the *Eagle*—the NAACP had been preparing for a final showdown on covenants for several years. In July 1945, they called a national two-day legal conference to plan and coordinate a strategy for bringing a strong enough case before the Supreme Court to win a decision finding racial covenants unconstitutional. Thirty-three people attended, including Loren Miller of Los Angeles, with Thurgood Marshall serving as special counsel.

The NAACP and the Chicago Council Against Racial and Religious Discrimination sponsored a second conference on "The Elimination of Restrictive Covenants" in Chicago in May 1946, supported "by more than forty labour, civic, religious, housing, and veterans groups."[110] In January 1947, another meeting of key lawyers took place, where it was agreed to carefully select the case to be submitted to the Supreme Court, to ensure that it had the best chance of winning. Rather than waiting, however, the defense lawyers in *Shelley v. Kraemer* submitted their covenant case for certiorari, prompting the NAACP to do the same with the most promising case of their own. The two teams were friendly, but worked separately. In September 1947, another one-day conference, with forty-four people in attendance, was held to plan the best strategy for the Supreme Court argument. Many of the arguments and supportive briefs were sociological, establishing the claim that covenants were not a private but a public issue.[111]

With test cases on the constitutionality of restrictive covenants pending before the Supreme Court, it finally seemed that the tide was turning. A local progressive judge, Stanley Mosk, threw out a total of ten restrictive covenant cases.[112] More good news came when the US attorney general filed a plea with the Supreme Court in support of the NAACP position.[113] This was the first time the federal government had interceded in a case involving racial discrimination, and the *Eagle* notes the national and international pressure required to bring forth such an action, particularly the NAACP's filing of an appeal with the United Nations against Jim Crow.

In the aftermath of World War II and under a Cold War politics in which the Soviet Union could point to unarguable human rights abuses against African Americans in their condemnations of American capitalism, pressure was on the government to demonstrate some movement.[114] These international forces had little effect on US citizens, however. Even as the legal battle played out in the Supreme Court, a mob of more than 100 people formed on the lawn of Mr. and Mrs. King with the following message: "We don't want n— here. [sic] This time we are giving a peaceful warning. The next time it won't be so peaceful."[115] The drives to blanket neighborhoods with restrictions continued; in February 1948, the *Eagle* highlighted such an attempt by the West Pacoima Park Property Owners' Association, meeting in the Pacoima Chamber of Commerce building.[116]

In spite of widespread grassroots opposition and horror, the Supreme Court ruled restrictive covenants unconstitutional on May 5, 1948, in the landmark case *Shelley v. Kraemer*. Originating in St. Louis, it would be argued by Thurgood Marshall and LA's own Loren Miller for the NAACP and stand as a victory for the nation. It was the result of decades of litigation against restrictive covenants by lawyers nationwide, years of specific strategizing by NAACP attorneys, and of course mass action and pressure directed at the federal government through the war, challenging the US's role as the defender of equality and democracy across the world.[117]

Chapter 3

White Reaction

Old Walls Torn Down and New Ones Raised

It is to be noted how lapses in the administration of justice make an especially disastrous impression on the public: the hegemonic apparatus is more sensitive in this sector, to which arbitrary actions on the part of the police and political administration may also be referred.

Antonio Gramsci

The battle was won both in the courts, through pointing out the contradictions between restrictive covenants and constitutionally guaranteed rights, and through political and social pressure around covenants' discriminatory and dangerous social impact.

In this case, the public was to a limited extent the American people, but the international community played a key oversight role as it worked to form a broadly envisioned United Nations to stand against fascism and move toward world peace. In this conjuncture, Black communities proved visible and strong enough in their legal challenges to provoke a reversal by the US government in both policy and law around race and property to maintain a semblance of legitimacy as a champion of democracy abroad. African Americans felt jubilant. In June 1948, the *Eagle* reported the move-in day of a Black family to a restricted tract as front-page news. White feeling, however, was so strong that Mr. Kelley used a police escort to take the family in.[1] Singer Nat King Cole also made front-page news as he moved into his own new home in exclusive Hancock Park, in the teeth of vocal protest from that neighborhood's homeowner association.[2]

This shift in government policy did not correspond to an economic or ideological shift, even though it undercut the legitimacy of openly white supremacist viewpoints and the state-sanctioned ability to maintain exclusively white areas. White neighborhood organizations continued to fight the legal battle to save racial covenants. In *Barrows v. Jackson*, a group of homeowners brought a lawsuit against the white seller for damages rather than the minority buyer. It lost before the California Supreme Court in January of 1951.[3] Eleven homeowner associations from Los Angeles filed official briefs in support of the plaintiffs when the case reached the Supreme Court. When it lost once more, the LA-based attorneys filed a petition for a rehearing that betrayed the level of desperation felt by their clients. It stated that the covenants were not due to simple "wilfulness" but based upon "facts of life." It quoted statistics, showing that murder and crime rates were higher in nonwhite areas, and ended:

> Every national Negro magazine known to petitioners on the news stands this month, June, contains one or more articles, either featuring or displaying intermarriage between Negroes and whites and in other ways illustrating the example being set for Negroes. There is no room in the philosophy being taught to Negroes for the white man's personal freedom of choice of associates. This attitude among Negroes who move into white neighborhoods adds to the other factors which, equally understandably, make them unwelcome neighbors.[4]

Most white response to the loss of *Shelley v. Kraemer* was not in the courts, however. The HPA also continued in operation into the 1950s, working to protect African Americans from violence after moving into their new homes, along with other organizations such as the South Interracial Council.[5] Following the May decision, seventy-five whites watched a twelve-foot-high cross burn in Eagle Rock, while others made threatening phone calls and committed acts of vandalism.[6] They hurled milk bottles from fast-moving cars, burned more crosses and formed mobs of 150 people to repeatedly threaten another family.[7] In the last instance, police refused to disperse the mob, but confiscated the homeowner's gun. The *Eagle* reported the leaders of the group to be a C.C. Collins, white realtor, and Ben Fisher, apartment owner, and described how the police harassed those present to help protect the family:

> Six members of the Southeast Interracial Council were present Saturday night. Whenever they tried to speak they were denounced as Communists. When two of them left the mob scene, they were followed and stopped by deputy sheriffs. The deputies, who had made no move to search any of the mobsters, frisked the council members, examined their identification data, and ordered them out of the neighborhood with the warning, "Don't come back. We know you guys just want to stir up trouble."[8]

In September of the following year, six people stood in front of a house while flames licked at the back and a family slept inside—the house had earlier been peppered with buckshot and the windows broken. They had started the fire next to the gas main; the only reason it did not explode was that the gas was not due to be turned on until the next day. The police and arson squad took hours to arrive after being called, and only after the *Eagle* had been called and several carloads of men had arrived to protect the home.[9] There were many more cases of threats, intimidation, mob activity, and arson.

In March 1952, a home on Dunsmuir Street was bombed, destroying the front of the house while the family slept in the back, and part of the home across the street. Police stated that the work had been professional, and it was the third bomb to have been exploded on the street. Residents had also received dozens of crude warnings, which they had turned over to the police. No arrests were made.[10] The attacks, threats, invocation of the KKK, use of broken bottles, and tacks on lawns and driveways continued through the 1950s. While the state could no longer openly maintain the spatial boundaries of the community of consent, it maintained neutrality as white communities took coercion into their own hands even as they blamed African Americans themselves for all the violence. White supremacy continued hegemonic, and continued to prioritize the maintenance of white space and privilege, despite both the withdrawal of support for covenants by the state, and the shifts in moral consciousness brought by anti-fascist struggle. Police seemed to agree with the sentiments expressed by one of the leaflets being distributed en masse by one of the many white protection groups: "It is true that Negroes have brought upon themselves criticism, hatred and distrust by forcing their way into neighborhoods restricted against them."[11] Local papers had headlines like "Migration Causes Big Jump in LA's Negro Population," and graphics, such as that from the *Mirror-News* showing "Negro migration":[12]

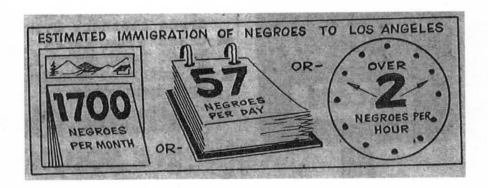

The housing crisis deepened, with increasing violence against those moving into white neighborhoods. Map 7 charts the worst incidents against recognized racial faultlines and the HOLC map to indicate the homogeneity of race and class, showing that only a few conflicts occurred along the fiercely held boundaries as could be expected. Instead, some of the most destructive anger was found in wealthier neighborhoods, where owners had more to lose. Most acts also seemed directed against families moving into the middle of recognized white areas. The one recorded case of a family of four being burned to death occurred far to the east, in the suburb of Fontana, after two of the town's deputies visited issuing warnings that they were "out of bounds" and needed to leave the town.[13] These incidents show exactly why movement out of the ghetto would still hug its boundaries, where the support and protection of other African Americans could be the difference between a fighting chance at keeping a new home, or being forced out through isolation, more extreme violence and possibly death. This in turn ensured that rather than achieving integration, the ghetto simply spread, the spatialities of struggle further entrenching white fears of "invasion" and their desperate search for possible ways to rebuild the political, legal, and ideological supports for preserving white privileged space.

A series of interviews about this period carried out by Chicago sociologist Rose Helper in the mid-1960s give some sense of how the white community and the real estate professionals who served them experienced racial turnover in the neighborhoods where such a wave was about to occur:

> As the Negro movement comes closer, as rumors circulate about their having bought or being about to buy in the area, and as Negroes walk or drive up and down the streets, the people of the area become "concerned," "excited," "jittery," "disturbed," "troubled," "worried," "apprehensive," and "up in the air." Some owners and tenants leave. White people who ordinarily would buy in the area begin to hesitate. The broker's sales decrease or stop. This is the "doldrums," "twilight zone," "stagnation period," "stalemate period"—when white people will not buy and Negroes are not yet buying. Speculators begin to buy. Then a house or property is sold to a Negro, and the block is "broken." The exodus begins. Negroes may now occupy only two or three properties in the block, but, since probably a larger number of families are living there than before, there seem to be many Negroes in the area. White people become alarmed, put properties up for sale, and vacate housing. Some people cannot leave. Some remain on principle—those who will not sell their properties to Negroes, and those who see social good in an interracial community. Others who remain believe that they can "manage" the area so it will not go Negro or hope that some quota can be maintained.[14]

CORE member Bruce Hartford belonged to one such family of activists. His memories of growing up in Leimert Park—recorded as a blue area on the HOLC maps, and once a model of how to maintain a segregated high-value neighborhood through covenants, deed restrictions, and a neighborhood association—corroborates this story.[15]

Just under ten years after *Shelley v. Kraemer*, the "ghetto" had moved from Main to the borders of Leimert Park, and Hartford's story shows just how quickly a whole block could change:

> So when we moved in, the South Central ghetto was about seven blocks away. And over the course of time, each year it moved a block or two closer to us. So then one year, I remember one spring, I think it was '56 or '57, they "busted" our block. Meaning they sold a home to a Black family. And then every weekend over that summer, I'd be mowing the lawn and I'd see these real estate people come up and say, "Oh, Mr. Hartford (to my father of course) I am sure you know what's happening here to the neighborhood. I know you have concerns. I see you have children,

and you know what's going to happen to the schools. And we really want to help you. We will buy your house, right now, today, write out a check for—" I guess it was around $30,000. Now the house was worth $40,000, probably. These are ballpark figures from a kid's memory so probably not accurate . . . over that one summer, just three months, they turned over every house on that block except ours and this Swedish family next door who refused to move. Now during that time, the white kids who were moving out, and the Black kids who were moving in, there was enormous tension, because the white families were losing the most valuable thing they ever had in their lives. They're white working-class people. They're being driven out—as they see it—of their homes and losing a quarter of its value. Meanwhile, the Black families coming in, trying to get rid of the ghetto, and the ghetto is coming.[16]

He describes a process of panic and loss and anger, in which fear of the ghetto and economic investment are inseparable but where speculators are really the "bad guys." Hartford's vantage point as a committed civil rights activist allows him to see the tragedy of the inexorable expansion of the ghetto given white fear and the immense profits to be made buying from owners willing to sell at a loss, then selling to buyers willing to pay a premium. This only became possible in a market where there existed the dually reinforced belief that race defined a neighborhood's value and whites' fear of all nonwhites, alongside a population still trapped in overcrowded, unsafe, and dangerous housing willing to pay more than they could afford to get out. Racial boundaries certainly meant big money to speculators, but it was more complicated, not least because most realtors and community builders distanced themselves as men of ethics from speculators and block busters.[17]

At least in some cases, the initial process of neighborhood change seems to have been motivated by homeowner profit rather than panic. This was explained in 1950 by a representative from Neighborly Endeavour, Inc. of Leimert Park to a meeting of the Normandie Avenue Protective Association—a gathering so crowded that it had to be split and held in two sessions of about 150 people. It was chaired by a realtor named Ted Roko.

The trouble is not with the Negroes for wanting to live in a good neighbourhood. The trouble is with your selfish neighbors who want to sell for an abnormally high price . . . That is why you must talk to your neighbors. Don't assume that they are going to do the right thing. Make it clear to them that you wouldn't hurt them by selling your property to a non-Caucasian and you expect them to play fair with you . . . We're going to have to be good neighbors in this . . . This experience has drawn us much closer together in Leimert Park. We had to buy up one piece of property and we're going to sue the person who sold it to a Negro. There are a lot of constructive things that we can do now that we are organized . . . We chose the name Neighborly Endeavors, Inc. because we realize that it is only through loving our neighbors that we are going to be able to protect our community . . . You will have to buy up this first piece of property which has been sold to a Negro. You may have to buy a few more.[18]

There was not yet talk of speculators—rather, of greedy neighbors. But it is the 'neighborliness' of it that disturbs most, because it is so clearly a matter of loving your *white* neighbors, protecting your *white* community—and the boundaries of the community of consent could not be more clear. The threat from outside brought its members closer together. It is not simply their property values that they are protecting, but their whiteness. They are not alone in cloaking their racism in such Christian language of brotherhood.[19]

Tracking the operations of such groups through their experience of the backhand of such "loving" organizations, the *Eagle* gives the following list:

The Neighborly Neighbors. The Neighborly Endeavor. The Ministers Association, the Margaret Hess Association and several others. The single purpose of all these groups is to prevent Negroes from moving into certain areas considered restricted by the leaders of the organization, or to force Negroes out by fair means or foul.[20]

Nor had the organizing activities of Neighbourly Endeavour, Inc. to prevent sales to nonwhites gone unnoticed.[21] When a Black family did move into the neighborhood, the friendly people of Leimert Park responded by running a hose through a window one day while they were away, flooding the kitchen and cellar. Through the intercession of Bass, a twenty-four-hour guard was mounted over the home.[22] Perhaps this was the same family cited above who allowed their good neighbors to buy them out.

The responses of white homeowners that remained roughly within the law were remarkably parallel to that of the real estate profession, even down to language—not entirely surprising given the number of groups documented by the *Eagle* where realtors held leading positions. The response of the CREA was, on one hand, to emphasize that the Supreme Court had not invalidated the restrictions themselves as owners were free to discriminate as they chose; the state simply could not enforce such covenants.[23] On the other hand, they launched a short-lived campaign to obtain a constitutional amendment to secure race restrictions. President Alfred Rea's address on the subject, mailed in a letter to every NAREB member board, is worth quoting at length:

For many decades prior to this recent decision the principle of law was well established that such restrictions, under proper conditions, were valid, and enforceable by the Court. Acting upon this long-established principle of law, millions of home owners of the Caucasian race have constructed or acquired homes in areas restricted against occupancy by Negroes. The practice of surrounding homes in such area with the security of such restrictions has become a traditional element of value in home ownership throughout this country.

The recent decisions of the Supreme Court abovementioned have destroyed the values thus secured. The threat of occupancy by Negroes of property in such areas depreciates the value of all home properties and constitutes a direct deterrent to investment in the construction or acquisition of homes of superior quality whether large or small.

The unfortunate feature of the situation is that those who suffer most are the owners of comparatively modest homes.

The magnitude of the economic and social loss with which we are confronted is appalling. The widespread depreciation in value of homes, the instability of home ownership, and the discouragement of construction and acquisition of homes are conditions that menace the family life of the nation as we have enjoyed it in the past. Additionally, the insistence of some Negroes upon moving into areas previously restricted exclusively to the occupancy of Caucasians will necessarily create racial tensions and antagonisms and do much harm to our nation's social structure.[24]

While the constitutional amendment proved unworkable, the California Real Estate Board did not change its beliefs or practices. In 1950, the board was asked for its legal opinion on whether a board could discipline a member for selling property in contradiction to its racial restrictions; the answer was a resounding yes.[25]

They were also very open in the August 1948 issue about how they could continue to restrict areas by race (and class) without using covenants:

Several proposals have been made for securing restrictions on ownership or occupancy which will not run afoul of the Supreme Court decisions.
1. Vesting title to an entire tract in a corporation owned by the residents of the tract.
2. Putting up a cash bond with a homes association which would be subject to forfeiture in the event of occupancy of any home site by a person or persons not approved by the homes association.
3. Forming a homes association, the members of which are the owners of building sites within the residential tract, and prohibiting occupancy except to those persons or families who hold an occupancy permit issued by the homes association.

The advantage of the last alternative is that it will permit exclusion of undesirable whites. If fairly administered so as to exclude undesirable persons irrespective of race or color, no difficulty should be encountered in its enforcement.[26]

The white families like those remembered by Bruce Hartford (and members of Neighbourly Endeavours, Inc.), did not move to the suburbs through a happy process of choice and social upgrading. They felt they had been invaded and robbed by African Americans, pushed out of a community they had believed was protected by legal contract and had worked hard to defend. It seems natural that most would approve of all of the above measures suggested by CREA, as they would undoubtedly be seeking out new homes even more defensible than the old. Block by block, struggle to maintain the racial boundaries "scientifically" supported both by professional appraisal practices and a white nationalist–Christian rhetoric of patriotism and community caused a traumatic hardening of the lines between "us" and "them." Capitalizing on the fight against fascism in Germany, Black struggle had forced varying levels of retreat from open white supremacy at home and neutrality from the law regarding segregation, a breach in the legal definitions of white community rights, but it did not remove the economic foundation of such common sense nor the desire for separation. It must have made it easy to accept, even welcome, increasing privatization and the reduction of personal freedom to try and maintain the white neighborhoods of an earlier status quo: the protection of both use and exchange value, white wealth and privilege, along with its social reproduction.

Capital rolled into the building of exclusive and restricted suburbs. Charlotta Bass had always recognized residential segregation as one of the key issues facing the African American community, and this spatial awareness of the struggle only increased through her growing radicalization over the decades. Writing in 1960, she also noted the commitment of whites to maintain this segregation as the next frontier of struggle:

> And it also became apparent that some way of dealing with the tract developers of suburban communities had to be found. One after another of these large new suburban areas was built and the developers were at great pains to make them all-white. Restrictive covenants were not even needed.[27]

WHAT WAS WON AND WHAT WAS LOST

In spite of forces pushing for their containment through the first half of the twentieth century, there occurred widespread individual resistance against the formal and informal mechanisms that sought to force and keep African Americans tight within the ghetto. The 1920s saw the first coordinated effort to win the right of Black homeowners to live anywhere they could afford, through an alliance of homeowners and a propaganda effort to prove the worthiness of African Americans of wealth and status. This pragmatic collective effort that tried to take capitalism at its word, organized and given voice by Charlotta Bass in the pages of the *Eagle*, would come to grief against an unyielding white racism that refused to see African Americans as equals, and that would fight at every level to keep white neighborhoods white.

Beginning in the 1930s, new efforts arose to end racial covenants and segregation as part of a broader struggle to end racial discrimination and Jim Crow in all of its forms. In the post-World War II climate, these marches, demonstrations, and carefully fought legal cases would pick up enough social and moral force to end the legal enforceability of housing covenants, as well as usher in the final period of decline for Jim Crow.[28] Instead of ending segregation, however, the new neutrality of the government and the removal of the legally enforceable props of housing segregation, along with World War II's challenges to fascist ideologies, would bring about a new articulation of strategies and racial ideologies to maintain white space; this in turn articulated with the investment of capital and materials freed by the end of the war into the construction of immense suburban housing developments. In so doing, whiteness remained the key factor recognized by developers in the creation of commodified social space, the building and selling of a "place of privilege" and "place of happiness."[29] To preserve and defend white residential space, CREA looked to the privatization of neighborhood developments and the creation of mechanisms that allowed developers and neighborhoods to discriminate against peoples of color without openly declaring race as the basis for discrimination. The results, and a further development of the potentialities of privatization and covertly discriminatory practices, are further explored in the next chapter. But this did not go unchallenged in the turbulent era of the 1950s and '60s, and a new generation of activists would emerge, drawing on theories of non-violence and direct action to fight against segregation.

Part II

1960s

Bringing Down the Hate Wall

Chapter 4

CORE and the Testing of the White Suburbs

Without a doubt, the Supreme Court victories of 1948 and 1953 had shaken the ideological, legal, and political articulations of segregation, and the African American community took advantage of this crack in the walls of white hegemony to expand beyond its earlier racial boundaries. Yet the racialized economics of land values remained intact. After the racial covenants that had protected a de jure segregation were rendered powerless, white homeowner associations, professional realtors, and developers worked to connect and build new spatial, ideological, legal, and political supports for segregation to protect white space and privilege. But a new kind of justice movement was rising that would try to end this hegemony once and for all by striking out into the newly expanding suburbs—with all of the militancy and direct action associated with the civil rights movement of the late 1950s and '60s.

Charlotta Bass wrote her last *Eagle* editorial in April of 1951 at the age of seventy-seven, control of the paper being wrested from her in what Scott Kurashige describes as "the most historic Cold War shift in Black community leadership."[1] She had not bowed before the anti-communist witch hunts that would destroy so much of the left, but they had their impact on both her and the *Eagle*. Her final editorial expresses her frustrations with being pushed out by the group taking over the paper, headed by civil rights lawyer and former editor Loren Miller. While Bass had steadily moved to the left, Miller had moved to the center and the Democratic Party.[2] The *Eagle*, like LA's other Black newspaper the *Sentinel*, continued to cover the movement for racial equality, but it was now explicitly anti-communist and lost the immediacy of Bass's touch and sense of movement. Even so, it continued to be an invaluable resource until 1964, when it failed within months of being sold by Loren Miller to a consortium of local investors.[3] Released from her duties at the *Eagle*, Charlotta Bass ran for president of the United States in 1952 on the Progressive ticket and continued to be politically active until her death in 1969.[4]

In some ways, the Congress of Racial Equality (CORE) represented a clear break with this past. Led by a new generation of activists—many of them white—CORE members adhered to a national intellectual and spiritual organizational vision, one that determined both goals and strategy guidelines for achieving widespread integration. CORE emerged through work to develop new tactics for eradicating racism through direct action, building on Gandhi's philosophies of non-violence. In the

1950s and early '60s, CORE, like the SCLC, saw racism as primarily a moral issue and worked to unite groups of activists embodying the integration that they worked toward in the community. Their belief that the lived experience of integration was the best way to break down racial barriers led them to target segregated social and residential spaces, and put pressure on individual developers in wealthy suburbs who refused to sell to African Americans. This represented a rather different kind of movement than those driven solely by the needs of the Black community and led by that community, raising both problems and possibilities.

While this section looks to some extent at the breadth of CORE's organizing around segregation, it focuses on what would be their largest campaign in terms of both resources expended and the numbers of protestors involved—the picketing of developer Don Wilson. Wilson's practice embodied the way developers translated racial hierarchies as spatial hierarchies. In their massive campaign to end such discriminatory practices and dissolve LA's racial boundaries, CORE mobilized integrated picket lines, where hundreds were arrested demonstrating their belief in the justice of their cause, gaining considerable mainstream press coverage of the fight for integration for the first time. This forced a grudging acceptance of their moral rights even from the developers, and helped create political will for the passage of California's Fair Housing Act to prohibit discrimination.

Yet despite these victories in further shifting political and legal structures, they fell short in achieving any meaningful spatial integration or a shift in the economics linking race with land value. This section shows some of the ways in which the commitment to segregated white communities and the maintenance of privilege was renewed and strengthened in the face of this determined struggle. White supremacist beliefs were ideologically reframed to counter and reincorporate key aspects of the moral arguments posed against them. This withdrawal into a coded language of racism, buffered by a discourse of individual property rights, articulated with a like desire for withdrawal into the more insulated suburbs.

Changes in discourse did not shift the deep sense of need to defend the whiteness of property, as such racialization had already been encoded into its value—both the residential use value in terms of common sense understandings among whites of the best environment in which to live and to raise children, and the exchange value cemented into place through appraisal policies, mortgage regulations, and professional codes for both developers and real estate dealers. The city was already divided along invisible but fiercely held boundaries of white and Black territory. As these boundaries began to shift after the victory against racial covenants and white flight began, new strategies to defend white property articulated with the capital flowing into real estate development after World War II. Capital's need for a "spatial fix"—solving the problem of overaccumulation of capital through its massive investment in suburban development—intertwined with the new strategies for defending white communities, driving new forms of control and privatization.[5]

This is illustrated particularly well through examining CORE's campaign against community builder and developer Don Wilson, whose business practice of creating different developments for different races exploited to the full the city's racial hierarchies. While his policy was to sell homes to Asians, Mexicans, and whites in Dominguez Hills, and he completed a development for African Americans near Compton to deflect CORE's criticisms, he succeeded in withstanding a campaign to maintain his Torrance development for whites only, through an alliance with local homeowners, the police, and city government. Torrance City Council ultimately passed a resolution closing the entire neighborhood to strangers—essentially gating the community. This action forced CORE to discontinue direct action in favor of what would prove a fruitless effort through the courts. CORE's campaign helps put into context LA's uneven racial geographies and the deep inequalities found from one suburb to the next—how and why did the color line yield in places like suburban Compton after the victory against racial covenants, but continue to be maintained in other suburbs like Torrance against all odds? This pivotal conflict shaped both future civil rights struggles and efforts to preserve the hegemonic equation between white space and privilege as communities came to define themselves through ever more substantial walls.

CONGRESS OF RACIAL EQUALITY

CORE was established in 1942 in Chicago as a small, tight-knit organization. Particularly in the early days, people joined CORE almost as a vocation, and non-violence was viewed as a way of life for many of its early members—they often lived collectively, devoted considerable time to debating philosophy and strategy, while carrying out almost all decision-making through collective membership meetings.[6] Formed around a detailed memo about organizing a Gandhian-style "confrontation with American racism" from James Farmer (who would become CORE's future director) to his then-boss at the pacifist and antiwar Fellowship of Reconciliation (FOR), it was taken up by a group of student members of FOR at the University of Chicago and made a reality.[7] From this beginning, CORE had a clearly articulated vision for achieving its goal of racial equality: "CORE has one method—interracial, nonviolent direct action."[8] This strong identification with Gandhi's teachings continued to be central to CORE's practice, and his image featured on the cover of one of their key pamphlets.

CORE grew steadily under the auspices of FOR, organizing itself through small chapters around the country and forming a national board in 1943. Activities focused primarily on direct actions to desegregate commercial establishments such as restaurants, theaters, and skating rinks. A branch formed in Los Angeles, with a small group operating on a modest but consistent scale until 1948 brought red-baiting and charges of communism from the loyalty board. A group of about ten revived LA's CORE in 1955, but after two years of limited campaigning around employment discrimination, it almost folded. Organizing work started up again in 1958, still on a shoestring budget with some paid organizing time by an employee of CORE's national office, but with no office space.[9]

CORE came to national prominence in 1960 through its sponsorship of the Freedom Rides—courageous actions in which African American and white activists undertook direct action to integrate travel through the Deep South. White mobs greeted them at every stop as well as at state lines, their bus was firebombed and they were both beaten and jailed for refusing to recognize segregated bus facilities. CORE had already been in existence for almost two decades when the Freedom Rides sparked the national imagination and catapulted it into the civil rights spotlight.[10] They became one of the most iconic actions of the fight against Jim Crow in the South, receiving widespread media attention and interventions to support the Freedom Riders from President Kennedy himself.

Newly invigorated both by members who had participated in the Freedom Rides themselves and a large influx of new members inspired by them, CORE had its own LA office by 1961. When studied by a young graduate student in 1965, it had expanded far beyond its earlier core of twenty to twenty-five members to encompass officers and ten committees staffed by its membership, though this was falling from the heights reached in 1962–63. Peter Ralph Bartling's chart (below) shows both the structure of the LA chapter as well as its relationship to CORE as a national organization through representation at the district, regional, and national levels.

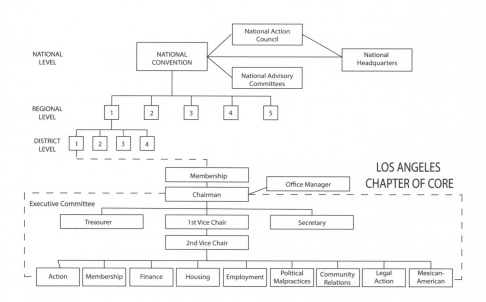

Above all else, CORE worked on an ideological level to challenge and transform racism, although when discussion and negotiation failed they put their physical bodies on the line through direct action. Drawing on Gandhi's works on non-violence and Thoreau's writing on civil disobedience, CORE's principal tactics became direct and nonviolent actions such as sit-ins and pickets.[11] They believed this to be a clear break from earlier race campaigns. A 1960's CORE pamphlet states: "A dramatic change in American society was plainly in the making, and it was the result of a dramatic change in anti-discrimination tactics."[12]

Some of these direct and confrontational tactics had clearly been used previously by other organizations. CORE, however, brought to the struggle a philosophical foundation, organizational resources, and a documented historical memory far more focused and collective than could be recorded in the pages of a newspaper or the stories of a handful of activists. Over time, CORE developed a refined and clearly articulated organizational way of thinking and of running campaigns. CORE believed in direct democracy and its goal was always to be driven and directed by its membership, but within the parameters of its identity, mission, and commitment to nonviolent action reinforced through membership orientations.[13] Ideally, chapters distinguished between active members who were allowed to vote—they used a register to track presence at committee and membership meetings—and supporting members who simply paid dues. These ideals, of course, often fell through, and internal reports show systems straining to keep up with new volunteers or track voting members.[14]

To ensure fidelity to their central vision, the national organization raised money and put together pamphlets outlining their goals, strategies, and principles of action as formulated over a period of almost twenty years. They held a long-range goal of complete social integration achieved through an integrated movement, and believed that ultimately to achieve this goal it was opinions and emotions that needed to change more than concrete political and economic structures.

> CORE seeks understanding, not physical victory. It seeks to win the friendship, respect and even support of those whose racial policies it opposes. People cannot be bludgeoned into a feeling of equality.
> CORE sees discrimination as a problem for all Americans. Not just Negroes suffer from it and not just Negroes will profit when it is eliminated. Furthermore, Negroes alone cannot eliminate it. Equality cannot be seized any more than it can be given. It must be a shared experience.[15]

They shared this approach with other civil rights leaders. Martin Luther King, Jr. wrote as part of the foreword to a CORE pamphlet published in 1961:

> We can and must win the mind of the prejudiced person. Force doesn't change minds. Anger reinforces fears. And that is why it is so terribly urgent to work out the techniques of changing people's minds, of allaying their fears about integration. CORE puts before people's eyes a new way of acting. You say and you show that feelings about segregation are silly, that customs can change without disaster following, and that this is the time to change them. And you proceed to demonstrate. Here is a method of achieving social change which we all may use.[16]

This is not to deny the concrete changes for which CORE fought—desegregated jobs, cafes, schools, public spaces, neighborhoods—nor that they used both political and economic leverage to achieve these things through legislation and legal action, alongside boycotts, pickets, and shop-ins to stop business as usual. Their central principles of nonviolent interracial action, however, were geared to changing hearts and minds through the winning of the moral high ground, and would become increasingly contested within the organization as frustrations rose around limited successes.[17]

This moral focus was also cause of (and caused by) their active antagonism toward communism—an animosity that during the McCarthy era and the Cold War spread to include all avowed socialists. Where the Great Depression and World War II had brought working relationships between the radical left and civil rights movements through the NNC and labor struggles, 1960s movement leaders felt it important to distance themselves for very practical reasons—usually because Communist Party members gave their first allegiance to the party and used their influence to control civil rights organizations according to party dictates.[18] Members of Black freedom struggles had long had connections to and held membership in the Communist Party, and they had thus experienced a number of changes in the party's line around race and revolutionary struggle. Many Black activists felt deeply betrayed by the party's abrupt shift from fusing struggles against racism and segregation with organizing grassroots direct action around unemployment and housing, to the creation of the popular front and a changing party line that ignored race to focus on class and the labor struggle once again.[19] Undoubtedly a second, and even more practical, reason was the efficacy of the state in using red-baiting to destroy organizations as exemplified by McCarthy and the House Un-American Activities Committee, among others. It is hard to tell how much this distancing was seen as a practical yielding to an American political reality, and how much was the result of differences in practice and ideology. After the loyalty board's investigation of LA's CORE for their work in coalition with communists, the 1948 National Convention unanimously approved a statement on communism that both "deplored the Red Scare" and found communism "destructive" to their principles.[20] CORE made their distance very clear and public, as in this pamphlet from the 1960s:

> The only people not welcome in CORE are "those Americans whose loyalty is primarily to a foreign power and those whose tactics and beliefs are contrary to democracy and human values." CORE has only one enemy: discrimination, and only one function: to fight that enemy. It has no desire to complicate its task by acquiring a subversive taint, and it avoids partisan politics of any kind.[21]

Along with partisan taint, CORE as an organization appeared to have also jettisoned all analysis of racism as connected to structural economic roots.

EARLY HOUSING CAMPAIGNS

In LA, early CORE actions focused primarily around discrimination in hotels. Chairman Earl Walter claimed that after testing seventy hotels and taking a dozen to court, they were able to ensure that by 1963, more than 65 percent of hotels would accept African American patronage as opposed to the 70 percent who would not accept it only seven years earlier.[22] They also formed an emergency committee to support African American families moving into white areas as a number of other groups had done before them (though this appears to have been relatively short-lived):

> When the first Negro family moves into a previously all white neighborhood, there may be threats of violence. CORE action can help stop such threats from being carried out. Los Angeles CORE in 1958 had an emergency committee, prepared to stand nonviolent guard duty. This committee established an all-night vigil when violence was threatened against a Negro teacher and his family who had bought a home in a formerly white area. There was no violence.[23]

It was not until 1961 that they formalized a new housing campaign for integration, and the Los Angeles chapter started meeting with sister organizations to inform them of their new campaign to "initiate integration in previously segregated areas."[24] Breaking the earlier patterns of expansion, this strategy targeted the large suburbs distant from established "safe" African American areas, striking into the heart of white space and its privileges of safe homogeneity, high property values, and local amenities, particularly higher quality education. The Centinela Bay Human Relations Commission agreed to help CORE by asking members to provide housing listings as they appeared, and their real estate members agreed to create "a simple checklist of the things a buyer should do to facilitate the orderly transfer of property, so that at no point in the transaction could a technicality frustrate the efforts to conclude a purchase."[25] Their optimism is almost contagious.

The CORE "Rules for Action," a thirteen-point list to guide members' actions, opens with: "1. A CORE member will investigate the facts carefully before determining whether or not racial injustice exists in a given situation."[26] A key part of CORE's housing strategy was developing testing procedures to prove the existence of discrimination—always there was a sense that establishing the facts of racism's existence would allow a rational confrontation and an end to racism itself. They put together a three-page instruction guide for volunteers who agreed to be checkers, in which peoples of color looking to buy or rent would partner with whites to establish if discrimination were present. A nonwhite applicant would first approach a landlord, agent or broker, to be followed closely by a white applicant in the case of their being turned away, giving a very similar family and income profile. The confidential instructions opened with a strong statement about standards of behavior and dress, as each volunteer would be "representing yourself, a technique, and the ethics of CORE."[27]

By early 1962, CORE had tested thirty-three buildings, and was involved in litigation and campaigning around several of them, among them an apartment building in Venice, and a family called Kennedy that was refused a home in an FHA-financed tract in Rolling Hills.[28] CORE was at the same time fighting to maintain the quality of their external work in spite of ongoing internal issues. An internal report describes the chapter as a "chaotic mess" due to "their rapid and uncontrolled expansion from a cosy little in-group prior to the Freedom Rides to a large, disorganized, amorphous group just after." National organizer Genevieve Hughes goes on to say:

> A source of continuing tension and a reason why my constructive work to resolve these problems is difficult is that the housing program has been plunged without previous planning into high gear. There is no time to find a breathing space to sit down calmly and plan and organize. The committee is simply not up to the demands placed upon it. Members lack time, training and transportation—at the same time they have six cases requiring some kind of action and new ones come in all the time. They cannot seem to get together to plan what to do to take care of these cases in an orderly fashion. As the pressure mounts and the cases are not taken care of tension and animosity reach the breaking point. The meeting I attended broke down into charges and counter-charges when the crying necessity was for planning for the future.[29]

In spite of this, the CORE housing campaign continued to grow through a series of large pickets. Leafletts were distributed on behalf of a nurse unable to rent an apartment on Venice Boulevard. When CORE opened negotiations with management, the reply was that if they rented to an African American, the other tenants "might not like" it.[30] CORE sought to dispute that fact, interviewing all of the tenants, attempting to convince them of the need for their support and giving them concrete actions to carry out.

FROM MONTEREY PARK TO WILMINGTON

CORE's testing strategy also established discrimination in the case of developer Montgomery Ross Fisher, after Bobby Liley and his family inquired about buying a home in the Monterey Park tract and "the salesman was quite frank in telling them that their race would be a hindrance to the development."[31] The *LA Times* quoted the developer as stating that "he supposed the company could be 'forced to sell to a Negro,' but prophesied that such a sale would cause 'perhaps a hundred persons to move out. I hope that bridge never has to be crossed.'"[32] When picketing achieved no result, a sit-down strike of ten to twelve people was initiated in the tract sales office the first weekend of March. That Monday, the Monterey Park City Council passed a resolution that, in the words of the *LA*

Times, "deplored" such discrimination.[33] The *California Eagle*, now under Loren Miller, reported the whole resolution, which actually "unanimously condemned discriminatory housing and called upon all citizens to conform to an open-housing policy."[34]

City council's support of CORE and the Liley family was to at least some extent due to the residents of the housing tract also joining in support of the campaign against the developer.[35] A Dr. Henry Burton and Luis Lopez circulated a petition pledging to accept "neighbors of good character . . . without regard to race, creed or country of origin" and that they as homeowners would not sell if an African American entered the neighborhood.[36] It certainly seemed to be a period of hope, as the *California Eagle* made room on the front page for both the Monterey Park City Council's statement in favor of open housing and the visit of Robert C. Weaver, head of the Federal Housing Agency, stating that it was only a matter of time before President Kennedy signed an executive order banning discrimination in housing with federal financing.[37]

In spite of the political pressure, the developer refused to budge. On the tenth day of the sit-in, management entered the office to lock the protesters out of the bathroom, and shut off the water and power. A series of pictures on the front page of the *Eagle* captured the moment, and showed some of the sit-in participants, African American and white, including Mrs. Liley and three Freedom Riders. To overcome the problems posed by a locked bathroom, neighboring households as well as a local filling station offered the use of their facilities, allowing the sit-in to continue.[38] Farrell notes that this was the first "prolonged overnight demonstration in CORE's history and is reminiscent of sit-down strikes in factories during the 1930s." While only the *Eagle* covered the story as front-page news, even the *LA Times* carried a note to the effect that the sit-in continued, though the story was buried on page 29.[39]

On the thirty-fifth day, the Lileys finally went into escrow to buy their new home—a deal made by a new seller who had acquired the property through a foreclosure sale.[40] Fisher had chosen to go bust on the development rather than sell to an African American family. No firm evidence provides the reason for the foreclosure, but in piecing information together it seems possible that having his own home much closer to the consolidation of the African American community in South LA might explain such obduracy, and economically the month-long occupation of the sales office must have played a significant role.

In its very limited coverage, the *LA Times* portrayed both the discrimination and the sit-ins as isolated problems leading to an individual victory, and gave minimal space for comment to Earl Walter, head of CORE. Walter contextualized the Lileys as one family among many: "At the moment, however, we must remind ourselves that only one Negro family, at the cost of great effort and sacrifice, has acquired a new home."[41] This is very different from the excitement and sense of movement building in Black newspapers like the *Sentinel*. In its pages, Walter is allowed to confront the full problem of segregation—only two percent of new building was then available to African Americans—and he goes on to clarify the difference between a token victory and CORE's ultimate goal. "[T]oken integration is only disguised segregation unless it is recognized to be the first small step toward the final goal of complete equality of opportunity in all phases of community life."[42]

CORE framed the Liley's purchase as a victory of collective human spirit and energy, as well as a privileging of human and civil rights over other rights. CORE's newsletter, celebrating the victory and raising much-needed funds, outlines just how much work went into maintaining the thirty-five-day picket:

> Such a simple occurrence [the Lileys moving into their new home], but how much effort has gone into making it a reality. How many hours of picketing, how many dinners and lunches and snacks and hot drinks for ten prepared and delivered, how many phone calls, how many blankets and sleeping bags and flashlights cheerfully loaned, how many personal services (transportation, baby sitting, sign painting) willingly donated, how many good people working together to demonstrate that we do live in a world where human values must outweigh all other values.[43]

It underlines the larger organizational goals behind the Monterey Park campaign (obviously to maximize fundraising appeal), and the larger victory in securing a home for the Lileys:

> But through the wide publicity this action received, CORE achieved its primary purpose, to throw light upon an incident of injustice in order to stir the moral conscience of a community or perhaps of the nation so that eventually the law or prejudice or institution from which the injustice arises may be eliminated. And as an immediate, tangible reward, we expect that here in the Los Angeles area other minority families are already assured a smoother path when they seek to buy homes in previously segregated areas ... Already calls have come in from people who have suffered discrimination in other areas of the city, and already we have started the work of careful investigation which will be followed by attempts to negotiate. We feel that now, in many cases, negotiations will succeed, but we know that we will have some stubborn cases which will demand direct action such as picket lines, boycotts, sit-ins.

The impact of the sit-in and victory in Monterey Park seemed to have the effect that CORE hoped for. An apartment block in West LA agreed to rent to a Black technician after negotiations and threat of a picket line.[44] A developer in Rolling Hills sold a home to a family of color, while another in the South Bay agreed to cease all discriminatory restrictions after CORE convened meetings between them and civil rights organizations, including local chapters of the NAACP and American Civil Liberties Union (ACLU). Supporting organizations like the Centinela Bay Human Relations Commission clearly hoped that this successful direct action would be the first and last, stating, "The Sit-In focused attention &

was essential to knock a large enough hole in the barrier thru which the mainstream of amicable mediation can now flow. Both are necessary to eliminate the barrier."[45]

Walter had noted the need to avoid tokenism and to make the Liley's case simply a step in an ever-expanding campaign to achieve full integration. To maintain the momentum and increase the numbers of people involved (particularly increasing the African American participation and expanding beyond it to other peoples of color) and communities put on notice about their lack of integration, LA's CORE initiated a program called "Operation Windowshop." A small article on the second page of the *Eagle* on May 31, 1962, announced the project for a weekend in late June that would "find members of all minority groups demonstrating their legal right to live anywhere in the city. They will seek to buy or rent houses or apartments in areas where discrimination has been widespread." One of CORE's manuals highlights their belief that part of the solution to segregation was helping convince African Americans to be bold in their housing choices and demand integration:

> A. Discrimination is widely practiced, and members of minority groups are often reluctant to face rebuff and discouragement in seeking housing.

> "Operation Window Shop"

> 1. may be directed at urging people to move out of ghettoes and familiarize themselves with housing market;

> 2. may be aimed at securing applicants;

> 3. requires considerable publicity, leafleting;

> 4. urge[s] large numbers of people to get out on same day or same weekend and look at housing whether they plan to rent or buy immediately or not.

> B. Purpose of "Operation Window Shop" in Los Angeles area of California was to help overcome this reluctance and accelerate housing integration.

> It also acquainted people of minority groups with the types of housing available in other areas, so that by the hundreds and thousands, we would get the habit of exercising our right of free choice.[46]

The last sentence seems to imply that initially organizers believed it was simply the absence of such a "habit of free choice" rather than violence and structural and institutional constraints that served as the greatest barrier to integration. The *Eagle* urged people to come along, whether or not they planned to move, to "demonstrate their determination that discrimination in housing must come to an end."[47] That African Americans still feared to go to the outlying white suburbs—and they, therefore, formed the principal targets for CORE—is made clear in the array of support they brought together: The Centinela Bay Human

Relations Commission, the San Fernando Valley Fair Housing Council, the San Gabriel Valley Council on Discrimination, and the Orange County Fair Housing Practices Committee.

CORE continued to support the Lileys through a drawn-out home-buying process—the developer, using a tactic that would become increasingly familiar, appeared to accede in a sale only to back out through the dragging out of paper-work and rejections for small technical faults. A second major campaign also began after CORE pressured the developer of Sun Ray estates in Wilmington to sell to an African American couple—the McClennans—after its initial refusal. Sun Ray accepted the application but submitted it to the Veterans Administration without noting the large down payment; it was eventually turned down after months of delay. The couple was told the house was no longer for sale, while white testers were immediately thereafter offered a chance to buy it. CORE's press release, dated October 14, 1962, announced a "new form of non-violent direct action—the 'dwell-in,' to prevent the house from being sold to anyone else before a lawsuit could be filed."[48] None of the mainstream media picked up the press release on the dwell-in until the *Eagle* reported the arrest of all seven "dwell-inners" on October 25. The arrests ended the dwell-in and CORE turned it into a "dwell-out"—camping on the lawn in front of the house.[49] Police arrested five more the following week. Unlike Monterey Park, the campers in South Bay faced violent harassment from the community:

> Yells, curses and taunts were shouted at the "campers" by white persons driving slowly by. Clods of dirt and rocks were thrown at them. Firecrackers were tossed into their midst and, on occasion, a lighted flare was hurled in their direction.[50]

The arrests escalated. On November 3, the *LA Times* reported the arrest of ten protesters, and the following day seventeen more were held under citizens' arrest by two neighbors who complained that their playing the guitar through the night was waking their children.[51] By November 8, the tally stood at forty arrests as CORE sent a call for support from the Freedom Riders in their hous-ing campaign.[52] While an injunction was granted against the developers to keep them from selling the home on Baypoint and to prevent discrimination against the McLennans, the loitering charges brought against over a dozen protesters were not dropped.[53] Apart from the immense organizational costs of dealing with bail and legal support for so many, the continuing case of the Lileys showed just how much work remained after any initial victory. The thirty-five-day sit-in at Monterey Park that had ended in April with "victory" continued to drag on, and the sale did not fully close until early December, allowing the Lileys to finally move in just before Christmas.[54] For the McLennans in Wilmington, it was nine months before an agreement was reached, and the discrimination lawsuit and the developer's counter lawsuit against the CORE sit-in participants were dropped as the house entered escrow.[55]

DON WILSON AND THE BATTLE FOR SOUTH BAY

CORE's major housing campaign of the period—against Don Wilson—was thus just one of multiple cases, even as CORE expanded their pickets to include all three of Wilson's tracts that, as we shall see, together embody many aspects of the articulation of space, race, and development in LA. CORE's campaign started in July 1962 in Dominguez Hills, where Wilson's policy was to sell to whites, Asians, or Latinos, but not to African Americans. CORE expanded their pickets to include Wilson's developments of Southwood Riviera Royale in Torrance, a strictly whites-only development, and Centerview Estates near Compton, which would sell to anyone of any race.[56]

Map 8 shows the three Wilson developments in relation to each other, the other sizable CORE campaign in the area at Sun Ray Estates, and their distance from previously reported attempts to break the color line. Most revealing are the differences in the three advertisements for the tracts. They fall more or less within the same price range, with Dominguez Hills as the cheapest, from $21,650 to $24,500, the Centerview homes running from $22,950 to $28,250, and Southwood starting at $25,700. The plans for the Dominguez Hills and Torrance developments are almost the same, with only slight differences in amenities and similar square footage for both houses and lots. The primary difference lies in the requirement for money down: Compton's Centerview starts at $695, Gardena's Dominguez Hills at $995, and Torrance's Southwood Riviera Royale is two to three times the previous amounts at $2,500. As the down payment is negotiable between builder and seller, the differences in the levels of up-front cash required arguably served to both increase the prestige of the Torrance neighborhood as an expensive and exclusive district while also acting as a flexible barrier to both Torrance and Gardena that could be lowered for the right kind of family if needed, but remained to justify refusing applications by families of the wrong race or class.

The difference in how Don Wilson as a developer treated these three different areas, and the racial boundaries he personally enforced for all three, is closely bound to their different histories. It is yet another reminder of how our present is so deeply shaped by our past and the openly legislated racism that defined it.

DOMINGUEZ HILLS AND COMPTON

The whole area was originally known as the South Bay, a series of suburban small towns alongside agricultural and oil-rich land about fifteen miles southeast of downtown Los Angeles. For the first half of the century, its agricultural potential drew early Japanese and Filipino migrants, as well as Mexican agricultural workers. While the Alien Land Law prevented Japanese families from owning property, their children signed short-term leases for land to grow vegetables and flowers. Families were regularly moved from their farmland every three years, and the Alien Land Law ensured that they could be moved from productive land for development subdivision or oil drilling at any time. Dominguez Hills was part of a large swathe of then-unincorporated land central to Japanese flower and vegetable cultivation for market, with the Japanese commuting to their farms from residential clusters closer to Compton or Gardena, where there were fewer restrictions.[57] Some Japanese families moved back after being interned in concentration camps during World War II. Among the irreparable losses they suffered was the razing of the Japanese community center in Gardena, which had possessions from many families being stored inside.[58] The Filipino community remained in place, along with small Mexican barrios that had survived the mass deportations of the 1930s on unincorporated and unrestricted lands.[59] When Don Wilson among others began developing the area into housing subdivisions in the early 1960s, it already contained a somewhat diverse population that Wilson continued to cater to.

To the north and east lay Compton, on land bought from a Spanish landowner to build a small farming and dairy community in 1866. It incorporated in 1888.[60] As Los Angeles's population boomed between the 1920s and '50s, Compton steadily grew into a working-class suburb of affordable homes close to manufacturing and industry, but also close to the growing communities of color living in the uncovenanted areas of Watts. A large, destructive earthquake in the early years of the Great Depression had saddled the small town with crippling debt, but it also built a tight-knit community invested in protecting its own. This investment included immense efforts to maintain Compton as white, blanketing the entire town with race restrictive covenants in 1921.[61] In conjunction with realtors, developers, and residents, the city council opposed public housing developments outside the city limits but near enough to them for residents to grow nervous. In 1947, the Compton Chamber of Commerce started a new drive to update the race restrictions for another ninety-nine years in what the *Sentinel* termed a "Ghetto Plan."[62] Both the *Eagle* and the *Sentinel* covered the drama arising from this and a proposed mixed-race federal housing development in Sativa, which elicited large meetings in opposition, grassroots covenant campaigns, and rumored backroom deals between Compton politicians, brokers, and FHA representatives.[63]

The census paid for by the town showed the success of their efforts to keep Compton white. In 1940, out of a total population of 16,198, only seventy-two were classified as nonwhite.[64] By October 1947, after the Second World War's internment camps, this had dropped to fifteen out of 32,254. Mexicans—still classified as white by the census at that time—were confined to what was known as the "barrio" in Compton's northern tip, next to a more diverse Watts and Willowbrook.[65] The transformation of Compton from a white town into a majority African American town over two decades is above all a story of fiercely and often violently contested geographies, a street by street battle for territory that created a series of racial faultlines (see Map 9). An African American realtor testified before the Governor's Commission on the LA Riots that 120th Street was once the northern border that whites attempted to hold. In 1947 the *Eagle* reports it as 126th Street.[66] The overturning of racial restrictions in 1948 proved an immense blow to resident and development interests, but it was hardly the immediate death knell. A few years saw the boundary move only a few more blocks, as the *Eagle* reported Compton realtors rallying behind the slogan of "Keep the Negroes North of 134th St!"[67] Loren Miller recalled in testimony before the Governor's Commission on the LA Riots that the slogan became "Keep the Negroes North of 130th St!"[68] This continual movement south represents the hard-won pushback by peoples of color, forcing the continuous redefinition of exclusionary space—by 1952 the nonwhite population had climbed to 5,807, an increase of 2,592 percent, making them about 9 percent of the total population.[69]

This expansion occurred house by house, street by street. In 1948, the *Sentinel* reported the smashing of windows and the use of paint bombs against newly purchased Black-owned homes, as well as against those of whites believed to be selling out their neighbors. More than ten incidents were reported in September and October alone, including three to four cross burnings.[70] Five years later, angry mobs met others like Alfred Jackson, a World War II veteran who faced down the angry members of the Compton Crest Improvement Association with two colt .45s. His wife, Luquella, kept firearms handy at all times, often in the pocket of her housecoat.[71] In 1956, a cross was burned into the grass at Compton High School after a fight between two students.[72] As they had in Leimert Park, Compton whites fought every inch of the way. Yet much of Compton lay west of Alameda—possibly the longest and most strictly held racial boundary in Los Angeles, such that even today almost no African Americans live in the communities to the east of it even though they are now predominantly Latino. At the time, the street was commonly referred to as the Berlin Wall; it divided South LA's neighborhoods of color as well as the small incorporated towns to the east such as South Gate, Maywood, and Lynwood—the early center of LA's major manufacturing and the stomping grounds of both the KKK and white gangs like the Spook Hunters.[73] The area of Compton lying east of this boundary was the last to experience racial changeover.[74]

Compton's importance in encompassing both sides of this key racial boundary in assessing its defensibility—and thereby both the use and exchange value of its property—lies in the fact that Compton also shared a school district with residents of Watts and Willowbrook. As a result, white children attended schools that were increasingly integrated, and for many of their parents this was a primary factor in their leaving.[75] As Becky Nicolaides demonstrates so clearly in her study of South Gate, whites were as concerned about their children attending schools with those of other races as they were about living next door to them. They fought to ensure these intimately connected spaces of social reproduction remained white, and when this failed they fled.[76] Neighborhoods became prey to familiar block busting tactics and panic selling, as African Americans moved into a neighborhood and whites became willing to take whatever they could get for their homes.[77] By 1960, 40 percent of Compton's population was nonwhite, although whites continued the battle to maintain their neighborhoods—among them the two men in a car who put thirteen bullets through the Compton NAACP's branch windows in December of 1961.[78]

By 1962, Compton and areas immediately adjoining it were already recognized by developers as suitable for African Americans. In the conflict over the Lileys moving into their new home in Monterey Park, the *Sentinel* reported, "Fisher admitted he had sold to 'other minorities,' Orientals and a Mexican family. He said he felt it would be better for him to build a project 'in the Compton area for Negroes.'"[79] The larger and more established developer Don Wilson's response to CORE's picketing of Dominguez Hills was in fact to build the project in the Compton area, in what seems to have been a bid to deflect the pressure of civil rights demands by offering proof that he was selling homes to African Americans. He was quoted in the *LA Times* as calling it an "experimental interracial tract" and he invested heavily in a marketing campaign for the Centerview development through advertising in Black newspapers.[80] CORE members claimed "that salesmen at Dominguez Hills either flee from Negro customers, locking themselves in the sales office to avoid showing houses, or rudely direct Negroes to go to Centerview which they openly refer to as 'a tract for you people.'"[81] The new racial faultline between the African American ghetto to the North and the wealthier and whiter areas to the South had become the Artesia Boulevard Freeway.[82]

Civil rights gains had momentarily destabilized some of the legal structures, policies, geographies, and ideologies articulated to support white supremacy, which allowed African Americans and other peoples of color to force a shift in the racial boundaries of LA. Their moral and legal civil rights victories made clear that additional urban space had to be yielded to them along with a minimal show of service; thus began a scramble to forge new structures in support of white privilege and space. To prevent full integration in this period of radical change, choices had to be made: the holding of certain race walls became paramount to protect communities with more privileged history, location, and class background, even as others were allowed to fall. Compton, a working-class town crippled by debt, unable to maintain a segregated school system, and straddling a long-held and recognized racial faultline, was essentially abandoned as real estate interests and developers began actively funneling people of color there as a way of keeping them out of more exclusive tracts with greater prestige and amenities. In the face of this decision, and the repercussions of redlining and falling property values that followed it, white residents abandoned the city to African Americans, although only after years of bitter struggle.[83] As Derrick Bell, a father of critical race theory notes:

The plight of black mayors reminds us that we, as black people, gain access to political positions the way we gain access to all white neighborhoods—when the housing stock is run down, maintenance is expensive, and there is every likelihood that past abuse and mismanagement by whites will make effective governance impossible for blacks who, of course, will be blamed for the failure, which is made even more inevitable by the past practices over which black people had no control.[84]

By 1970, Compton was 71 percent African American, and while it has grown more diverse since that time, this has been caused by an influx of Latino residents, many of them immigrants. The inner suburban city of Compton is as representative of the disinvestment, poverty, and violence as any inner-city neighborhood.[85] The brutal economic and political reasons behind this shift were concealed behind the rhetoric of simple human nature. Eighteen years after the end of de jure discrimination, the National Association of Real Estate Boards and the California Real Estate Association president, Charles Shattuck, stated in sworn testimony before an assembly committee in Los Angeles that "if they [African Americans] move in, the white people just move out. That's all. They move out. They just don't care to stay there."[86] It is only as he continues to state how his colleagues refused to be part of "the salt and peppering of the whole community" that he acknowledges some of the institutional agency involved.[87] As Stuart Hall states: "Appeals to 'human nature' are not explanations, they are an alibi."[88]

TORRANCE

Torrance, as distinct from Dominguez Hills and Compton, represented a still-developing and more exclusive area that real estate interests seemed determined to keep white—its history exemplifies the shift in this period from the defense of racial boundaries that confined people of color within compact areas to a defense of defined white neighborhoods with mechanisms to keep unwanted people out. It began as a "completely new kind of company town," planned by Llewellyn Iron Works, the Union Tool Company, and the Pacific Electric Railway.[89] Clothed in the language of industrial location, the decision to build the town most likely had more to do with the recent labor strife in Los Angeles, which had resulted in the bombing of the *LA Times* building and Llewelyn Iron in 1910. An early article listing the benefits of moving to Torrance stated: "the absence of paternalism or welfare work, the availability of jobs from different employers, and the benefits of homeownership."[90] Yet from the beginning it was also restricted, not simply in terms of race, as almost all similar industrial suburbs were, but also in terms of class.[91] The companies were open in their beliefs that "there are some classes of workers of better character than others. Therefore it is desirable to attract the one and discourage the other."[92]

To this end, they hired garden city architect Frederick Law Olmstead, Jr. to draw town plans for the 2,000 acres that had originally formed a part of the Dominguez Land Grant from the Spanish Crown.[93] Zoning separated land uses, confining industry downwind and on the opposite side of the tracts, while restrictions ensured that nonwhites lived "in a 'foreign quarter' outside of the city limits."[94] By 1912, Olmstead had withdrawn from the project, citing the difficulties of supervising from Boston and growing complaints about curvilinear streets and irregular lot shapes. His prestige remained with the project, however—1920s booster advertising highlighted residences and gardens in close proximity to good jobs promised by modern industry.

The opening issue of the *Torrance Enterprise* on November 5, 1920, reflects the initial corporate and anti-union idealism of the enterprise:

> The basic reasons for the establishing of Torrance were to provide practical, spacious, moderately-priced locations for the ever-increasing number of industries of the growing city of Los Angeles; and also to create and develop a manufacturing idealistic along idealistic lines, [sic] or in other words to establish an environment that would produce maximum efficiency in the men as well as in the factories.[95]

The nature of such efficient men and their community is further established on the same front page, where an article headlined "Japs Licked in Torrance" states that the vote for the Alien Land Law represents "the most complete repudiation of the Japanese invasion of California, even to renting them land."[96]

By December 1920, the *Torrance Enterprise* was boosting the city as the home of the Union Tool Co., Llewellyn Iron Works, the Pacific Electric shops, Torrance Window Glass Co., American System of Re-enforcing [sic], California Carbon Co., Salm Manufacturing Co., and Alumnit Viterous Facing Co. There was clearly no shortage of jobs but rather of workers; four front-page news items in the same paper dealt with new housing, and one article lists the buyers of new lots and announces the building of eleven new homes, six by Pacific Electric for its own employees. There was no need to openly discuss race; the Dominguez Land Company early on inserted racial restrictions into its deeds to ensure that their new city remained white.[97] In 1924, the front pages of the *Torrance Herald* still regularly announced the arrivals of new families by name and address, and the building of new homes. It was a newspaper belonging to a small town that was proud of its growth, industry, and the wealth of the new oil fields that had been discovered.

Torrance played its own role in the 1920s rise of the KKK, as covered by the *Torrance Herald* on August 24, 1924:

> Several thousand persons witnessed a "naturalization" ceremony of the Ku Klux Klan east of Western Avenue in Torrance Saturday night. The ceremony was conducted by Torrance Klansman under the light of a large electric cross. About

100 candidates were "naturalized." During the ceremony an aeroplane with four lighted "K's" circled over the field. The ritual of the Klan was distinctly heard by the thousands who stood outside the ropes . . . The Klansmen used loud speakers. All of the Klansmen were unmasked . . . Before the ceremony proper started a Klan speaker delivered an address on Klansmanship.

Klansmen clearly had little fear of trouble with the local authorities or the disapproval of their neighbors as they borrowed the discourse of citizenship—reinforcing the idea that "true" Americans are white—to celebrate their induction of new members into white supremacy on a mass scale.

Throughout decades of struggle against restrictive covenants and discriminatory housing, Torrance remained untouched and primarily white, though it had grown to include a small residential area for Asians and Mexicans working in agriculture. In 1940, a special census reported the nonwhite population as 1,209, dropping by 57.4 percent to 515 after the internments of World War II, even as the white population increased by 93.7 percent to 17,450.[98] By 1952, the white population had almost doubled, reaching 31,252 while only 582 nonwhites lived within its borders.[99] An illustrative incident occurred in 1951, when a group of fifteen picketed a minstrel show and performance in blackface at Torrance High School. A *Press* article claims no discrimination was intended, then goes on to quote a local resident who states: "I think the picketing was disgraceful, particularly when there are no Negroes living in Torrance."[100] Part of the privilege of exclusionary white space is its ability to insulate itself from its own exclusionary nature—for example, the feeling that discrimination only occurs when there is someone immediately and physically present to experience the discrimination. In 1963 at the height of CORE's campaign, Torrance's mayor, when interviewed, reputedly stated, "Torrance has no Negro problem. We only have three Negroes in the city," though he later denied this.[101] Alongside the town's stated desire to continue growing was always the addendum—often implicitly understood rather than stated, as it had been in the 1920s—that to continue to be successful it had to have the "right kind" of people.

While no longer printing the full names and addresses of newcomers to Torrance by the 1940s and '50s, the local papers continued to show the city's vital interest in expansion and building additional homes. The sale of a large piece of land to developers Wilson and Kauffman for a new tract of 1,900 homes in the community of Southwood made front page news of the *Torrance Press* on May 12, 1955. A two-column article on the second page of January 17, 1960's *Press* is headlined "Don Wilson Builders Dedicate Spanking New Office Structure," a measure of the prominent social positions held by the larger housing developers such as Don Wilson, certainly one of the "community builders" studied by Marc Weiss and others.[102] A single office building housed "all divisions of the corporation: Southwood Construction Co., Escrow Division,

General Accounting and corporate offices." As much an advertisement piece as anything else, it quotes extensively from Wilson, who states:

> Our new facilities will enable us to continue to lead the building industry by building better quality homes more efficiently. Every phase of a development, from acquisition of land to finished homes ready for sale, is handled under one roof by our integrated operation. This assures buyers of our homes high quality standards, excellent construction, a fine land value, all at the lowest cost possible.

Despite emphasizing value for money, the article does not skimp on descriptions of dated luxury in the offices themselves, giving extremely detailed descriptions of walnut panelling, alternating stripes of deep blue, white and orange carpeting in Wilson's office, and the 6,000 square feet of paved private parking. It worked to boost both Torrance and its development, giving a sense of civic pride in both the building and the business, and noted that the 465-unit development at Southwood Estates was 92 percent sold out, and a 335-unit development at Southwood Del Amo was about to begin construction.

By October 16, 1960, no longer was proximity to work, the presence of factories, or Torrance as a modern industrial city the highlight of the sales pitch; the *Torrance Press* advertised the 192 units of Southwood Riviera Royale with a half page ad for a "bold . . . exciting new concept in living" in a "selective community" that is "secluded, private and desirable." It lauded its selectiveness, its defensibility, and its proximity to conveniences such as the marina, major shopping centers, churches, schools, and recreational facilities. Even so, Torrance had always been (and continues to be) close to high-paying manufacturing jobs closely guarded by the white community.[103] CORE briefly picketed the Vickers Corporation—just down the road in Torrance from their pickets at Southwood Riviera Royale—after the unjust firing of an African American lathe operator in 1963. The man fired was one of only six or seven African Americans of 600 employed at the plant.[104]

On March 25, 1962, the *Press* profiled Don Wilson and his importance to the city of Torrance. Since its beginning twelve years before, Wilson's firm had grown to 100 employees and constructed over 50,000 homes in fifty complete communities. Of these, the firm built over 5,000 homes in Torrance alone, providing housing to 35 percent of its then-population. The picketing of Wilson's developments as part of the growing national civil rights must have come as quite a shock to Torrance's white citizens.

Chapter 5

The Second Salvo

Don Wilson and the Battle for the South Bay

From an initial picket in Dominguez Hills, CORE's campaign slowly began to grow. By August 1962, the *Sentinel* reported of a "Pastor to Pray on Gardena Picket Line," but the blessings of a number of pastors from Compton and other communities availed little in the campaign to integrate Don Wilson's developments.[1] By autumn, CORE's campaign strategy of steady escalation of direct action resulted in a sit-in at the Dominguez Hills sales offices.[2] In an impressive display of membership strength, CORE was able to maintain three separate picket lines and a sit-in at the Wilson properties, even as they began the dwell-in in Wilmington and continued working with the Lileys and on other cases of discrimination coming to their attention.[3]

CORE was working on refining their public argument around segregation, both the reasons for its existence and what would bring about change. In a press conference held at the end of 1962, CORE passed out a statement on the housing problem:

> We now have concrete knowledge that this is a segregated city as we have always known from the statistics put out by the County Commission on Human Relations and other agencies . . . We have a growing conviction that there is a definite plan to this. The lines of the Ghetto are drawn. There must be a secret illegal agreement between the builders, realtors, developers and money lenders to attempt to hold these lines.
>
> It seems to CORE that the newspapers and other media have failed to convey the extent of discrimination in Los Angeles County. It may be that the press is subject to pressures from advertisers. On the other hand, it may be that CORE and other civil rights groups are failing to get the facts across, and that is why we have called this News Conference.[4]

This is as close as LA CORE got to a public analysis of how the spatialities of housing discrimination worked. Through analysis of their experiences in trying to achieve integration, they arrived at the same conclusions presented throughout these chapters—that segregation was a goal consciously and collectively pursued by banking and real estate professionals who worked to maintain these racial faultlines. In a leaflet from late 1962 or early 1963, CORE begins calling the racial faultline of Alameda the "Hate Wall," which functioned to keep undesirables in rather than out. The flyer's language shows their awareness that such a wall does not simply separate Blacks from whites in space, but it also functions ideologically to wall them out of a shared sense of community, to make of them "second-class citizens." CORE argues that they are walls in which all whites are culpable. Through breaking down these walls, CORE clearly understood its goals to be both spatial and social integration across the city. The leaflet manages to be both narrow—in limiting segregation to a few bad actors—and yet sweeping in its indictment of those forming the "hate wall." It is clearly a call for residents in segregated tracts to choose sides and support those fighting against segregation—a call that the residents of both Torrance and Dominguez Hills would choose to ignore.

Leaflets used to rally the African American and Compton community also highlight the complicity in discrimination of those who chose to buy in racially segregated tracts. More than simply a call to conscience, these leaflets were also a call to dignity and economic interest:

SEGREGATION IS DEGRADING

If you let Don Wilson tell you where you may or may not live, you are accepting second class citizenship for yourself and your children. Housing which is *not* segregated is available.

SEGREGATION IS EXPENSIVE

When Negroes are denied the right to shop around for the best buy, they can be forced to pay higher prices. Don Wilson's salesmen are quoting prices on houses at Centerview *$1000 to $2000 higher* than are being asked for *identical* models at Dominguez Hills.

SEGREGATION CAN BE STOPPED

Make Segregation unprofitable. Refuse to buy from those who engage in racial discrimination. Don't cooperate with racial injustice!! Don't look at housing here. Go to Dominguez Hills or Southwood Riviera Royale.[5]

Such leaflets, backed up by the pickets and sit-ins that showed the individual and organizational determination to fight Wilson's practices until he changed them, aimed to galvanize a larger moral outrage and movement to win full integration.

In January 1963, Don Wilson contacted CORE via the state attorney general, stating that he wished to negotiate a settlement. Underlining the direct democracy with which they tried to run their campaigns, CORE's representatives attended the meeting between Wilson and two negotiators with the power only to bring a proposed settlement back to a larger meeting of whole active membership.[6] They also decided to continue picketing throughout the negotiations—which the *Sentinel* blamed when the negotiations faltered.[7] Yet Attorney General Mosk clearly felt that Wilson had not been negotiating in good faith, as Mosk filed discrimination charges against Wilson in March and obtained a temporary restraining order forbidding further discrimination.[8]

LOS ANGELES HAS A "HATE WALL" - AN INVISIBLE WALL, BUT IT'S AS UGLY AND INHUMAN AS THE WALL WHICH DEFACES BERLIN.

IN LOS ANGELES, THE WALL IS AN UNWRITTEN AND FURTIVE AGREEMENT BY WHICH A FEW REALTORS, DEVELOPERS, LOAN COMPANIES, AND OWNERS OF RENTAL PROPERTIES ENFORCE A SYSTEM OF HOUSING SEGREGATION, TELLING ONE-FOURTH OF OUR CITIZENS WHERE THEY MAY AND MAY NOT LIVE.

THIS "HATE WALL" VIOLATES STATE AND FEDERAL LAWS.

THOSE INSIDE THE WALL ARE DENIED A BASIC FREEDOM AND ARE TREATED AS SECOND CLASS CITIZENS.

THOSE OUTSIDE THE WALL ARE WILLINGLY OR UNWILL-INGLY FORCED TO COOPERATE IN A CRIMINAL CON-SPIRACY AGAINST THEIR FELLOW CITIZENS.

DON WILSON - TRACT DEVELOPER - IS ONE OF THE ARCHITECTS OF THE LOS ANGELES " HATE WALL".

AT HIS SOUTHWOOD RIVIERA ROYALE TRACT, DON WILSON WILL NOT SELL TO NEGROES, MEXICANS, OR ORIENTALS.

AT HIS DOMINGUEZ HILLS TRACT, DON WILSON WILL NOT SELL TO NEGROES.

AT HIS CENTERVIEW ESTATES TRACT, (LOCATED JUST INSIDE THE "HATE WALL") DON WILSON IS WILLING TO SELL TO MEMBERS OF ALL MINORITY GROUPS, CYNICALLY ASSUMING THAT MINORITY PEOPLE, LIKE DOCILE SHEEP, WILL ALLOW THEMSELVES TO BE HERDED INTO A JIM CROW TRACT.

CORE, THE CONGRESS OF RACIAL EQUALITY, WILL CONTINUE ITS PROTEST AGAINST DON WILSON WITH PICKET LINES, SIT-INS, AND OTHER FORMS OF NONVIOLENT DIRECT ACTION UNTIL HE CHANGES HIS POLICY IN ALL TRACTS.

DON'T BE A PARTY TO RACIAL INJUSTICE! GIVE CORE YOUR SUPPORT !

WRITE DON WILSON AND PROTEST HIS POLICY! JOIN OUR PICKET LINES!

DON'T BUY FROM
DON WILSON

Congress of Racial Equality - 1115 W. Venice Blvd. - DU 9-4444

Despite the order, Wilson did not sell any homes to African Americans outside of Centerview. An injunction against discrimination lacked the power to force the developer to sell a home.

POLICY CHANGE IN SACRAMENTO

While CORE's main focus was direct action and concrete victories, they worked concurrently, as they had in earlier campaigns, to support the legal and political strategies for institutional and policy change led by other organizations. The local chapter of the NAACP had drafted a fair housing ordinance to bring before the city council that would "ban discrimination by real estate brokers, banks, lending institutions and individuals in the sale or rental of private housing."[9] The ordinance was sponsored by Council Member Ed Roybal and brought to the health and welfare committee on June 21, 1962. Speakers from CORE, the NAACP, the West LA Fair Housing Committee and San Fernando Valley Fair Housing testified to a packed room about specific cases of discrimination, along with a Black real estate agent describing his experience of trying and failing to become a member of the LA Realty Board.[10]

The California Committee for Fair Practices held a state-level conference in Fresno in December 1962. The 148 people present, representing more than 100 civil rights groups, made legislation barring discrimination in all rentals and sales of housing their number one priority for the 1963 legislative session.[11] Assembly Member Rumford would sponsor the legislation as Assembly Bill 1240; the document essentially mimicked a fair housing bill that had failed to pass the committee in 1961. It barred discrimination in all privately or publicly funded housing, gave enforcement powers to the Fair Employment Practices Commission, and banned discrimination among lending institutions, mortgage brokers, and realtors.[12]

Marlon Brando and Paul Newman would (briefly) join the sit-in organized by CORE as it took up the struggle to pass Bill 1240 with all of its customary vigor. The actors symbolized the wider support from those in Hollywood and the broader left who had been energized by the civil rights struggle in the South, but CORE carried out the sit-in in the face of internal opposition from more moderate civil rights groups and their allies, who wanted to distance themselves as much as possible from CORE's confrontational tactics.[13]

The sit-in began with ten CORE members establishing themselves in the capitol's rotunda on May 29, 1963. Rumford himself is quoted in the *LA Times* stating that the demonstration was "well-intentioned but misdirected" and that "it certainly won't encourage the enactment of legislation. I don't want the senators to think we're trying to pressure them."[14] Three days after the sit-in began and a call was sent out for a "Freedom Ride" to the capitol, the participants had swelled from ten to fifty.[15] The *Sentinel* clearly sided with the traditional civil rights advocates who shared in mainstream disapproval of CORE's actions. It waited until June 6 to cover the action with three short paragraphs, and even Brando and Newman's presence resulted in the story expanding to only four paragraphs.[16] An *LA Times* article gives it more coverage but with a negative slant. Headlined "Sit-ins Fill Capitol Foyer with Litter," the reporter notes the "flag-draped area looking more like a campground than a legislative hallway."[17]

The sit-in would last over three weeks. Blocked by two powerful senators—Democrats Gibson (originally from Alabama) and Burns, who were both strongly opposed to fair housing legislation—the bill sat in the Committee for Governmental Efficiency as the two worked to stop or water down the bill in negotiations. Support from Rumford and the governor ensured the bill's passage, but the senators still achieved the exclusion of owner-occupied dwellings of four units or less and the removal of specific references to minimum fines or jail time for violation.[18] Over the weeks that the bill was held up in committee, more than 300 people and sixteen CORE chapters from around California participated in sit-in relays.[19] Escalating from the sit-in, CORE had launched a hunger strike, as well as what they called a lie-in, in which twenty-five members lay down and blocked both sides of the door upon the adjournment of the session. The bill passed in the last few dramatic hours before the session's close. Burns, who had worked to block the bill in committee, threw the firecrackers traditionally lighted in celebration at the end of session at the protestors.[20]

The American Friends Committee, in their published report on the bill, noted that external factors had played a role in its passage; the first factor being CORE's sit-in to protest to ensure that the vote was taken:

> The quiet group sitting around the rotunda railing for three weeks did seem to serve this purpose: It was a daily reminder to all passing by that the fair housing issue had not been settled, and the resultant publicity in the press reminded the voters that the Senate was stalling.
>
> In the meantime, daily reports of violence in racial conflicts in the South, and especially news of the use of fire hoses and police dogs against the Negro people of Birmingham, gave legislators a new sense of the urgency of AB 1240.[21]

Passing the Rumford Act certainly marked a milestone in fair housing legislation, giving concrete means of enforcement to anti-discrimination provisions and expanding this enforcement to lenders and realtors. Before 1948, the state and federal governments had actively supported segregation through policy and regulation; after 1948, they were required to remain neutral. The passage of the Rumford Act, along with other civil rights legislation, meant that the government now had to take sides *against* segregation. While it proved too weak to have a real effect on CORE's ongoing disputes with Wilson, the Rumford Act still signified not just the removal of a previous pillar of a segregated society but a potentially active force against segregation. The easy use of government force and policy to maintain white space and privilege would no longer be possible without the act's repeal (a vigorous campaign led by CREA did spring up and is discussed at the end of the chapter), but the twists in CORE's Torrance campaign would point to alternative strategies of sidelining government interference, or articulating it in very new kinds of ways.

THE CONFLICT ESCALATES

Back in LA, CORE was making no headway against the united forces marshaled in support of Wilson's company policies of segregation. One of the part-time salesmen working for the company was Torrance Police Sergeant Philip Wilson, and CORE filed complaints against him with the Torrance Police Department, mayor, city attorney, and city council for threats and harassment, particularly of interracial groups.[22] In May, CORE accused Sgt. Wilson of knocking two CORE members to the ground and kicking them repeatedly while they were attempting to sit-in at the Centerview tract escrow office. Five colleagues from the Firestone Police Department responding to the call refused to arrest him or call an ambulance, and the Compton District Attorney refused to file charges.[23] The connection between Wilson and the Torrance Police was cemented when he hired an additional off-duty police officer, Lt. Don Cook, as a security guard during demonstrations.[24] Like Wilson himself, both policemen (and undoubtedly most in the department) lived near the disputed area, and thus all had their own personal stake in the conflict through work and home. Trouble between CORE and the police would only escalate as the number of arrests mounted.

Even as the Rumford Bill sat blocked in committee and their colleagues were conducting a sit-in in Sacramento, sixteen demonstrators were arrested on June 16 in two groups during their attempt to sit in at Wilson's Torrance sales office.[25] This is the first time that the local papers covered the story in real depth; *The Press's* coverage displayed photos of the demonstrators being arrested. It opened with an acknowledgment of national unrest suddenly become local: "Torrance today was facing a role as target in the nationwide demonstrations for integration."[26] Direct actions in LA and Sacramento brought CORE both a large increase in members as well as a higher profile in the mainstream press. The *LA Times* covered CORE's next training in "picket-line conduct," followed by a demonstration of about 125 people to "confront the public with the fact there is a racial problem in Torrance."[27] While in some ways this did actually begin to present CORE to the mainstream white public in a meaningful way, the caption underneath the large accompanying photo marginalized their impact, stating: "Sit-in ignored—Couple talk with Southwood Homes salesmen in tract sales office as CORE sit-in demonstrators sit side-by-side on the floor before desk."[28]

At around 1:30 a.m. on Sunday morning, Wilson made twenty-three more citizen's arrests of CORE members continuing the sit-in at the sales office. The *Sentinel* reported the brutal handling of those arrested, with the women "subjected to indignities," and one pulled by the hair and thrown headfirst into

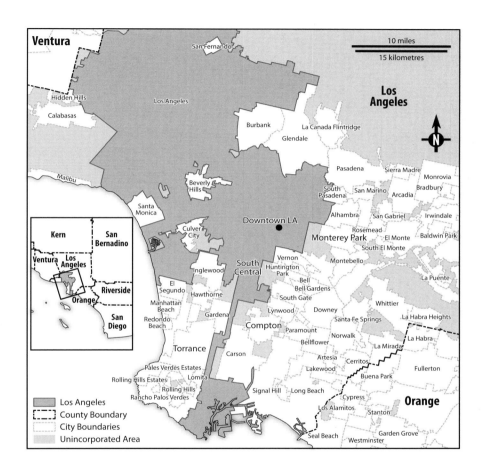

Map 1. The greater LA area

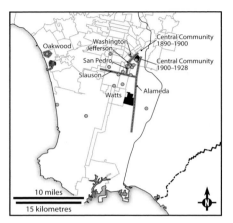
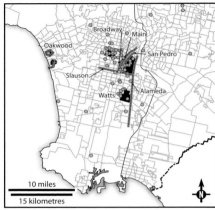
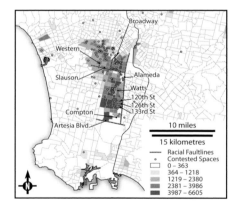
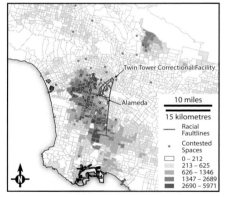

Map 2. LA's African American population, 1890–2010, mapped against points
of contestation and showing shifting racial faultlines

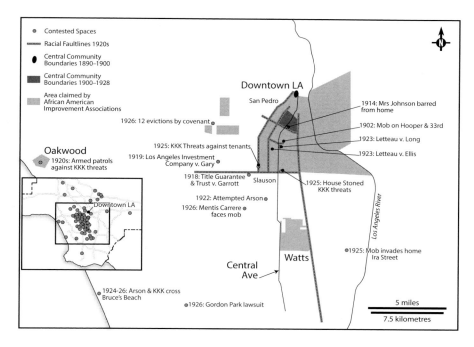

Map 3. "Disciplinary" actions against African American families outside of the Black Belt, 1902–1926

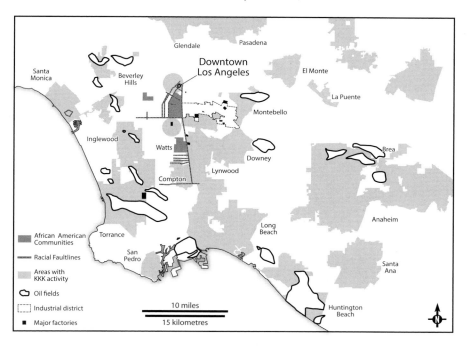

Map 4. Known KKK areas and industrial areas in 1920s LA and Orange County

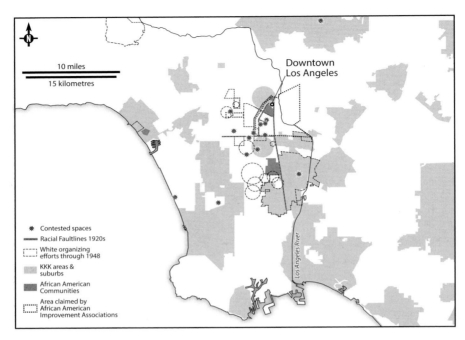

Map 5. African American homeowner associations, homes of prominent white realtors, and early spaces of contestation through 1927

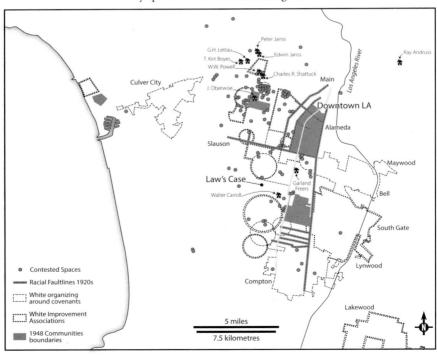

Map 6. White organizing efforts through 1948

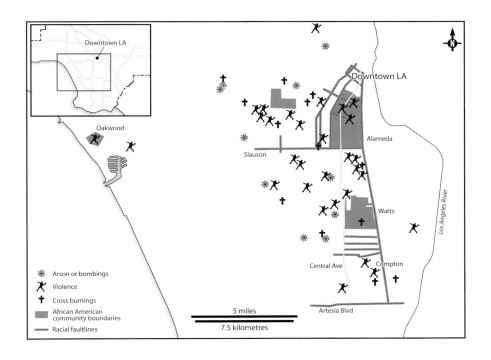

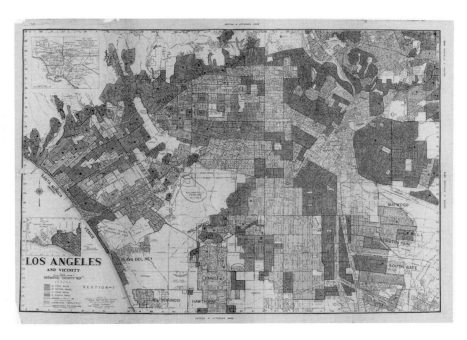

Map 7. Incident map (top) showing the worst violence in relation
to the 1939 LA HOLC map (bottom)

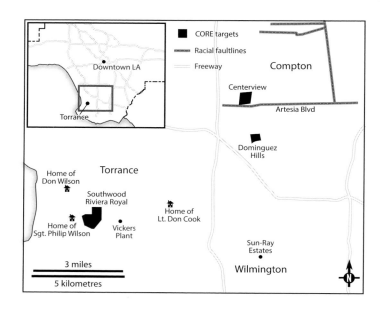

Map 8. Developer Don Wilson's tracts and advertising campaigns

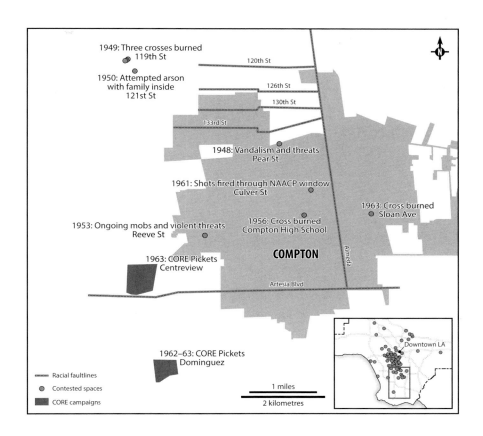

1949: Three crosses burned
119th St

1950: Attempted arson
with family inside
121st St

120th St

126th St

130th St

133rd St

1948: Vandalism and threats
Pear St

1961: Shots fired through NAACP window
Culver St

1963: Cross burned
Sloan Ave

1953: Ongoing mobs and violent threats
Reeve St

1956: Cross burned
Compton High School

COMPTON

Almeda

1963: CORE Pickets
Centreview

Artesia Blvd

1962–63: CORE Pickets
Dominguez

Racial faultlines
Contested spaces
CORE campaigns

Downtown LA

1 miles

2 kilometres

Map 9. Principal racial incidents in Compton

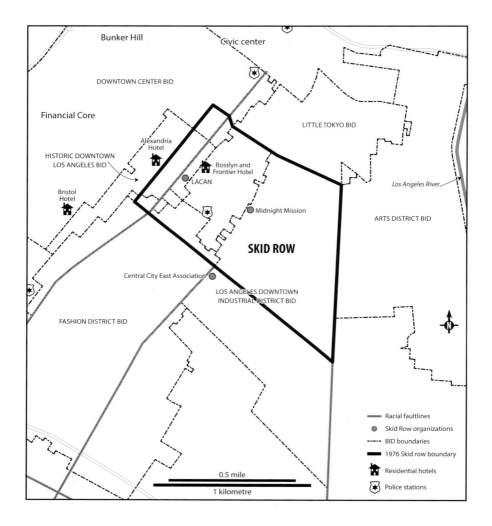

Bunker Hill

Civic center

DOWNTOWN CENTER BID

Financial Core

LITTLE TOKYO BID

Alexandria
Hotel

HISTORIC DOWNTOWN
LOS ANGELES BID

Rosslyn and
Frontier Hotel

LACAN

Los Angeles River

Bristol
Hotel

Midnight Mission

ARTS DISTRICT BID

SKID ROW

Central City East Association

LOS ANGELES DOWNTOWN
INDUSTRIAL DISTRICT BID

FASHION DISTRICT BID

━━━ Racial faultlines
● Skid Row organizations
┅┅┅ BID boundaries
━━━ 1976 Skid row boundary
🏠 Residential hotels
✴ Police stations

0.5 mile

1 kilometre

Map 10. Downtown LA Business Improvement Districts (BIDs)
with Skid Row boundaries from 1976 plan

the paddy wagon before she was tipped over.[29] The arrests (without any report of police brutality) made it all the way to page two of the *LA Times*.[30] This increased visibility in the mainstream press had partly been spurred by the growing militancy and cooperation among more of LA's Black organizations. They now joined with CORE in demanding immediate equality. Dr. Taylor, head of the LA branch of the NAACP, was joined by other civil rights organizations, including CORE, to announce demands and deadlines for actions toward "total integration" in the area, "holding in reserve Birmingham-type demonstrations if their goals are not met."[31] CORE was no longer alone in militantly demanding total integration.

African American struggle around segregation in Los Angeles was finally obtaining prominent and somewhat favorable coverage in the white mainstream press. White reporter Paul Weeks was the first employee asked by the *LA Times* to cover "the lives and concerns of blacks in the city," what reporter Jon Thurber would later call "a groundbreaking assignment for the paper at the time." Thurber notes that Weeks had to work hard to gain entrance to the community, and that most of LA's Black leaders remained suspicious of the white press, asking only to be quoted anonymously in Weeks's articles.[32] Weeks covered LA's civil rights struggles with some sympathy, and in an article on the struggle for integration he used as a sub-headline "Not a Gift but a Right."[33] The next day Weeks quoted Wendell Green of the United Civil Rights Committee on the ways that residential segregation had "sealed off the Negro from the rest of the population," ensuring that whites did not know the struggle of African Americans better.[34]

Space and segregation were being recognized—as Bass had done years before—as principal forces in maintaining racial barriers. Wilson and the campaign for full residential integration would be taken on as the principal struggle of the new united front against discrimination, with LA's other civil rights organizations joining their efforts with CORE's. In preparation, the United Civil Rights Committee (UCRC) and CORE conducted three civil rights trainings in nonviolent tactics for more than 300 people. In spite of this, the NAACP's Dr. Taylor remained much more willing to cater to white sensibilities. He was reported as "inclined to blame both Negro and white communities for the burgeoning of the Negro housing situation in the past ten years. 'We were both asleep,' he said. 'We weren't aware of the population explosion to come.'"[35]

Throwing their weight behind CORE, the NAACP and UCRC also joined them in direct negotiations with Wilson, demanding acceptance of the following conditions:

1. Accept deposit from Odis B. Jackson [an African American who had volunteered to buy a home in the tract].
2. Hire a Negro salesman in Southwood office.
3. Move for a dismissal of the trespassing charges against 40 CORE demonstrators.

4. Issue public statement saying selling houses on non-discriminatory basis, place in advertising and post in sales offices.
5. Advertise the Centerview development in *LA Times* and the Southwood tract in *Eagle* and *Sentinel*.[36]

The conditions were discussed during a long, contentious meeting and decided upon later the same day as a meeting scheduled with Wilson—the NAACP/UCRC representatives turned up over an hour and a half late.[37] When the conditions were not met, an announcement from Dr. Taylor implied they were starting anew, saying "We will strike our first blow at housing bias with a strong demonstration at this project Saturday." Wendell Green, chairman of the joint NAACP-UCRC housing committee, stated hopefully, "We know that a major breakthrough on the housing tract is a certainty if we show we mean business by a large demonstration."[38] A large motor cavalcade was planned between the four main civil rights organizations.

RADICALIZING RESIDENTS, PRIVATIZING THE STREETS

After one march of 125 people and the promise of an even larger one to come, Torrance residents were as up in arms as the newly united African American civil rights organizations. Since April, the pickets in Torrance (and apparently only in Torrance, highlighting its broader importance to the white community) had been attracting counterprotestors, including over a dozen Nazi party members complete with armbands and placards such as "RACE-MIXING IS JEWISH, ZIONISM IS TREASON, COMMUNISM IS JEWISH."[39] While not picked up by the press, Nazi counterprotests had become part of CORE's recruitment talks at colleges, as member Bruce Hartford recalls from watching films of actions shown at a coffee shop near UCLA:

> In his movie there were more fully uniformed members of the American Nazi Party counter-demonstrating than there were CORE pickets. Jack boots, tan uniforms, swastika armbands, stiff-arm salutes, the whole megilla [sic].
> So when I saw those Nazis—"Holy shit! When is your next picket? I'll be there." And I went. And again there were more damn Nazis there than there were of us. They had about 50, we had about 20. And these were scary Nazis. These were not your three little Nazis surrounded by a mob of anti-racist protestors. This was a band of racist thugs surrounding a little CORE picket line. Way different from today. Way, way, different from today. And they were throwing shit at us, and you know, the whole bit.[40]

Not only were Nazis turning up in the neighborhood, but they were purportedly taking the side of the white residents there, causing no small discomfort. In a city council meeting held the Tuesday evening before the threatened mass march, over 250 "angry and disturbed home owners" demanded something be done about the "racial picketing."[41] One resident representative described the feeling of "sitting on a powder keg with a short wick. We don't know who's going to ignite it." They continued:

> We want to protect our property and secure safety for our children and ourselves. We want to take all steps to prevent a riot.[42]

The resident's language is, of course, remarkably race neutral, attempting not to take sides in the conflict, and instead focusing on the disruption caused by CORE's search for civil rights. A similarly neutral petition, reportedly signed by 100 residents in less than two hours, refers to the safety of their children and that they "have been unable to secure for themselves the full use and benefit of their individual property rights, peace and quiet." Yet when the representative of the Centinela Bay Human Relations Commission attempted to speak, asking for the council to use its influence to ensure all qualified buyers were allowed to buy into the tract and to investigate charges of "overzealousness" on the part of the police, the crowd booed and shouted him down. Instead the homeowners urged for "every available police support to break up people congregating in the area" and for the area to essentially be closed to outside traffic on evenings and week-ends—thus, the proposal to close off the community first came from the residents themselves.[43] One local newspaper published a picture contrasting the "Beatnik type" marching with CORE to the upstanding Torrance citizens attending the council meeting.

There seems to be an equation with outsiders, "beatniks" and counterculture, and Negroes—all things unwanted. Another article on the upcoming march notes that only one of the picketers is from the South Bay, and she is a "*divorcée*," underscoring gender norms and stigmatizing a perceived failure to succeed in building a nuclear family.[44] Taken together, the story is an ugly reminder of just who could be considered part of their community.

In the *Torrance Herald*, an editorial on the front page sums up local opinion—there is no discrimination and CORE is unreasonably stirring up trouble:

> the charges of racial discrimination are not backed by the facts, leading to the conclusion that the rightful demands of American Negroes for equal treatment, not only in law and civil rights but in social contacts and opportunities, are not involved.[45]

Here the *Herald* supports as true Wilson's statement that he had in fact never been seriously approached to sell a home, in the face of overwhelming evidence to the contrary. More curious is the way the editorial acknowledges discrimination as wrong and shows support for equal rights, while refusing to acknowledge that residents are involved in any kind of discrimination. It was a familiar papering over of the virulent and open racism of owner associations only a decade before but with a no less fierce defense of privilege. As in the *Press*, much is made of the majority of picketers being young college students who are not there to actually buy homes. Mayor Isen characterized as "ridiculous" CORE's attempts to "crack the community in our highest-priced neighborhood." He said there were homes of more modest price "they could have sought."[46] The continuing unquestioned commonsense connection between whiteness, exclusivity, and exchange value could not be more clear. Meanwhile, providing lip service to this new equality without accepting it in practice, Don Wilson insisted on his willingness to sell a home, but stated no African Americans were able to qualify as buyers. The UCRC, NAACP, Urban League, and CORE failed to get anything more than a repetition of this statement in negotiations with Wilson, even while pressuring him through a meeting between the developer, four civil rights groups, three clergy representatives, and Torrance city officials.[47]

On the Friday before the big march, Mr. Jackson—an African American buyer—drove to the sales office to put a deposit on a home. The manager stated that his cheque was rejected because his wife was not present; "it is not a case of discriminating."[48] On a visit to the tract with the city manager and a councilman that same afternoon to plan the emergency blockading of the streets to cars, forcing protesters to park and walk the final mile to the picket lines, the mayor told the *Sentinel*, "The demonstrators aren't barred . . . This is a free country." He described how Torrance had grown from 20,000 to 120,000 in just over a decade, and yet, "so far as I know," he said, "the only Negro residents are two persons whose spouses are colored." He advised patience and a removal of pressure, "if these people, through their white advocates, would calm down."[49] Like the residents, he provides generic support of civil rights while essentially denying the existence of discrimination in Torrance. He also implies that any impasse is the fault of the protestors and that African Americans are little more than the pawns of white outside agitators. These would become familiar themes.

While the organizers of the march had expected 200 to 300 people, at least 200 cars met up for the cavalcade that first drove to Centerview Estates and Dominguez Hills before reaching Torrance, where about 700 marched in total.[50] They paraded before a sales office closed at the request of city authorities to prevent another sit-in.[51] Of an estimated 250 spectators not from the actual development, the American Nazi Party—carrying a large banner stating "White Men Unite"—and about 50 people from the Committee Against Integration and Intermarriage appeared among the curious and hostile.[52] From the residents themselves, there was a scattering of American flags on front lawns, as though to say the protest was un-American. Barbara Dimmick of CORE writes of Torrance residents lined up at the intersection of Sepulveda and Anza Boulevard. While occasional encouragement of the marchers was heard, no one joined them—on the contrary, most of the remarks remained "censored" in her account.[53] A *Sentinel* article describes:

Across the street, on the corners ahead, unsympathetic white crowds waited . . . Half-naked white youth sent up a chorus of boos. "Don't you get the message? We don't want you here," shouted a man. The corner was overcrowded with white people. They spilled into the streets.[54]

Another notes a group of neighborhood youth reciting the Pledge of Allegiance to the marchers, and signs saying, "Without property rights there are no human rights" and "We have civil rights too."[55]

In the aftermath of the protest, a family returned to their car to find all of the windows smashed, and that evening a sniper shot three bullets through the plate glass window at CORE headquarters while people were meeting inside. No one was hurt.[56] The following day, CORE resumed its normal picket, and the twenty people on the "freedom lines" stood far outnumbered by the fifty police present to keep order.[57]

Tensions increased. A CORE photographer had his camera smashed when he was assaulted and knocked down by a Torrance resident.[58] Two students, one Black and one white, reported a white Cadillac making three attempts to run them over in an alley. A resident witnessed the assault and called the police with the license plate number.[59] Although the police initially stated they would arrest the driver with a charge of assault with a deadly weapon, no arrest was made, even after CORE members attempted to conduct a citizen's arrest.[60] The two police officers in charge of the investigation were reportedly Sgt. Phillips and Lt. Cook, both of whom worked for Don Wilson.[61] The body of a Black man shot in the back of the head three times was found in an empty lot nearby, provoking even more fear. Four CORE representatives visited the hospital where he was taken.[62] While the murdered man was ultimately proved not to have been known to the protestors or to have participated in the march, given the openly white supremacist presence there, along with the terrorism being faced by civil rights protests in the South, this must have been traumatic.

In spite of this, CORE had such an influx of new volunteers that they had to fight to ensure that all were trained in CORE's principles, particularly nonviolence, and search for larger places to hold meetings.[63] On the other side, homeowners protested at another packed emergency meeting held by the city council, with William Uerkewitz, president of the homeowner's association, arguing for a city injunction to secure their community from strangers. "Many moral implications are brought up," the *Torrance Herald* quotes him as saying, explaining that men and women are sleeping in the office in view of the neighboring houses. He did not need to underline that not only was it men and women, but men and women of mixed race. The council rushed through an emergency injunction, closing Southwood Riviera streets down to all but residents and their guests on evenings and weekends.[64]

A CORE press conference announced that they planned to defy what the *LA Times* called Torrance's "sit-in law," noting that the fine was higher than similar ordinances in the Deep South. They planned both to challenge its constitutionality and to continue preparing for the largest protest yet on July 28, to mark an entire year of picketing against Wilson's policies of discrimination.[65] The Los Angeles Superior Court granted an injunction against the Torrance ordinance, even as the *Press* reported that the city council was contemplating repealing the ordinance only a week after it had been passed. This came on the heels of an announcement that an agreement had been reached between Wilson and the NAACP and UCRC. Charges against the thirty-nine people arrested by Wilson during the sit-ins were dropped. The agreement detailed that: 1. Wilson had received the deposit of an African American and would work "diligently to complete the sale"; 2. The African American salesman employed by Wilson at Centerview would be "utilized" in all of his tracts; 3. No discriminatory advertising would be used.[66]

An editorial in the *Torrance Herald* under the title of "A Welcome Agreement" plays the NAACP and UCRC off unfavorably against CORE, implying that calm negotiation would have solved everything from the beginning.[67] It notes that CORE did hail the announcement, but insisted on maintaining minimal and token pickets present at both the Torrance tract and Centerview until the sale had actually been completed. The memory of the attempts of the developer in Monterey Park to frustrate the sale to the Lileys served as a cautionary experience. With only one placard and a handful of picketers, they passed out a statement, which included the following:

> CORE has discontinued its sit-in demonstrations . . . However, CORE will maintain a token picket line until all steps of the agreement are put into effect and until the Negro buyer is assured ownership of the home. CORE hopes that this interim vigil will be brief so that we can turn all our energies toward ending discrimination in other areas of Los Angeles County.[68]

The NAACP and UCRC were fairly public with their feelings that the months of pickets and weeks of sit-ins conducted by CORE did not carry the force of the joint effort they had launched. Dr. Taylor played the role of the moderate saving the day, stating, "I think this thing might have been settled if I hadn't had to leave town for a week to attend the NAACP convention in Chicago."[69] The *LA Times* continued to support claims by John A. Buggs, executive director of the County Commission on Human Relations, that "[w]hile demonstrations are more spectacular, real progress has been made in quiet negotiation."[70]

Maintaining their picket in spite of criticism from other civil rights organizations, CORE also sent in white testers to attempt to buy homes from Wilson when he failed to contact Jackson about the sale within a week as promised. They found that the deposits on the remaining homes were from other Southwood residents and friends of Wilson, and white families were told they were still available.[71] CORE's report to a meeting with the NAACP and UCRC resulted in all three jointly accusing Wilson of reneging on his deal, followed by an announcement of a mass public meeting to decide on next steps.[72] Wilson then claimed that Jackson's check had not gone through and that he was rejecting his offer on the "ground that Jackson was not financially qualified." CORE announced that the sit-ins would continue.[73]

The following weekend more than 150 people picketed Torrance, including Marlon Brando and Pernell Roberts from the popular TV Western *Bonanza*. Ninety-five policemen were waiting for them, working in twelve-hour shifts.[74] Although still unable to enforce the emergency ordinance passed by the council closing streets down to non-residents, sixty-nine people were arrested over the weekend in what the *Press* titled "Arrests by the Busload." The police department obviously looked to up the ante, charging picket captains not just with trespassing but with counseling others to break the law and contributing to the delinquency of minors.[75] The city attorney, homeowner association, and Wilson worked together to each file a separate lawsuit against CORE, requesting essentially the same thing: increased legal restraints on those picketing in Torrance.[76]

In the leaflet distributed by homeowners, they clearly viewed themselves as mere innocent bystanders in a drama that was not about civil rights but publicity, and unfairly targeted at their neighborhood. They distanced themselves as much from right-wing white supremacy groups as from civil rights groups, categorizing both as "attention-seekers."

> It is painfully obvious that CORE does not in fact stand for what they say they stand for. They certainly don't seem to be genuinely interested in either civil or human rights. They agitate, demonstrate and disrupt for the sole purpose of keeping a normally quiet residential area in a constant state of turmoil. Many of our neighbors are in a state of near panic.
>
> Baby sitters refuse to accept jobs in the area where all night lie-ins take place.
>
> Expectant mothers are nervous, upset and distraught. Our wives and mothers are afraid to go out after dark, not only because of the demonstrators, but for fear of the trash they attract as well . . . Nazis, gangs of teenage bums spoiling for trouble, sneak thieves and others of that ilk. Our children are being taught that disobedience and disorder is the way to attain goals and that law officers represent evil. If these are the aims of CORE, then they have certainly been successful.
>
> The homeowners of this area have been plagued by these demonstrations and the publicity seekers they attract for a full year. We are fed up with them and with their tactics. We want for ourselves the same civil rights they claim to be demonstrating for. We want to be left alone to enjoy our homes and our families. Is that too much to ask?
>
> We are not wealthy people. To many of us, our homes represent most of what we own and hold dear. Many in the area have made substantial sacrifices to purchase homes in this neighborhood. Now we want to live in them in peace. We respect the civil and human right of every individual, whatever his race, creed or color and we ask that our own rights be respected as well.

After a long paragraph explaining why they believed that Jackson was not a serious buyer and never intended to purchase the home, the statement continues:

> All of these factors have convinced the 600 homeowners in the Southwood Riviera section that it is not Don Wilson being demonstrated against, but the individual residents themselves.[77]

Here the residents recast themselves as a beleaguered minority, their own rights under attack, without making any attempt to try and answer the question of why this might be. This letter shows how they worked to overcome the destabilization of the old ideological certainties of white supremacy that Torrance was founded upon to find new forms of discourse to justify their untroubled enjoyment of its exclusive (and expensive) space. They take up a similar discourse of civil rights as the protestors, but privilege those of property (being already in possession of it) and security rather than those of justice or equality—thereby helping to forge the new ideological supports of white privilege strong enough to survive in this new historical moment.

An *LA Times* article gives a more revealing view into what lies behind this new discourse. It opens with the reactions of tract residents describing children playing a new game: picketing. An angry mother blamed the mass protests for "disturbing our children, upsetting our lives and chang[ing] our way of thinking about Negroes." Residents believed that protesters were being used in some way by communists, related rumors that they were being paid, questioned their motives as being self-glorifying or driven by personal grudges, and they worried about the safety of their children. One described his wife as "a nervous wreck." Another woman stated, "I'm very liberal minded and I couldn't care less if a Negro lived next to me. But, I don't like to be pushed around like we have been in past months." A third: "We're tired of people saying we have to put up with everything just because someone is mad at Don Wilson. We have rights too." All of them seemed sure that Don Wilson did his best to sell a home to an African American, and that it was not the developer's fault the deal fell through.[78]

OBSTINATE TO THE END

In a follow-up article covering the protestors' point of view, the *LA Times* quotes picketer Reverend Samuels: "It's monotonous, hot, tiring work to spend hours every Saturday or Sunday trudging up and down a sidewalk under the eyes of police and the disdainful glare of homeowners." He was one of 152 who had by then been arrested in protest at the tract. In response to the charge of communism leveled at them by homeowners, another CORE member responded: "CORE is totally non-political. We have only one aim and that is eliminating racial discrimination. Any member whose allegiance is to a foreign power is automatically expelled." According to CORE, Jackson did indeed wish to buy the home, and eight other African American couples had attempted to purchase in the tract. While members were sympathetic toward the homeowners' complaints, they felt that human and civil rights were more important than property rights. The article highlights that through the entire year of picketing, CORE had encouraged residents to join them in asking Don Wilson to stop discriminating. Only in the past week had one homeowner out of the tract's 650 joined the pickets in support.[79]

And still the picketing continued, even as CORE, the NAACP, and UCRC sought additional leverage against Don Wilson. In terms of understanding the economics of Wilson's business practices, the closest the groups came was in their analysis of where leverage might lie that could force him to sell a home. The NAACP/UCRC had already announced their request that the governor take the steps necessary to revoke Wilson's building licence.[80] CORE announced in a press conference that they would begin an around-the-clock sit-in of the Torrance sales office, defying further arrests. At the same time, they requested that the Home Savings and Loan Association issue a statement that they would cease to support Wilson until he acceded to CORE's integration demands. As CORE explained: "Since 1960, Wilson has never found a Negro who 'qualifies financially' for homes in his all-white tracts, but he has sold equally expensive homes to Negroes in his Centerview tract."[81] Seeking more powerful leverage from those with money, CORE then expanded their pickets to include the Home Savings and Loan Association's Beverley Hills and LA offices.[82] The Southwood pickets continued, with sixty demonstrators appearing the following weekend and another twenty-five arrests. A *Sentinel* reporter describes Wilson being visibly affected by the sight of so many white people: "To one group of sit-ins with only one Negro, he said: 'One black. Look, only one black!'"[83] Such an unconscious utterance of surprise that Black and white should fight together for equality underlines the impossibility of Wilson even imagining such an ideal.

In the first week of August, the court upheld the city's curfew law and lifted the injunction. The weekend following, Torrance police made seventy-two arrests, thirty-one of them for violations of the new law as CORE members conducted a "walk-in" to test the ordinance.[84] The sheer volume of trials was proving difficult for Torrance to handle, with the single city prosecutor's request for help refused by the district attorney, even as the trials themselves were being scheduled in batches of twenty-five in the Redondo Beach Council Chamber to accommodate the size.[85] Barbara Dimmick of CORE wrote:

> The time is now . . . 1963. The place is a quiet, residential street in Torrance, California. Which is in America. The land of the free, the home of the brave. It's 7 p.m. on a Sunday evening. Marring the quiet scene are roadblocks and the armed policemen and a crowd of curious onlookers. What's happening . . . why, nothing much, just some people. About thirty, walking single file toward the roadblocks and the police. They go through the roadblocks. Now the police leap onto their

motorcycles and follow them. They stop the walkers. A huge bus rumbles over. The walkers are arrested. The police put them in the bus. The charge? It's against the law to walk down that street after 7 p.m. on weekends if you are not a resident of Torrance. This happened last Sunday in America . . . land of the free . . . home of the brave![86]

Even as this massive effort was happening in Torrance, CORE was mobilizing for a mass march on the board of education with the NAACP and UCRC, to be followed by a fundraising concert starring Nat King Cole. At the same time, the employment committee was concluding negotiations with Disneyland to hire on a non-discriminatory basis.[87] Their organizational resources must have been stretched to their limits.

The following weekend the national director of CORE, James Farmer, walked the picket lines both at the Torrance tract and in front of the Home Savings and Loan Association, and a new student group affiliated with CORE picketed the Torrance police station itself in protest of the more than 200 arrests made over the past year.[88] The police reported the weekend's total as twenty-six arrested at the tract, and five more at the Torrance police station.[89] In what appears to have been retaliation, the twenty protestors arrested on the Saturday were said to be transferred to the Los Angeles County Jail, with its longer processing times, though the bondsmen believed them to be in Torrance.[90]

The following week, the judge ruled on the first of the three lawsuits filed to restrict picketing, issuing an injunction against sitting, standing, lying, or squatting on the property. It placed no limits on the number of picketers, but insisted that they continue moving and remain at least ten feet apart and on one side of the sidewalk.[91] That same week the same judge ruled on the "public nuisance" lawsuit of the homeowner association, and ordered an even more severe injunction, stating that protesters could only picket for ten minutes of every hour, and not before 8 a.m. or after 7 p.m. These stipulations proved to be severe blows.

Meanwhile, ACLU attorneys had completely tied up the courts—not one CORE picketer had yet come to trial after days of jury selection, with only twelve of 125 peremptory strikes used by the defense.[92] They also filed affidavits for seventy-three protesters requesting a change of location, as they could not obtain a fair trial in Redondo Beach or Torrance.[93] The number of cases put immense pressure on the entire South Bay legal system; a new division was added to the South Bay district to help deal with the cases and Torrance was forced to hire additional help for the prosecution.[94]

After three days of negotiations between the attorneys, the city of Torrance and CORE, an agreement was reached: the city of Torrance agreed to drop charges against the 234 persons arrested who were still facing trial, while CORE agreed to limit pickets to two, one day a week, with no sit-ins or mass demonstrations unless a court found Wilson guilty of refusing to sell a home to anyone based on race, creed or color, and the home in question had not then gone into escrow within thirty days.[95] The city emphasized that it had only been working "to protect the peace of the neighborhood and to uphold law and order," and was not engaging in the actual dispute.[96] The city's "non-engagement" cost an estimated additional $8,000 a day to cope with the added legal costs of prosecuting protestors, other staff, and policing costs, and it continued to pursue a permanent injunction against picketing.[97] While CORE continued small pickets at Centerview, this was essentially the end of the direct action campaign, although the discrimination lawsuits against Wilson continued to move through the courts.

An article in the *Sentinel* gives CORE's tabulations of the cost of their thirteen-month campaign against Wilson. They estimated:

- Over 11,700 manhours [were] volunteered by 3,500 persons.
- The demonstrators walked 5,600 miles at [the] tract and drove more than 80,000 miles to get there and home.
- They also consumed 230 gallons of coffee; 1500 soft drinks; 600 loaves of bread; 250 lbs of cold cuts; 300 lbs of hamburger; 12 cases of tuna fish; 16 crates of lettuce; 270 lbs of cookies; and 1354 candy bars.
- During the demonstrations, 62,600 leaflets were distributed and 249 arrests made.
- Bail totaled nearly $100,000, however that expense was largely erased when all charges against demonstrators were dropped as a result of an agreement reached by CORE and the City of Torrance.

The article notes that the Torrance tract "still has no Negro residents."[98]

Homeowners were clearly angry, not just about the picketing and the sit-ins, but that their position on racism was being questioned at all. The police shut down the Centinela Bay Human Relations Commission's forum on civil rights at Torrance High School, declaring it an unlawful assembly and ordered the crowd to disperse, as they believed "the temper of the crowd created a possibly riotous situation." Panelists blamed members of the John Birch Society, who heckled, booed, and all coughed at once when the panel moderator attempted to start the discussion.[99] They also led the entire audience in the "Star Spangled Banner," though the reporter states that the crowd did not go along with the "Battle Hymn of the Republic." Yet the depth of bad feeling was clear when Torrance Council Member Sciarotta blamed CORE for the incident, stating that it was "fixed to make this city look bad."[100] A Torrance resident writing an editorial on the event notes that "the forum turned into a Neo-fascist demonstration of Pro-Birchers and Radical Rightists":

This demonstration in Torrance, the "All American City" was a most frightening experience . . . Members of the Torrance Police Department were present at the meeting and they did NOTHING. While the Radicals hooted and leered the speakers, they just watched. Couldn't they have removed the undesirables and thereby set an example for the rest?[101]

The week during the council deliberations to approve the extra support for the legal department, Council Member Drale asked the council to "study the possibility of adopting a resolution on civil rights." Council Member Miller violently opposed the idea, as he believed that the issue did not exist. The *Torrance Herald* reports his statement as "everything the city has done has shown that everyone receives equal rights in Torrance." The president of the Southwood Homeowners Association protested that "the council would even think about a resolution," fully backing Miller's statement that the actions spoke for themselves.[102] It is hard to see just what these actions were. After the signing of the agreement with CORE, an editorial claims the city's accolades rest, rather, on its lack of action:

> A situation which was distasteful to both sides has been resolved and the civil rights of both demonstrators and residents of the Southwood tract have been protected by provisions of the agreement. The city does not belong to the dispute between CORE, and builder Don Wilson, and it should be noted again that the city has never attempted to decide—or in any way inject itself into that dispute.
>
> The agreement is a product of reasonable men discussing common problems in an atmosphere of mutual respect and trust. The tension is gone and the neighborhood is again quiet.[103]

August 28, 1963 saw LA's largest ever civil rights march, held in conjunction with the mass march on Washington.[104] CORE shifted its focus to the Los Angeles education board, where members held a hunger strike for integration.[105] In December, the state filed charges against Wilson for discrimination under the Rumford Act.[106] There is no report of any African Americans moving into the Dominguez Hills tract, while the Centerview tract continued to sell. It was not until July 1964 that the *LA Times* reported that an African American family had moved into the Southwood Riviera Royale estate—not through the open purchase pushed by CORE and the state, but through the subterfuge of purchasing their home through a white intermediary with the help of the Centinela Bay Human Relations Commission.[107] This period saw tremendous moral gains won by the civil rights movement, and new laws and support of the state and federal government for integration, yet ultimately CORE's campaign failed in its efforts to integrate Torrance—a failure that likely reverberated throughout the Los Angeles area.

Chapter 6

White Reaction

Old Walls Torn Down and New Ones Raised

The ultimate failure of the Torrance campaign highlighted the limitations of a moral movement. As Julius Lester writes, "It was thought then that segregation was a moral issue, therefore a moral weapon—nonviolence, love, satyagraha—would bring the walls of the prison tumbling down."[1] But it became obvious that the walls of segregation weren't tumbling despite their victories, a realization that brought about huge divisions within civil rights groups like CORE. National director James Farmer writes of his limited success after being brought in to try and deal with the growing splits in terms of both race and philosophy: "CORE in California, like CORE in other states, continued to simmer over the fire of a widening racial clash and a strengthening of the spirit of black nationalism."[2]

The December 1963 active-member newsletter from Earl Walter, chairman emeritus of CORE, highlights the split while reaffirming the organization's dedication to its original values:

> In addition, the revolution itself has had its effect on the group . . . The high points and the low points, the stresses and the strains challenge the stability of individuals . . . the hazards of destruction are necessarily there also. Not every one of us in the movement has outgrown that conditioning which makes heroes out of the real villain in terms of human behaviour. If we are not fully committed to nonviolence, in a period of tension it is quite easy for us to become perpetrators of hostility rather than victims, and thus to lose the advantage that the philosophy offers.[3]

He is clearly writing to the growing number of advocates of "Black Power," and he does not seem sorry to lose the "some 20 or 30" people splitting from the organization. For those who stayed within CORE, the emphasis shifted more and more to community organizing within the African American community, by neighborhood. In November 1963, they launched the new project "Operation Jericho," aimed to bring the longest-standing and strongest-held racial faultline of the "Alameda wall" tumbling down.[4] Like Torrance, the invisible but powerful barrier of Alameda Street was able to hold throughout the revolutionary turmoil of the 1960s. CORE's campaign around integrating schools showed Alameda's importance as a school district boundary as well as a residential one. The battle to keep neighborhoods white was always also about control over key institutions and wealth—maintaining white dominance over social space.

The desperate importance of overcoming the segregation of space and institutions was intuitively understood as necessary for society's transformation by CORE's organizers and members. The intractable and united front presented by Torrance overshadowed their other victories, however. Despite the brief revival brought by a new campaign involving mass sit-ins at meetings of the school board, the organization was losing steam. White reaction, on the other hand, was steadily building.

Immediately after the Rumford Act had passed—making housing discrimination illegal—in 1963, the California Real Estate Association formed the Committee for Home Protection and began a campaign not just to overturn the law, but to amend the state constitution. Proposition 14 on the 1964 election ballot would make it unconstitutional to limit the right of any homeowner to sell, rent, or lease their property (or, more importantly, *not* to sell, rent or lease their property) to anyone they wished. Such was its perceived popularity, Republican candidates distributed supportive propaganda stamped with their names, such as William McDill running for Assembly membership in the 61st District. The predominant rhetoric of property rights, patriotism, and freedom continued, with a nod to these concepts' economic importance. The other side of the leaflet states that a "Yes Vote: Will restore rights basic to our freedom—rights that permit all persons to decide for themselves what to do with their own property." This is emblematic of the ways that CREA and their supporters attempted to mobilize the idea of freedom to reclaim and redefine the concept of rights to white neighborhoods as civil rights equal to those claimed by groups like CORE. CREA's is a discourse of privilege lost; American rights that had been taken away by an interfering government in service to minority groups. As proof of the resonance of such a recasting of whites as victims needing protection, Proposition 14 won in a landslide.[5]

The effect of such a major defeat for liberals and all communities of color cannot be underestimated. Meier and Rudwick found great disillusionment with CORE's tactics in the face of these defeats and the power of white racism. Quoting a member after the Watts uprisings, they write:

> nonviolence might well have been adopted by Los Angeles Negroes had they received convincing evidence of its effectiveness. Likely they saw, as we in CORE have learned, that the most persistent nonviolent campaign . . . can yield at best a puny gradualism. The laws we have won are grudgingly written, passed, and enforced.[6]

Dr. Cobb, staff member of the LA County Human Relations Commission and a UCRC member, stated in an interview with the Governor's Commission on the LA Riots that in the field of housing, "the CORE housing chairman had expressed the feeling that there was nothing that could be done . . . when the civil rights leaders take that attitude, this reflects a serious problem."[7]

In August 1965, Watts exploded. While much of the press reflected surprise and disbelief that such an uprising could take place after the civil rights victories of the period, the mood of everyday people in cities across the country proved to be very different. Even the internal politics of organizations committed to nonviolence like CORE showed a quickly growing anger and frustration with the slowness of real change. From the initial arrest of Marquette Frye, the uprising spread over five days to involve over 30,000 people. It resulted in thirty-four deaths, over 1,000 injuries, over 3,000 arrests, and tens of millions in property damage.[8] It is not coincidental that the Watts uprisings followed hard on the heels of Prop 14—indeed, the Governor's Commission noted its passage several times in the hearings as a principal cause of discontent along with police brutality—and graphically illustrated the loss of hope in peaceful protest and the political process. Sears and McConahay conducted a study of opinions after the riots, and their findings showed this clearly:

> The racial polarization of local black and white leaders was duplicated almost immediately in the responses of the black and white publics. These descriptions of and feelings about the riot were as different as night and day . . . Most blacks perceived the riot as (1) a purposeful symbolic protest; (2) against legitimate grievances; (3) designed to call attention to Blacks' problems . . . When asked directly, a majority felt the riot did have a purpose or a goal, felt that the targets deserved attack, and agreed that the riot constituted a black protest. Also, when given a free choice of descriptive terms, a surprisingly large minority [38 percent] chose to talk about it in revolutionary or insurrectional terms.[9]

They also found of Black respondents that "most thought Whites had become more 'aware of Negroes' problems' and more sympathetic to them as a consequence of the riot."[10] This stands in tragic contrast to whites and Mexicans interviewed:

> [Fifty-two percent] reported feeling a "great deal" of fear. Fear among whites was greatest in Baldwin Hills and Leimert Park, two integrated communities on the edge of the Curfew Zone . . . but, even in affluent Pacific Palisades 20 miles from the riot, 12 percent reported "a great deal" of fear.[11]

Watts and its aftermath radicalized the community, driving deeper the rifts between and within traditional civil rights organizations as some continued to promote nonviolent struggle while others, frustrated with the pace of change, turned to new strategies. The division over urgency, tactics, and Black nationalism would pull CORE apart.

Much of the debate was over the role of violence, and the role activists should play in the community to create meaningful and transformative change.

The words of Robert F. Williams ring with such force in the light of LA's many decades of struggle—and even more so for Monroe County, North Carolina, where he worked to end segregation and nearly lost his life. Above all, they serve to re-center violence where it has always belonged: in the maintenance of white supremacy.

> The existence of violence is at the very heart of a racist system. The Afro-American militant is a "militant" because he defends himself, his family, his home and his dignity. He does not introduce violence into a racist social system—the violence is already there and has always been there. It is precisely this unchallenged violence that allows a racist social system to perpetuate itself.[12]

He advocated the use of guns for self-defense as well as a broad program of economic justice rooted in the working class community. He would prove an inspiration for the Black Panthers, who briefly created a revolutionary moment joining Blackness together with political and social liberation beginning in 1967.[13] As Panther member Elaine Brown explains:

> They were a new generation of black men, divorced completely now from the old, the civil-rights movement of the NAACP and the Urban League and Martin Luther King's Southern Christian Leadership Conference. They were young black men no longer concerned with the business of segregation or integration. They were young black men who were calling for an end, not only to discrimination, an end not only to the denial of civil rights, but to all forms of oppression of blacks—social, political *and* economic—on all fronts.[14]

They were able to politicize and channel a widespread collective understanding of how far African Americans remained socially and ideologically outside of white definitions of citizenship and community, just as they were contained physically outside that community's borders. They spoke of almost universal anger and alienation revealed through the uprisings, particularly among the youth and gangs, who felt this most keenly (particularly through constant police harassment). For a moment, they seemed poised on the brink of revolution.[15]

The civil rights movement had pushed to the limits for change via legal rulings and legislation without achieving full equality. The Watts uprising and similar explosions in ghettoes across the country seemed to show how well African Americans understood this, particularly after the assassination of Martin Luther King, Jr. in 1968. It is hardly surprising then, that the FBI carried out their intensive, and successful, COINTELPRO program to destroy both the Panthers and their revolutionary program. J. Edgar Hoover's 1968 memo called on all field agents "to exploit all avenues of creating . . . dissension within the ranks of the BPP . . . recipient offices are instructed to submit imaginative and hard-hitting counter-intelligence measures aimed at crippling the BPP." This involved an array of anonymous phone calls and notes, the use of infiltrators and provocateurs, and targeted raids and assassinations, which left the Panthers' programs in tatters.[16]

The red scare of the 1950s had earlier marginalized figures like Charlotta Bass and destroyed viable organizations joining community with labor, and class with race. COINTELPRO's destruction of the Panthers in LA and across the country worked similarly to prevent new currents within the sweeping wave of Black nationalism from drawing on a more broadly revolutionary experience and history.[17] This left the field open for Black nationalist groups, such as the Black Muslim movement led by Elijah Muhammad, who—particularly after the split with Malcolm X—called for a narrow separatism without challenging capitalism itself.[18] As Horne writes:

> LA elites recognized that the nationalists could be accommodated in a way that their militant predecessors of the left could not. As long as separatism was decoupled from reparations, the NOI [Nation of Islam]-influenced nationalism not only did not present a threat to private property, it could even be helpful—along with racism—in keeping apart those who might want to unite jointly against the LAPD and the elites it was sworn to protect.[19]

Nor did Black nationalism achieve much breadth or staying power, in South Central at least. Sonya Winton quotes South Central activist Robin Cannon as saying:

> When the Panthers died, black political activism in my community died. CCSCLA [Concerned Citizens of South Central Los Angeles] is awakening the old and new guard in our community to confront the same issues that plagued our neighborhoods in the 1960s and 1970s. But this time, no matter how hard the dominant system tries to get rid of us, we're [CCSCLA] not going anywhere![20]

The white community reacted very differently, feeling itself a victim while in fact emerging a victor. While the passage of Proposition 14 shows that the period of "white backlash" was well under way in 1964, the fear caused by the Watts uprisings certainly deepened it. But as Julius Lester details:

> The "white backlash" was nothing new to the black community. They knew all about the backlash, the frontlash, the sidelash and all them other lashes . . . it simply meant that white folks were a little tired of picking up the papers and seeing niggers all over the front page . . . The average white person didn't know what niggers wanted and didn't much care. By now they should have gotten whatever the hell it was they said they didn't have, and if they hadn't gotten it, they either didn't deserve it or didn't need it.[21]

The homeowners of Torrance would not frame their feelings in such a way, but their angry patriotism along with their demands for their own security and the ability to just be left alone to enjoy their own rights, property rights in particular, expressed the same sentiments. Developers and realtors helped lead the development of this discourse. Before the passage of the Rumford Act outlawing housing discrimination, Earl Anderson, executive secretary of the Los Angeles Realty Board, was quoted in the *LA Times* as citing reverse discrimination—that forcing a landlord to take someone in was in fact discrimination "against the majority" and that realty board members are "only agents of the public. We do what they tell us to do."[22] The winning of limited political and legal protections for the civil rights of people of color was enough to make most whites feel threatened in their privilege as well as victimized. These civil rights gains eroded even further their existing abilities to protect what they believed to be the use and exchange value of white neighborhoods (activists never broke the link between property values and the race of occupants), but segregation's necessity only increased as anti-discrimination legislation, and particularly *Brown v. Board of Education*, made segregation seem the primary strategy to "naturally" maintain white institutions for social reproduction.

The conflict in Torrance also held many lessons for other cities and for other builders trying to sell the social space of "home." When CORE threatened to picket the Home Savings and Loan Association to ask them to pressure Wilson, top executive Ken Childs convened a meeting of the largest housebuilders in Los Angeles, ostensibly to try and convince them to end discrimination in unison. The effort failed.[23] Clearly, however, other builders were keenly aware of the pressure being brought to bear against their discriminatory policies and were discussing it among themselves and watching the conflict closely. A few lessons could certainly be drawn from Wilson's defeat of CORE: the lack of the government's ability or will to enforce anti-discrimination legislation; the ways in which a verbally expressed desire to sell to African Americans could then be neutralized in the complications of the home-buying process; and perhaps most of all when compared to CORE's victory in Monterey Park, the importance of local government support of white developments and the use of their power to control access and levels of protest within such developments. Through their ordinance, Torrance's city council effectively privatized the entire neighborhood and created policed walls to protect Southwood's white population from uncomfortable protest. When courts upheld this legality, CORE was forced to yield, presumably drained from supporting the over 200 people already arrested. Privatized, gated communities accomplished the same goal from their very inception, ensuring that any future picketing would only be able to occur at the neighborhood gates or in city halls. CORE had been fighting the "ghetto wall," remnants of the covenant fight built to contain African Americans inside a small area. Soon activists would be facing walls that completely enclosed a neighborhood here, a city there, erected to keep them out.

The movements of the 1940s had forced concrete changes in law and policy, thereby removing ideological and financial support for de facto segregation by the US government. The civil rights struggles of the 1960s solidified these gains in transforming unchallenged expressions of white supremacy, winning laws against discrimination enforced by the government, and creating a fairly widespread consensus that Jim Crow racism was wrong. These victories increased token representation in business, civil society, and politics, yet left essentially untouched any real political power and economic dominance.[24] As Derrick Bell writes:

> The symbols change and the society even accepts those symbols we civil rights advocates have urged on it, but our status remains fixed. Society's stability is enhanced rather than undermined by the movement up through the class ranks of the precious few who too quickly are deemed to have "made it."[25]

Spatially, the changes that allowed African Americans and other people of color to escape agonizingly tight ghetto boundaries imposed on them by whites— what Soja describes as the fractal landscape—are a testament to the new freedom to buy homes and the shifting racial hierarchies that opened up different geographic areas to diverse populations.[26] This required new ideologies and spatial practices if white privilege and spaces were to be maintained—and no better example proving the desire for this on the part of developers, politicians, police, court officials, and white residents can be found than Torrance in 1962 and '63 as they worked together to help forge a new praxis for the preservation of their neighborhoods and their privilege.

The seeds of these new spatial practices, now widespread in cities across the country, can be found in the lessons learned through the victory of developer Don Wilson and the good people of Torrance. The clearest long-term strategy has been putting control of streets and public spaces into residents' hands—in any common interest development, or CID, a homeowner association can shut down their streets in the same way that Torrance did, without requiring a city ordinance and police. In CIDs, individuals own their own homes (though their use is incredibly restricted by covenants placed to preserve the character of the neighborhood and property values), and they hold in common and control the development's streets, amenities, and public spaces. Membership in a self-taxing homeowner association, usually known as a resident community association (RCA), is mandatory, and it both enforces covenants and carries out many of the services traditionally belonging to a municipality, including street paving and lighting, security and garbage removal.[27] The United States Advisory Commission on Intergovernmental Relations reported that the new phenomenon of CIDs "probably accounts for the most significant privatization of US local government responsibilities this century."[28]

In 1964, there were fewer than 500 of these associations. The explosive Watts uprising occurred in 1965. The National Fair Housing Act, which passed in 1968 and made housing discrimination illegal for the first time, was only made possible in the immediate shock that followed King's assassination. By 1970, there were 10,000 RCAs. By 1992, 150,000 associations governed an estimated 32 million Americans, and homes within CIDs composed 11 percent of the housing stock.[29] These numbers reflect the fact that an enormous amount of surplus capital was being channeled into real estate development through this period.[30] The most profitable real estate development still followed the model laid down by HOLC in the 1930s—new tracts of homogenous housing protected to the greatest extent possible from "adverse influences."

Some, like lawyer Sheryll Cashin, argue that while "homogeneity is not intrinsic to the CID concept, in practice CIDs tend to be highly homogeneous by income and race."[31] Yet contextualized within the ongoing struggles over space, the rise of new, homogenous suburbs are closely tied to the desire of whites to live among their own.[32] Along with other civil rights won in the 1960s, advocates argue that through such mechanisms, the protections available under fair housing laws have been consistently whittled away.[33]

Along the same principles as neighborhood CIDs, more and more suburban areas were protecting their tax bases and ensuring control over their public spaces in another way—through municipal incorporation. A host of small cities sprang up beginning in the late 1950s in a process documented in Miller's *Cities By Contract*.[34] Using an innovative approach labeled the "Lakewood Plan," they contracted with the county for vital services such as police and fire protection. This allowed them to reduce their city taxes to a fraction of what LA was forced to impose, often charging absolutely nothing in the early years based on the strength of sales taxes. This was followed in 1977 by the passage of Proposition 13, another part of what is termed the "property owner's revolt." Prop 13 froze property taxes at their 1975–6 levels, with only 2 percent increases allowed per year unless the property changed owners, at which point the new tax assessment would become the new base level. An ex-city council member described this as *the* principal issue for the city of LA; debt and bankruptcy were the factors preventing LA from acting as a city, and the repeal of Prop 13 was necessary for the city to competently provide its required level of services.[35] Thus LA settled into a new articulation of space and privilege labeled as the "succession of the successful" by Robert Reich.[36]

WHAT WAS WON AND WHAT WAS LOST

The victories of the post-World War II period partially destabilized the political and social supports for white space and privilege, and challenged widespread acceptance of white supremacist ideologies. The civil rights movement of the 1960s against Jim Crow brought this destabilization to a head, and for a moment, wholesale structural change seemed possible and revolution was in the air. Instead, a set of limited, however real, concessions were won. Openly expressed sentiments of white supremacy and biological racism have continued into the present, but the 1960s achieved their marginalization along with widespread acceptance of at least a generic political and social equality. The government legitimated this movement—forced by these victories to abandon its neutral stance on segregation, it actively (though with widely varying levels of willingness and effectiveness) began to support integration, taking measures to improve the position of oppressed "minorities" and prosecuting discrimination and hate crimes. Yet the economics of real estate continued to link race to both use and exchange values of land. Segregation only intensified with white flight, reflecting a dissonance between lip service to equal rights and loyalty to a community lived and understood in terms of race and segregated suburban neighborhoods.

Thus, despite these civil rights gains, new discourses of "freedom" and "color-blind" ideologies came together with the old real estate economics of land, where value continued to be defined by whiteness. This ensured that race remained central to the massive new suburban building programs that formed part of a new period of capital development centered on land speculation and real estate.[37]

Large developers made decisions about where the new racial faultlines would fall as they expanded into the suburbs. Older areas that were not seen as defensible (or worth defending)—such as Compton, with its heavy tax burden, integrated schools, and compromised position straddling the Alameda wall— were abandoned to peoples of color. Sales office staff and targeted advertising campaigns in Black newspapers like the *Sentinel* channeled them there and away from white areas. White homeowners, on the other hand, invested financially and emotionally in these neighborhoods, fought a tenacious and often violent rearguard action that ultimately—and most traumatically for families unwilling to live in integrated neighborhoods—failed to preserve their segregated nature. Resentment and a feeling of victimization became widespread— even among those successful in defending the whiteness and privilege of their neighborhoods.

The Torrance campaign showed homeowners themselves reaching for the rhetoric of civil rights and patriotism to defend their security and property values, prioritizing property rights over all else. CREA, too, consistently mobilized ideologies of the sanctity of property rights and a rhetoric of privatization and freedom, now opposed to a government that had betrayed it to support, even if only nominally, the same peoples of color that CREA had worked to protect neighborhoods from.

In the end, capital, resources, and most whites moved further into the suburbs, to newer, more defensible CIDs and gated communities, preferring the newly incorporated smaller cities with their well-protected tax bases. Thus, the connection between whiteness and land use and exchange values was further cemented, both materially and ideologically, rather than challenged. Segregated space remained unconsciously normalized for new generations, forming a buffer between them and the realities of poverty in resource-deprived central cities—a spatial fix not only for capital but also for a racial privilege that allowed overt forms of racism to recede into the background, their purpose achieved materially through new urban forms.

The results of this in the present are explored in the next section. It describes what has happened now that the physical limits of expansion have been reached and the development of the city center has promised higher profits for developers, who continue to apply these suburban understandings of white community and logics of land value to already existing poor communities of color.

Part III

Into the 2000s and Back to the Center

The Racial Cleansing of Skid Row

Chapter 7

Battle on Skid Row

Even LA had to hit some kind of limit in terms of just how far it could spread into agricultural land and desert. LA County now spans over 4,084 square miles, is made of up eighty-eight incorporated cities, and has almost 10 million residents.[1] It continues to be highly segregated—yet the patterns have been slowly shifting since a 2001 study showed whites in a high-property-value outer-suburban ring hemming people of color into the inner suburbs and city, and high levels of segregation between other communities of color even when they too expanded into the outer suburbs.[2] The limits of infrastructure, commuting distances, and land itself have for the most part been reached. Investment in real estate has not ceased to play a central role in California's economy, however. As Harvey and Smith describe, the process of uneven development has made the failing infrastructure of the center city a fertile ground for redevelopment, where the "rent gap" has been steadily growing.[3] Despite this spatial change in the direction of capital flows from suburb to center, the product has remained essentially the same—developers are still producing and selling social space, privilege, and happiness, which means that for the most part they are trying to sell 'white space'.[4]

This unbroken link between race and value has ensured the existence of a rent gap in communities of color as well as redlining practices, the withdrawal of resources, the practices of absentee landlords, and the like. Building on Harvey and Smith's theorizations of the gap, this section further grounds these theories in the contested histories of the US's urban spaces, acknowledging the central role that race has played in definitions of value and community. While some of the marketing discourse has changed to focus on selling points such as "live where you work" and the excitement of the big city, in both discourse and practice it has retained key features developed through decades of struggle over residential space: defensible exclusivity, homogeneity, security, narrow definitions of community and responsibility, and increasingly privatized control over public areas. Above all, it has tried to replicate the white spaces so necessary to the social reproduction of white privilege. Unlike the development of the suburbs, however, the creation of such exclusive spaces has entailed the mass displacement of the poor, primarily poor communities of color.

What we see today is segregation through an active displacement, rather than older, more familiar forms of exclusion through racial covenants and white flight into suburbs heavily protected by multiple forms of legal and illegal discrimination. The logic of white supremacy embedded in land valuation is now shaping financialization and development in the US, ensuring that racial cleansing is central to processes more commonly known as gentrification. This fact has transformed struggle. Where once Charlotta Bass and CORE fought for their rights to move into the neighborhoods they chose, now grassroots organizations in cities across the US are fighting to stay in place.

Those facing the enormous efforts to displace them and their families from downtown LA have not failed to recognize the racial logics that underlie this process, and this section details the ways in which their successful resistance has made segregation through displacement very different from simply discriminating against new occupants or building gates around new developments. Their success has provoked new articulations of ideologies, policies, and violence with the same dialectic of race and land value in a strategic search for something that works on behalf of space and white privilege, highlighting the contested boundaries between the two visions of community downtown, and between consent and coercion.

THE EARLY STRUGGLE FOR DOWNTOWN

Like many cities, LA has faced capital restructuring, where real estate and development rather than heavy manufacturing have become key to the urban economy.[5] Through the postwar years, real estate development expanded steadily outward into the suburbs. But a group of wealthy elite, represented by the Downtown Business Men's Association from its founding in 1924, continued to fight over the decades first to keep, and later to attract, capital back to the central banking and business district. Now known as the Central City Association (CCA), this collective of business interests continues to be among the most powerful forces behind the downtown's development. The main obstacle to this development was Skid Row.

Through the late 1970s and into the '80s, the size and racial makeup of Skid Row's residents changed remarkably from a small, mixed but mostly white male population to what Haas describes as the "mass homelessness" of primarily Black men.[6] By 2012, almost half of those homeless in Los Angeles—by conservative estimates, over 50,000 people—were African American, forming a majority in Skid Row.[7] A recorded transcript of a tour given to rapper Chuck D by Pete White and General Dogon of LA CAN emphasizes how viscerally this concentration is felt on Skid Row streets, as well as how invisible it has been to most people:

> Chuck D: I mean, am I crazy? All I see here for miles is nothing but Black folks. How can you not tell this story? Quote me on that because I am seeing Black folks

until the eye goes dim. How can you be a person in the media and not tell this story?[8]

The primary reason for this lies in LA's massive deindustrialization—the widespread closure of factories and industry through the processes of globalization, deinstitutionalization, and the dismantling of North America's limited welfare state—and the ways in which this hit the African American community the hardest.[9] Hired on in places like Boeing and GM only after years of struggle against discrimination, African Americans were lowest on seniority lists and the first fired, causing a massive wave of unemployment in the African American community as plants closed in the late 1970s and early '80s. While new industries replaced the old, the new plants required either highly skilled labor and located themselves even farther into the suburbs or were industries based around sweated labor such as the garment industry, hiring primarily immigrants.[10] The uprising after the Rodney King verdict in 1992 showed how little the anger over discrimination and bleak prospects had shifted since 1965.[11] Such restructuring combined with poor educational opportunities and lack of transportation, alongside interrelated factors emerging from concentrated geographical poverty such as substance abuse and mental illness, together formed the kind of community that is still visible today within these same Skid Row boundaries set as the boundaries of containment so many years ago. Skid Row's community is now formed by those living on the streets, those living in for-profit residential hotels, and those living in nonprofit-run single-room-occupancy (SRO) hotels, most of which provide supportive services. Depending on money and life circumstances, many cycle through all three (see, for example, *Jones v. City of Los Angeles*).[12] A 2005 report from the Los Angeles Housing Department analyzes the population inhabiting Skid Row's residential and SRO hotels as being:

> predominantly male (78%), African American (72%) and Supplemental Social Security (SSI) recipients, with a monthly income of $221. The average SRO "household" income is approximately 10% of area median income (AMI), or $4,588/year (based on current 100% AMI of $45,875, for an individual). Only 10% of SRO residents are employed. Among SRO residents there is a high incidence of substance abuse (70%), mental illness (45%) and other disabilities. Many SRO residents have chronic illnesses, including contagious diseases but lack proper medical care.[13]

This is fairly representative of the larger community, though reports from the Downtown Women's Action Coalition have shown increasing numbers of women and children on Skid Row.[14] The homeless counts conducted by the Los Angeles Homeless Services Authority (LAHSA) reported more than 4,000 people sleeping on the streets in 2011.[15]

In 1975, the city council passed the largest central city redevelopment plan in the US at that time; the 255-block Central Business Redevelopment Project was an effort to save the city from the decline being faced by city centers across the nation as globalization and deindustrialization hit.[16] The plan delimited areas for different kinds of development, and was highly specific regarding Skid Row, located in the area also known as Central City East. Don Spivack of the Community Redevelopment Agency in charge of the district summarizes the city's formal policy:

> The decision was made with the adoption of the redevelopment plan in 1975 that the program in Central City East would be to try to stabilize it, create and maintain a base of low-income housing and the delivery of social services following a policy that was subsequently referred to as a "Policy of Containment." The containment idea was not so much that you put a fence around Skid Row to keep people in, but you designate an area in which facilities and services will be encouraged to centralize and exist because you have a population in the area that needs the facilities and needs the services.[17]

Despite the focus on services, there is no getting away from the use of the title "policy of containment" found in the documents.[18] This city policy emerged from the nineteen-member citizen's advisory committee to the Central Business Redevelopment District, chaired by Harold L. Katz, founding member of the Century City Chamber of Commerce, one-time director of the Los Angeles Business Council and specialist reserve police officer for the Los Angeles Police Department (LAPD).[19] The plan notes that "[r]ehabilitation of this area is dependent first upon the achievement of a solution to the social and medical problems of the Skid Row population."[20] The decision was clearly to quarantine these "social and medical problems" in a small area while pouring development funds into its surroundings. Its impact on downtown's quality of life, however, was duly noted:

> The Project area living environment will also be improved by the implementation of measures to resolve the various social, medical and economic problems of the Skid Row population, which currently detract from the quality of the living environment for the many residents of adjacent areas.[21]

No care is given to the quality of the living environment for those most dependent on it for survival. Nor do either Spivack or Katz note that the policy of containment was also one fought for by homeless advocates. They believed it to be the only way to save Skid Row, if only temporarily, from wholesale destruction through redevelopment as called for in the original study produced by downtown business interests, especially after they watched the neighboring Bunker Hill community razed to the ground.[22] They advocated for preserving Skid Row through a combination of reasoning, protest and the skilful (if Machiavellian) use of the threat of Skid Row residents and agencies resettling in other council districts.[23] As individuals and academics who were part of this resistance effort, Haas and Heskin give their own view of what this policy physically consisted of:

> The basic concept of the Skid Row plan was the "containment strategy" that characterized the Produce Market, Little Tokyo, and the river as physical walls around the area combined with a human wall of "selective police enforcement" to discourage indigent people from entering the commercial portion of downtown . . . The police and the planner—the cops and the "soft" cops—would assure that the Skid Row population and creeping blight would be contained in one specific area of downtown.[24]

THE POLARIZATION OF SKID ROW

The difference between the Skid Row community and the new residents moving into the rehabilitated lofts and new luxury developments is staggering. A demographic survey of the new loft dwellers done for the Downtown Central Business Improvement District (DCBID) at the end of 2004 showed a majority between the ages of twenty-three and twenty-nine and "young professionals." Of these, 57.9 percent were Caucasian, with the next highest ethnicity being Asian/Pacific Islander at 17.1 percent. A presentation of the report presented to the DCBID board noted the low rates of African Americans (5.2 percent) and Hispanics (8.3 percent). This was followed by a note to "dig deeper" (though there is no mention of what they found). The median income of these new residents was close to $90,000, almost twenty times that of the average SRO resident. Close to 8 percent earned over $200,000. A second study commissioned by the CCA and the DCBID in 2008 found Caucasians at 54 percent, and an average income of $92,200.[25]

The amount of profit at stake in the development of housing and businesses geared toward downtown's new residents is startling, even after the recession. The charts that follow are from the DCBID's 2011 annual report:

DCBID PROPERTY VALUE INCREASE		
Year	Total assessed DCBID value	Percent + / -
1997	$4,211,364,587	
1998	$4,480,598,392	6.39%
1999	$4,838,421,305	7.99%
2000	$5,025,431,988	3.87%
2001	$5,260,525,694	4.68%
2002	$5,544,496,087	5.40%
2003	$5,688,391,189	2.60%
2004	$6,045,596,904	6.28%
2005	$7,002,900,943	15.83%
2006	$7,853,144,506	12.14%
2007	$8,695,487,916	10.73%
2008	$9,301,781,581	6.97%
2009	$9,326,410,136	0.26%
2010	$8,851,402,207	-5.09%
2011	$9,030,845,311	2.03%
2012	$9,213,781,118	2.03%

1 BR Condo Sales 2000-13		
Year	Avg price per square foot	Percent + / -
2000	$168.81	
2001	$191.44	13.5%
2002	$219.78	14.8%
2003	$275.59	25.4%
2004	$389.29	41.3%
2005	$462.51	18.8%
2006	$559.09	20.9%
2007	$527.54	-5.6%
2008	$475.49	-9.9%
2009	$340.31	-28.4%
2010	$329.58	-3.2%
2011	$320.39	-2.8%
2012	$373.78	16.7%
2013	$487.89	30.5%

The data on enormous jumps in the price per square foot for condos is perhaps even more telling—showing the drive for developers to go the extra mile. These prices also make these thousands of new units coming onto the market out of reach for most Angelenos, far less the population that has historically lived in downtown whose entire monthly income could not buy even one square foot after 2003.

The marketing director and vice president of the DCBID considers the massive developments of luxury housing and the influx of new residents one of his principal achievements in his time at the BID, and was working to bring two new schools—one public and one private—to downtown.[26] The amenities of the suburbs, principal among them quality schools and what is widely considered to be a "safe" environment for raising children, are thus recreated, the push for a public school helping to neutralize any opposition for the private one. The greatest single percentage jump in the price of condos, in 2004, gives some indication of the growing demand, making the BID even more sensitive to catering to the needs of new tenants. The DCBID minutes from October 6, 2004, note, "we need purple presence [the color of Historic District Security Guards] everywhere, especially with the residents moving in."

An examination of *DTLA Life*, a glossy magazine geared to downtown's new residents and published by LA Lofts Realty, reveals the importance of exclusivity and luxury as primary themes. A shop/gallery space opening on the top floor of a downtown skyscraper and calling itself "Please Do Not Enter" is described as "[a] new kind of *private* space . . . Please Do Not Enter invites a particular community to discover an eclectic array of exclusive, carefully selected and timeless goods."[27] Lofts are pictured as fully self-contained, with pool, spa, and gym; the other skyscrapers of downtown are their only background.

Articles on downtown property buying geared to both singles and young families, art collecting, interior and "curated" design, shopping and pets are clear indicators of the clientele the magazine aims to attract and the amenities it wishes to highlight.

The CEO of both the CCA and the DCBID notes another key aspect of downtown's development tied into the macro-circuits of capital:

> We also have a community that basically supports growth. People don't live Downtown unless they can handle commercial activity, noise, and all the things you find in the center of a big city. That all portends very well for development because we're not seeing the kind of no-growth behavior that you see in other markets in Los Angeles.[28]

To have wealthy people not just willing to live in high-density environments but be supportive of further development has been a dream come true, after decades of fighting the rise of the slow-to-no-growth movement among suburban homeowners looking to protect their home values, as documented by Mike Davis.[29] It is significant that businesses have identified the only check to expansionary growth in the downtown area as the poor and people of color.

This is the background for the struggle over Skid Row.

LOS ANGELES'S BUSINESS IMPROVEMENT DISTRICTS—
CLEANING UP AND MOVING OUT

The desire to "clean up" Skid Row is nothing new. The *Los Angeles Mirror News* reported in 1955 that boosters found Skid Row as limiting the creation of a revitalized downtown. A campaign initiated by the Downtown Business Men's Association (now the powerful CCA), resulted in closed bars and arrests. Urban renewal and redevelopment claimed 1,000 buildings, which included 20 percent of the housing stock yet remaining in Skid Row.[30]

For many years, however, downtown business interests were split.[31] Those of LA's older wealthy dynasties and downtown banking interests in the CBD, traditionally represented by the CCA, were initially well served by containment, though sweeps and encampment cleanups were carried out around the 1984 Olympics and 1987 visit of the Pope.[32] The CCA's support for containment in Skid Row was in contrast to smaller businesses who had located to Skid Row and in the neighboring districts for the lower rents. The Central City East Association (CCEA), located in the heart of Skid Row, officially formed in 1986 to try to deal with some of the issues of doing business within the containment area.[33] In line with city policy, the LAPD thus walked the tightrope between keeping the poor out of the CBD while at the same time responding to calls and concerns from Skid Row businesses.[34] From the time of its incorporation, the CCEA has pushed hard to clean up the area, lobbying the city, and working with the LAPD and other city agencies to conduct sweeps of the area targeting homeless encampments.[35]

Through conferences held by the International Downtown Association, the CCA had identified BIDs as a key piece of their efforts to revitalize downtown. As Carol Schatz remembers:

> I learned that every real downtown that had been successful in revitalizing itself had a business improvement district as a funding mechanism. So the first step in creating the BID was to get our then state assembly member, Louis Caldera, to author legislation that allowed for a property-based BID, because California had no authorizing legislation at the time. This was 1994. But 1995 was in the middle of this terrible recession, and the property owners in the central part of Downtown just were not interested at that moment.[36]

Thus, the first BID in Los Angeles was formed not by the more powerful CCA (the DCBID would start in January 1998), but rather by a small group of business owners who came together for that purpose in the fashion district south of down-town and Skid Row.[37] The letter below was discussed at the February 22, 1995, meeting of the new Downtown Property Owners Association (DPOA):

> Dear Downtown Property Owner;
>   For a long time, property owners in downtown Los Angeles have been concerned about the continuing physical deterioration of the area accompanied by a general decline in the value of their property.
>   Some of the factors contributing to this deterioration and decline are:
> - A continuing increase in criminal activity, including armed robbery, theft, vandalism;
> - An increase in number of homeless and unemployed, which helps contribute to the feeling of general deterioration;
> - Litter in the streets and alleys and graffiti covered walls.

Encampments were included in the long list of nonviolent misdemeanor crimes that the DPOA wanted targeted. In the same letter, the DPOA proposed the provision of maintenance services to "break down encampments and collect confiscated vendor goods in cooperation with security and LAPD," while these security services would be "supplemented by an armed vehicular night patrol which will aggressively patrol and protect the area from transient activities, relocate sidewalk and alley encampments." A 1994 press release from the DPOA seeking additional BID start-up funds based on the success of their pilot project, titled "Clean and Safe," states that they had been funded through their first two quarters by $210,000 of voluntary donations raised by local business, comple-mented by an additional $100,000 of public money. The BID launched in 1996.

The idea behind the BID is simple: through the self-taxing of business and property owners, they provide a level of services such as trash collection, street cleaning, and security that cash-strapped cities are unable to provide. In Los Angeles this occupation of the public realm by private interests has been greatly facilitated by the city's financial straits caused by the success of a white home-owner movement in passing Proposition 13 in 1975, which preserved their own assets by freezing homeowner taxes at the time of purchase. This decimated municipal tax bases available for public services.[38] While BID activities certainly represent at least the partial privatization of municipal services, this character-izes only part of their actual role and minimizes the size of their considerable impact on local politics and policy.

Study of the inner workings of the BIDs in downtown Los Angeles challenges much of the literature celebrating privatization by revealing how the line between public and private is murky at best, and more practical than ideological. BIDs often receive sizable public funding, although the bulk of the downtown BIDs' multi-million-dollar budget is undoubtedly raised through self-taxation. One of the reasons stated for the formation of the first BID in the Fashion District was the ability of such an organization to leverage additional government funds, and scattered through BID minutes there are notes of additional pots of municipal funding accessed that are not broken down in the budgets.[39] Examples of this additional funding are the CCEA's garnering $300,000 for public toilets to run their "Check-in Center" where homeless individuals could store their belongings, or trash bags from the city's public works department that the CCEA estimated to be worth approximately $35,000–$40,000 annually, or the CCA being offered $5,000 from the Community Redevelopment Agency to improve their kiosks.[40] More importantly, however, the formation of the downtown BIDs in Los Angeles has given a very practical and visible (some would argue intimidating) presence to business interests at street level.

This is mediated somewhat by different organizational structures. The DPOA, for example, hired an outside executive director to manage the Fashion District BID. With a master's degree in environmental design, previous experience working for the Canadian cities of Vancouver and Calgary, and a strong commitment to his position on the Los Angeles Chamber of Commerce/United Way's countywide Task Force on Homelessness, director Kent Smith has the ability to serve as something of a moderator between the demands of the business interests he represents and other stakeholders in the area.[41] This is in contrast to other downtown BIDs, where Estela Lopez, executive director of the CCEA, serves as executive director of the Toy and Industrial BIDs, and Carol Schatz, CEO of the CCA, is also president of the DCBID. Thus, these BIDs exist as separate and professional service-providing organizations in name only. They function under the immediate and day-to-day direction of the heads of the CCA and CCEA, whose only responsibility is for collectivizing and representing business interests.

The CCEA had formed its own two BIDs by 1999: the new Toy district and Downtown Industrial district BIDs. The response from organizations working with Skid Row's low-income community was immediate. In April, only a month after their red-shirted guards started patrolling, activists were blocking traffic to protest the actions of BID's security.[42] Their banner read "Private Security Guards = Homeless Harassment." No arrests were made, although a BID red-shirted guard was fired for cursing and threatening a protestor. Reverend Alice Callaghan, director of the local community organization Las Familias Del Pueblo, organized the protest, telling the *LA Times* that "A private police force should not be in control of public space."[43] Legal advocates agreed. That same year, the ACLU filed a lawsuit, *Cervantes v. International Services, Inc.*, on behalf of several homeless individuals for relief from private security guards hired by the BIDs. In summary: the "suit, the first of its kind in the nation, alleges that downtown property owners, through their support of the business improvement districts, bankrolled a 'systematic, concerted campaign' to chase homeless people off public property in violation of their civil liberties" and that "guards intimidated and harassed homeless individuals through illegal searches, seizures, detentions, and threats in an effort to coerce the individuals into leaving the BID."[44]

One of LA CAN's first campaigns was around the new BIDs and the ways in which they were impacting local residents. LA CAN started in Skid Row in 1999, growing out of the community organizing work of the Los Angeles Coalition to End Hunger and Homelessness and the desire of a group of downtown residents to form their own organization. Their current mission and goals emphasize the need of Skid Row residents to have power over their surroundings and their lives. Their mission is to "help people dealing with poverty create & discover opportunities, while serving as a vehicle to ensure we have voice, power & opinion in the decisions that are directly affecting us." Their three overarching social goals focus on process and people's ability to change things: first, to organize and through collective effort to "change the relationships of power that affect our community"; second, to build an organizing model that is consciously intersectional, seeking to "eradicate the race, class, gender barriers that are used to prevent communities from building true power";[45] and third, to eliminate the violence used against, but also found within, their community. This is a long-term project of transformation in the Freirean tradition, where the embracing of an individual's full humanity can only be found in collective struggle to transform an unjust world.[46]

They draw on social struggles from previous decades, particularly the decisions of civil rights organizations such as CORE members and other Black Power organizations, to root themselves deeply and organize in the community, to combine a sophisticated analysis of race, gender, and class with community organizing for concrete social change through a range of strategies, from advocacy and coalition building to direct action and protest. Some members and staff have direct relationships with former Black Panthers or are themselves former members; brought together with strong feminist voices this has ensured both a structural and historical analysis of how race, class, and gender intertwine with capitalist development and the resulting displacement downtown.

Direct democracy is both their goal and process, in which residents participate in all levels of decision-making on issues that impact the community. It is constantly built over the long term:

> Community organizing is the process of building collective "people power" that includes impacted residents defining problems, solutions, and methods to accomplish these solutions. In the process, people (members) will build a democratically controlled community organization that can take on future issues/problems and embody the will and power of their community over time.[47]

Although a membership organization like CORE, they are very different organizations for their work in a single community, their focus on challenging power through building structures of democracy, and the ways that they do this through ensuring that their work is led by membership from among the community they work in: the extremely low-income and homeless people of Downtown and South Central Los Angeles.

General membership in LA CAN is established by meeting two criteria: being low-income and making a commitment to advancing LA CAN's mission and campaigns. Members fall into three categories at any given time: *general, active, and core*. LA CAN, by design, is led and fueled by members and other community residents.

Core members comprise the majority of each decision-making body at LA CAN, and staff, interns and Board members are recruited from the core membership. Organizational decisions are made by Project Committees, Residential Organizing Committee (General Membership), Staff and Interns, and the Board of Directors.[48]

Thus, unlike CORE, which constantly struggled with the recruitment of Black members and an image of being middle class, LA CAN is firmly grounded in the needs of the community and has created a structure to give that community a level of power and control over it.[49]

This has caused them to take a very different approach from many other organizations on Skid Row, as they work to reframe debates in ways that actually grapple with the real dynamics causing homelessness downtown. Reporter Anat Rubin noted the importance of this:

I feel like we have to undo some of our beliefs about property and addiction and criminal justice, and those are much much bigger hurdles, but I think that groups like LA CAN have done a really good job . . . on that and they've never, they've never apologized for the actual community that exists here. They've never tried to paint it as a community that people would find more sympathetic according to their ass-backwards beliefs.[50]

In her opinion, this created the debate for positive change that is actually needed, starting with where people are without moral judgment. For LA CAN, empowerment is found through confronting the social, political, and economic structures that are the ultimate causes of homelessness. They do not cast blame nor look for the social pathologies and individual failings in their membership; rather, they work to transform the injustices in the world around them and through that process their members collectively transform themselves and move toward their full potential.

This is a vastly different approach than one that focuses on empowerment as simply building individual confidence or self-esteem to better succeed within the confines of racism and exploitation as usual. It also stands in opposition to discourses that focus on the hardships of the "deserving," with its connected willingness to write off those labeled as "undeserving." Such strategic decisions to fight only for those who can be portrayed as completely blameless, if not angelic, in the face of their oppression, is part of a long tradition that needs to be challenged. Such an approach fits easily into neoliberal and reactionary discourses of blame and punishment.[51] LA CAN fights such distinctions at every step, allows every voice to be heard and demands their right to do so. As Rubin continued, "there aren't a lot of organizations like LA CAN, there aren't a lot of other organizations who are fearless like that."

This fearlessness in confronting norms within the nonprofit world is echoed in the fearlessness of LA CAN's members in confronting power, and its efficacy is seen in their ability to fight to win:

> These developers was planning on making millions upon millions of dollars and we messed all of that up . . . We won the largest housing preservation in the history of Los Angeles. And we fighting against the largest police occupation in the history of Los Angeles and we winning.[52]

These victories are described in more detail in what follows—above all, there is a real sense of the power made possible by collective organizing, and pride in victories won. At the same time, the long-term goals of movement and true transformation of structural injustices are part of these collective deliberations. The words of another group member give a real sense of how LA CAN members and organizers view the struggle they are engaged in:

> I would say we're winning in an aspect but we haven't won—inequalities, social and economic inequities, we haven't won against that. That battle is still continued, there's still oppression, there's still repression, there's still a capitalist social-economic order that gives rise to these things . . . as long as you have capitalism you're going to have police abuse, police brutality. You're not going to get rid of that as long as you got a capitalist structure because that's what the police serve is the capitalist structure . . . Winning for me is bringing the people in, winning the hearts and minds of the people that are in need and mostly affected by what's going on. LA CAN is just one organization, one organization does not change everything, we need the masses of the people. We're talking about real change, LA CAN is a guide and can show, can give the people the models and examples that they will need, and the tools they will need to carry on the fight.[53]

Their very first report summarized the results of extensive surveys of Skid Row residents around their experiences with the new BIDs: 42 percent of 166 residents interviewed had witnessed harassment of other homeless by BID security, and 12 percent had been personally detained.[54] Author Pete White explains the ways in which BIDs were able to occupy and control space:

> Prior to the formation of the BIDs residents could move about as they pleased if the activity was lawful. Now such basic social interactions as resting for a spell on a street corner, eating lunch on a curb, or just standing on the street having a conversation with a friend result in hassle from Business Improvement Districts.[55]

The violence being used to remove the poor and homeless from the area was highlighted by a second suit filed shortly after the first by a security guard in the Historic Core BID who claimed that he was fired and then beaten by coworkers after complaining that coworkers were unnecessarily violent with people they encountered on the street. Guard Wilford Johnson was awarded a $595,000 settlement.[56] The CCA proceeded to take over security operations, thereby further centralizing their control of downtown LA's public spaces through their own operation of two BIDs—Downtown Central and Historic Core.

While LA CAN was not involved in the initial ACLU lawsuit in 1999, they joined it shortly thereafter, and helped to shape the final settlement out of court. The settlements included promises by the BIDs to establish guidelines for their security guards, train them to comply with the settlement, and provide money to a local nonprofit to monitor their conduct. They agreed that the guards would not "search, photograph, request identification from or order homeless people to 'move along' from public streets."[57] The ACLU also obtained a preliminary injunction to prevent security from confiscating personal property left on the sidewalks.[58] LA CAN created a community-based training program for BID security. It involved training around what guards could and could not do under the settlement, and also "breaking down some of the myths" about the community.[59]

This began a two-year relationship between LA CAN, the CCEA, and the Historic Core BID. Their position in relation to it and the other downtown BIDs, along with some of the key residential hotels mentioned below (which demonstrate the somewhat arbitrary boundaries of Skid Row as delineated by the city, given that residential hotels are scattered throughout the downtown area, although with a higher concentration in Skid Row), can be seen in Map 10.

Not only did LA CAN do trainings for new guards, but a complaint committee existed to solve any problems as they arose. Dennison states that there were substantial improvements in behavior. The lawsuit had ordered that the security guards stop carrying guns. The BIDs also made efforts to diversify their security teams to include women and people of color, whereas before they had been primarily white men. But after two or three years, Dennison states, this all changed again:

> Then when the redevelopment and gentrification push started happening, almost all of the BIDs over a 2 year period changed leadership because it was clear that the folks who had been working in skid row for a long time and who wanted to be good neighbors were no longer welcome in the business community, because the shift was yeah, we're not being friends with you folks, and pushed them all out. From that time, BID security became more and more adversarial towards the local community, as did the relationship between LA CAN and the BIDs.[60]

The real push to transform Skid Row came in 2002, to facilitate property development, and it became clear that CBD interests had aligned with those of

Central City East against containment to be in favor of "dispersal" from *all* of downtown. This was the year that the CCA reported "downtown Los Angeles is on the cusp of an urban renaissance," borne out by the steadily rising land values and price per square foot in condo sales.[61] What follows explains the three principal prongs of the mass offensive to facilitate this "renaissance" through the removal of poor people of color, the intensity and cost of the efforts showing how firm the belief remained in the necessity of a new homogeneity, and the links between race and land values. In addition to expanding security activities they could directly control through increased numbers of officers, cleanup crews and more aggressive patrols by the BIDs they directed, the CCA and CCEA also helped create political will and drove coordinated political action in the following areas: (1) a new downtown redevelopment plan that brought together private and public support to transform existing buildings into lofts and boutique hotels, thereby displacing housing for long-term and stable low-income tenants; (2) the promotion of a newly enforced rhetoric of public safety and health, demanding the eradication of any homeless presence with the attempted introduction of new public health ordinances effectively making homelessness illegal; and (3) fighting for the LAPD's Safer Cities Initiative and drug enforcement policies. These concentrated more than fifty police within Skid Row to focus on "quality of life" issues, with additional massive sweeps by narcotics and parole officers. Similar to the growing wave of violence that followed the overturning of racial covenants, it was not until close to 10,000 low-income residential hotel units were saved by community members and advocates in 2006 through passage of a residential housing ordinance that the full power of public safety enforcement and policing were visibly unleashed. To create a new, privileged, homogenous white space, the CCEA and CCA would mobilize a number of different policies and ideologies around homelessness, criminality, and health, seeking a new articulation strong enough to overcome resistance and recreate downtown as a preserve of spatial and racial privilege.

THE EMPTYING OF DOWNTOWN'S RESIDENTIAL HOTELS

In 2002, twenty-seven years after the first CBD redevelopment plan and coinciding with the CCA's shift to promote "dispersal" rather than "containment," the city pushed through two new and expedited redevelopment plans for downtown—the Industrial District and Central City redevelopment plans were created and passed within nine months rather than the typical eighteen or more, and many advocates found out about it in the newspaper.[62] The business community had been involved in its creation and was clearly in favor; Victor Franco, Jr. of the CCA testified before the city council and the CRA that "[i]n order to successfully eliminate blight, we believe public intervention through the redevelopment project is necessary."[63] Community advocates, however, sued the city shortly thereafter, charging a time frame and lack of notice that did not allow full participation. Barbara Schultz of the Legal Aid Foundation argued that the plan as structured was "actually going to exacerbate blight rather than alleviate it . . . What's going to happen to those thousands of people? If they're not getting relocation [assistance] and there's no replacement housing? They're going to be out on the street."[64] In a commentary piece for the *Los Angeles Times*, Alice Callaghan brought history to bear on the new redevelopment plans:

> Yet, in its new plan, the city seems not to think of skid row's human dimension. Indeed, it does not even mention skid row. Instead, as though struck by a collective short-term memory loss, the city divides Main Street in half and no longer regards three major hotels there as SROs. Instead, the three hotels can be turned into mixed- income housing.[65]

Clearly, like the CCA, the city's policy of containment and concentrating services had come to an end. According to a policy paper prepared by advocates, it was in fact four residential hotels cited as adaptive reuse projects: the Alexandria, Hayward, Barclay, and Cecil Hotels. This represented 1,785 units of privately owned housing affordable to the very poor to be lost to the community with the support of local government.[66] The passage of the plan spurred an even greater effort on the part of the private landlords of residential properties to cash in on downtown redevelopment.

Residential hotels, or single-room-occupancy hotels, known as SROs, are for the most part the expensive hotels of yesteryear, now rundown and providing housing of last resort. Traditionally home to older, single men, over the past few decades they have increasingly become home to couples and families. For many, they are the last stop before the street, and given LA's ongoing housing crisis, residential hotels have become sources of permanent housing rather than of the mythical transients so often invoked by business, landlords, and public officials.[67] With downtown's gentrification, landlords who had made their profits off of a variety of rent-collecting schemes but who universally failed to invest the minimum into the upkeep of their buildings suddenly found it much more lucrative to develop their properties into luxury units, or sell them to someone who could.

Both demolition and rehabilitation required empty buildings for maximum profit, thus avoiding the possibility of tenant struggle and costly relocation benefits required under law. A rash of evictions, primarily illegal, began. The Los Angeles Housing + Community Investment Department estimated that between 1995 and 2003, ten SRO hotels underwent this process, with a net loss of 1,087 units.[68] While this had clearly been occurring over a number of years, the implementation of a new redevelopment plan saw a larger number of hotels put at risk than ever before.[69]

An example helps establish the pattern of landholdings, primarily speculative and exploitative, prevalent on the cusp of the "urban renaissance" and what that meant for the low-come tenants residing in the buildings and the permanent loss of affordable units. The Morrison Hotel, just south of downtown, might have been made famous from its presence on The Doors' album of the same name, but by the 1980s it had lost even that faded grandeur and had become a relatively cheap residential hotel of 110 units. In 1989, it was bought and placed under the name of a holding company—1246 Hope STR—for $1,043,942. Rents were collected regularly and an additional $2 million loan was leveraged out of the property. When the owners walked away from the hotel after four building and safety inspections and owing more than $267,000 to the Department of Water and Power, it was put up for auction.

Bought for only $750,000 in 1997 by different owners through a newly formed limited liability company called Hope Pico LLC, they initially continued in the same pattern. Tenant complaints were registered with the city, but no action was taken. In 2001, two African American children were found with severe lead poisoning—the LA County Department of Public Health ordered the remediation of that single unit without informing other tenants or ordering the rehabilitation of the entire building. Further tenant complaints were recorded, while the owners leveraged more than $6 million in loans placed against the building. None of those funds were invested in the major repairs needed. Hope Pico LLC was, in fact, part of a much larger set of holdings belonging to two brothers, Sauli and Henry Danpour, who had a varied portfolio of real estate that included high-end rentals in Beverley Hills, multiple slum buildings with long histories of city code enforcement, restaurants, laundromats, and their own hardware store, which was used in later city hearings to provide receipts attempting to prove that building repairs had been made.[70]

In 2004, the building was fully occupied by primarily Latino immigrant and African American families and elders when managers started illegally refusing rent from tenants and telling them to leave. Within three months, over seventy units were emptied using a variety of tactics: payoffs well below the legally required amounts; threats of notifying immigration authorities, child protective services, and the police; and physical force. Tenants who refused to leave had mail withheld (including notices of eviction) and electricity in their rooms turned off; a tenant in a wheelchair living on the fourth floor was regularly refused access to the elevator; and others were confronted by a new armed guard at the entrance, and threatened with the manager's pit bull.[71] The owners applied for a permit to turn the Morrison into a boutique hotel and the building was put up for sale for $8 million as empty. When they acquired the neighboring lot, this was increased to $25 million.

The work of community groups and legal advocates convinced the city to act, and the remaining tenants worked closely with the city attorney's office to obtain a conviction of both the holding companies and the actual owners on twenty-one criminal counts. It was Henry Danpour's third conviction by the city for similar offenses. Yet within three years of their conviction, both were on a stage with almost the entire city council, the mayor, and the city and district attorneys celebrating summer in an event organized by the CCA. The Danpours had funded a large part of the festivities.[72]

Similar attempts by comparable holding companies to empty out residential hotels were occurring across downtown. Also in 2004, the management of the 100-unit Bristol Hotel illegally emptied its units over the course of three days just after its sale, despite an additional layer of tenant protection given by a loan of $850,000, which came with long-term affordability covenants, that had been granted to the owners by the CRA.[73] The resulting lawsuit brought forward by the city and the tenants stated that some of these evictions were carried out at gunpoint.[74] In the same year, the owners of the Frontier and Rosslyn Hotel began illegally emptying the top three floors of the hotel of more than 200 residents, converting the low-income units to lofts while resurrecting Jim Crow practices by putting in a separate entrance and elevator for the new residents. Under pressure from community groups headed by LA CAN and tenants, the city attorney filed a lawsuit against the Frontier and Rosslyn owners in March 2005.[75] Two of the hotels mentioned in the redevelopment plan, the Cecil and the Alexandria, were both part of a program organized by LA CAN and Legal Aid to enlist the pro bono aid of large law firms to represent tenants facing both harassment and eviction.[76]

The Legal Aid Foundation of Los Angeles filed lawsuits against the owners of a total of seven hotels in this period, as well as suing the city for its failure to include protections of, and requirements for, affordable housing in its redevelopment plan. The settlement of this lawsuit in 2005 ensured that the plan preserved all existing residential hotel units downtown and put in place a "no net loss" policy for all residential units.[77] Legal Aid also worked with LA CAN and other community organizations to pass what was known as the Residential Hotel Unit Conversion and Demolition Ordinance (RHO) in May 2006, putting a moratorium on all conversions of residential hotels.[78] As it was being debated, the Los Angeles Housing Department reported that seven hotels and 2,270 units were at immediate risk.[79] With the passage of the ordinance a moratorium took immediate effect, legally preserving more than 6,000 units of very low-income housing in Central LA, home to over 10,000 people.[80] Residential hotels such as the Morrison, already emptied in spite of the lawsuits and tenant organizing, were left to sit empty, no longer worth a fraction of their asking price and preserved as permanent affordable housing.

This was a huge victory for LA CAN, Legal Aid, and the low-income residents of downtown, although additional organizing and litigation was necessary to ensure implementation. Nonprofit organizations stepped in to redevelop the hotels, intentionally working to change the nature of the tenants in the buildings and supported by the city to facilitate downtown revitalization. In 2007, for example, an additional lawsuit against the CRA and the Amerland Group, owners of the Alexandria hotel, claimed that they "systematically and intentionally worked to remove the long-term tenants of the Alexandria and replace them with non-elderly, non-disabled and non-African American tenants."[81] In the 2009 settlement, the CRA and Amerland Group were required to pay almost $1 million and promised housing assistance to 100 current and previous tenants who had also had gas and electricity turned off and padlocks placed on their doors.[82] The Amerland Group became owners of the Frontier Hotel, which they renamed the Rosslyn Lofts. Just after the announcement of the lawsuit against them and the CRA in 2007 over the Alexandria, the city council awarded them an additional $8 million of city funds to rehabilitate the hotel, bringing the total to $20 million. This was in spite of the fact that the loan did not follow the city's own underwriting guidelines, that multiple open complaints had been filed against Amerland for illegal evictions and discrimination on the grounds of race and disability, and that the city was in the process of suing the previous owner for illegally emptying the top three floors of the hotel.[83]

In spite of this, the larger victory was sweet and had ripple effects in both the low-income and the business communities. It almost immediately created a backlash. In the words of an LA CAN activist:

> every for profit hotel tried pulled some kind of scam to illegally evict tenants so they could jump into the loft-building craze, that's what they wanted to do, and when we won that housing preservation ordinance, that preserved the housing for the next 50 years, the first thing that come out they mouth again was ok, well you won your housing, but when you come out your housing, come out in the streets, we got Sergeant Crook and Lieutenant Paulson right here that's going to throw you up against the wall, you better be straight, you going to jail. It's like I say that in six months they expected to sweep this community clean, but because of the work here at LA CAN we're still here, 6 years later we're still fighting, not only are we fighting, we're teaching cultural resistance to community residents, folks learning how to fight back.[84]

Legal Aid staff also noted the direct connection between winning the fight to preserve residential housing for the very poor and the implementation of the Safer Cities Initiative (SCI) as well as massively increased police presence in the community.[85] But before looking at SCI, this chapter will first turn to the increased efforts to rid downtown of its population living on the streets to support market forces and facilitate the redevelopment ridding downtown of its population living in residential hotels before 2006. The continued presence of between 2,000 and 4,000 people on the street on any given night also formed part of the urgency the CCA and CCEA felt in getting the SCI in place and folding it into their efforts.

"CLEANING UP" DOWNTOWN

In 2002, as the redevelopment plan for the Downtown Industrial District was being voted into place, the CCA published a report titled "Downtown's Human

Tragedy: It's Not Acceptable Anymore: A Public Health and Safety Plan." It is a remarkable document for the ways in which it attempts to reframe the debate around housing and homelessness, separating those who were temporarily homeless and able to benefit from shelters, supportive services, and increased housing (those they term the "real" homeless) from the "Service Resistant Addicted (SRAs), Mentally Ill, Panhandlers, Parolees, Drug Dealers and Other Criminals."[86] Such titles "naturally" call upon and reinforce racialized stereotypes, equating African Americans with "Parolees, Drug Dealers and Other Criminals" built over the previous two decades of the "war on drugs," thus utilizing an ostensibly color-blind discourse while the racial objects of such discourse are clear.[87] The report set the tone for every subsequent communication from the CCA and CCEA on the subject. Remembering the goal of developers as creating and selling "the context, the setting, the means of your happiness," it is not difficult to understand why business should wish to erase these embodied reminders of vast racial inequities and continuing desperate poverty.[88]

Building on lessons learned from earlier struggles, they also adopt some of the empowerment and movement rhetoric of civil rights groups like LA CAN to use against them:

> Notwithstanding our support and compassion for those who are in need, we believe it is necessary for society to "take back our streets" from those who cannot help themselves or refuse help and contribute to the deterioration of our community and their own health.[89]

In describing what "compassion" consists of, the report returns to a more traditional neoliberal rhetoric in which services enable rather than resolve:

> SRAs choose to live in encampments . . . CCA believes that by allowing people to live in encampments, the city becomes an enabler that promotes drug abuse, crime, self-destruction, disease and death.
>
> Thus the roots of the public health crisis lie not in a lack of housing, but: "The consequences of allowing the mentally ill and SRAs to live on city streets are manifest in the public health crisis that is created when all bodily activity is left unchecked."[90]

Framing homelessness as caused by individual choices makes enforcement the solution, shutting down any possible need for more structural analyses. By their own choice, "SRAs," their humanity removed by the title itself, have set themselves outside of the community of consent, and their coercion into vacating newly valuable space is legitimated by neoliberal ideologies of individual responsibility and the market's ability to determine land's highest and best use. In addition to arguing for dispersal for the first time, the CCA is also asking for a harsh new light to be shone on those providing services as potential "enablers" and their potential negative impact on property values.[91] The report states:

Only by dispersing "homeless" services throughout the city can we properly manage the public health and safety. In the short-term, service providers should be held accountable for their funding and, thus, document the services that they provide, and their benefits. Moreover, service providers should be accountable for how they manage the street environment outside their facilities, including food distribution and trash clean up.[92]

Through mixing neoliberal rhetoric of individual choice and financial account-ability with that of "taking back the streets," the CCA also attempts to lay claim to a discourse of rights in a way that stretches back to white homeowner claims of the 1960s, stating that the "the public has rights, too":

However, we strongly condemn ACLU's strategies that purport to protect the "civil rights" of individuals at the expense of the rights of the general public. As stated, we condemn these legal strategies because they are inhumane and cruel for the very populations the ACLU is claiming to protect. As well, we argue that law-abiding citizens have a right to use the public right-of-way without fear of harassment, intimidation, or endangerment of their health.[93]

A powerful discourse of resistance has thus been reappropriated, its priorities reassigned to the protection of white space (coded as belonging to "citizens"— part of the longstanding equation of citizenship with whiteness) and privilege, and thus rearticulated to the benefit of business interests in its support of the mass displacement of the city's most vulnerable populations of color. This reframing, together with their proposed solutions, lay out the framework for both the CCA and CCEA, and the respective BIDs managed by them, in the following years. Among some of the recommendations:

- Stop policy of releasing all parolees and prisoners onto Downtown Streets.
- Enact an Anti-Encampment Ordinance.
- Enforce Aggressive Panhandling Ordinance.
- Encourage citizens to press charges against panhandlers and trespassers.
- Make public defecation and urination illegal.
- Create homeless facilities across the County.
- Create an LAPD Street Crime Patrol in Downtown.
- Strengthen laws that allow forced intervention for the mentally ill.[94]

The CCEA and CCA, together with the LAPD, proposed passing a new anti-encampment ordinance along with ordinances banning public urination and defecation (even though the CRA had demolished the last public toilets some time before), while Council Member Jan Perry introduced motions to prevent the homeless from sleeping in business doorways, and to limit free food distri-bution.[95] Such ordinances that criminalize the activities of daily life for those who find themselves homeless have been widely criticized, and LA CAN and other community members organized a strong opposition to prevent their passing.[96]

A law already existed on the books with similar intent, however, and at the end of 2002, the LAPD started stepping up their enforcement of LA Municipal Code 41.18(d), an ordinance that prohibits sitting, lying or sleeping on any sidewalk or alley.[97] Two massive sweeps of the Skid Row area were conducted in November 2002, causing many service providers in the area to respond with anger. Mark Casanova, executive director of Homeless Health Care Los Angeles, is quoted in the *Los Angeles Times* as saying, "I'm all for getting crime off the street . . . but putting homeless people in jail is not the answer. It appears that [LAPD chief] Bratton is acting on behalf of businesses."[98]

Business was certainly acting in concert with government sweeps (having pushed for them). November of 2002 also saw the CCEA launching their own campaign in the press connected to the new redevelopment plan, making Skid Row into "a battleground, with billions of new redevelopment dollars at stake" in the words of one reporter, as "developers and business people have vowed to 'take back the streets.'"[99] The head of the CCEA followed the same line laid down in the CCA's report:

> "People down here feel there's not enough pressure put on this population," said Tracey Lovejoy, executive director of the Central City East Association, which oversees two business improvement districts.
>
> "This is a huge public health tragedy. For a society to say this is OK is wrong. People die of exposure, they're sick. It's not OK."
>
> Lovejoy said the city's failure to enforce laws has allowed what is estimated to be up to 3,000 homeless people to live on public sidewalks, while some social service providers enable them with free food, toilets and clothing.
>
> Her group has hired International Services Inc. to provide private security to make sure the homeless obey the law.[100]

Her words underline the assumption that the public health tragedy is caused by the homeless themselves, who are choosing to defy the law and live on public sidewalks. They have voluntarily placed themselves outside of community norms, thereby endangering the neighborhood, and must be policed accordingly. The article also makes plain the underlying effort behind the rhetoric to grant more power to both the LAPD and BID private security forces to forcibly remove people from the area. When asked what a comprehensive solution to the problem might look like, Lovejoy apparently told the reporter "We're the business community, for God's sake, we're not a social group. Come to me if (you're going to) distribute toys in China, and I'm there for you."[101] Barrett's interview with the assistant police chief immediately after a Christmas Eve police raid on an encampment is just as revealing.

It's no crime to be homeless. The spirit is not taking anyone to jail on Christmas Eve, but you're looking at Toy Town (also on Skid Row), and it's their biggest day of the year.

What do you do? Many homeless are mentally ill. You tell them, just move on, but they don't understand.[102]

In response to the sweeps, the ACLU filed *Jones v. City of Los Angeles* in February 2003 to prevent the city from enforcing the ordinance while no other options were available to the homeless. Carol Sobel, lawyer for the ACLU, connected this increased law enforcement against those who could not comply as directly connected to the rising property values in the area, saying "Now that skid row property has a high value, they want to sweep the homeless out of view . . . Everybody agrees people shouldn't be sleeping on the street, but the answer isn't to put them in jail."[103] The court granted summary judgment for the city. Although this was immediately appealed, the city continued its sweeps.

Another *Los Angeles Times* article describes what these enforcement sweeps looked like:

"We do it every day, Monday through Friday," said Officer Jason Lee, a spokesman for the Los Angeles Police Department.

Shortly after dawn Thursday, officers descended on Towne Avenue between 4th and 5th streets, rousing about half a dozen people sleeping on the sidewalk and advising them to move on.

There were no arrests or citations, but the departing homeless, and those who had moved on earlier, left a mound of makeshift bedding that a city public works crew swept into a pile with a skip loader and carted off to a dump.

"These people were blocking a sidewalk," Lee said. "The officers advise them to move on. If anyone refuses, they are cited or arrested. They're advised to take their belongings with them. If they don't, the stuff goes in the trash."[104]

Bedding is key to survival on the streets, and personal possessions, photographs, and paperwork for supportive services were also being thrown away.[105] Ethnographic work on homeless encampments by Bourgois and Schonberg, and by Gowan demonstrate the ways in which these losses make precarious lives immeasurably more insecure, often causing a further spiral down into desperation and making a transition out of homelessness even more difficult.[106] This is demonstrably not a tactic to end homelessness, however it is spun— rather, it is an effort to move those who are homeless elsewhere.

This is supported by the ways that the public face of "compassion" presented by the CCA, and attempted by the CCEA, breaks down in private communications and meeting minutes as much as it does in actual practice. In the sweeps conducted by the LAPD and other municipal agencies, BID crews often helped with the "cleanup." In the DCBID's meeting minutes, encampments and personal belongings kept on the sidewalks are discussed under maintenance with garbage disposal, and noted as part of their "trash track." The operations reports contain sentences such as "[w]ith help from the CHP (California Highway Patrol) and Caltrans, the Trash Track team was able to completely eliminate the street encampment."[107] Successfully avoiding any acknowledgment that the "trash" collected in fact consisted of the personal possessions of the homeless, the minutes show a mutually supportive relationship between BID "trash track" teams and both the LAPD and county transportation workers. The Toy and Industrial BID's operations director reported in their March 9, 2004, board meeting: "BID Security officers are working with LAPD to decrease the number of encampments in the Toy District. We have assisted the LAPD by picking up 12 carts in February." In the May 25, 2004, board meeting, the Toy and Downtown Industrial BID reported that encampments were down 50 percent from March— they were clearly effective in forcing the homeless somewhere outside of their district.

On June 2, 2004, the DCBID notes that shelters had to turn away referrals for lack of room. Yet in August, CEO Carol Schatz's argument to the board that not enough was being done had nothing to do with providing additional beds or homes:

> a package of legislation regarding sleeping on the streets, shopping carts and aggressive panhandling needs to be produced. She stated that if these issues were not approached, the problem would never change. City Council needs to be educated on these issues and everyone must attend the hearings.[108]

In terms of displacement, the BID seems to be reporting success after success. The targeting of encampments continues, and in September the minutes record the following:

> Trash Track operations continue through the district. Maintenance and Safety recently targeted Weirden Place and the 8th Street underpass. "Hot spots" are identified on a weekly basis.
>
> On Sunday, September 12th, the Maintenance Team performed a Caltrans cleanup. Although scheduled as a follow-up to the August 22nd clean up, over 100 bags of trash were picked up. Dismantled encampments generated much of the trash. Transients are relocating their encampments onto freeway access ramps and shoulders as the BID responds to encampments on 8th, 9th and 2nd Streets.[109]

Caltrans and the Downtown Central BID are clearly and knowingly pushing people to camp in ever riskier and more dangerous positions.[110] The consistent use of the term "transients" dehumanizes them even further.

Perhaps still feeling that not enough was being done, Carol Schatz encouraged property owners to contact the BID "for any quality of life or other issues impacting them."[111] In July 2005, the operations committee notes, "The Maintenance crew picked up a total of 52 bags of trash and shopping carts from an encampment at Main Street and 5th Street. The SET Team and BID officers protected the maintenance workers as they cleaned out the area."[112] While BID security cannot ticket or arrest people for violations, they are no longer just clearing out behind the LAPD or California transport police, but becoming more aggressive in their own clearing of the homeless and their possessions from public sidewalks. A moving appeal from Reverend Alice Callaghan, director of Las Familias del Pueblo in Skid Row, describes the actions of LAPD and BID security:

> For more than a year now, police have been enforcing an ordinance against sitting, sleeping or lying on public sidewalks. Security guards hired by property owners order people off public sidewalks and take the belongings of the homeless when they go inside a mission to eat. It is, the guards insist, abandoned property. The homeless must choose between losing their precious belongings and eating. Street maintenance workers, in violation of city policy, remove the belongings of the homeless, insisting that backpacks and rolled-up bedding stashed against a wall are abandoned. Shopping carts laden with belongings are dumped in the street and scooped into city trucks for disposal.[113]

A new strategy emerged in 2005 for further reducing camping and sleeping on the streets: the provision of bright street lighting. In September, the board minutes for the Toy and Downtown Industrial BIDs notes that the executive director, Estela Lopez, and the operations director, Tara Devine (formerly of Mayor Riordan's staff), had met with the head of the Los Angeles Department of Water and Power's (DWP) economic development group to develop a plan for lighting. By December, staff reported back to the board that:

> DWP is expediting the wiring and installation of the lighting. With the pressure from LAPD and increased visibility through media coverage, emphasis is being placed on "Lighting up Skid Row." McCormick expressed encouragement that the lighting would diminish the issues of narcotics and encampments that are presently "comfortable" along 5th Street.[114]

Work with the DWP would continue over the next few years. Another target was churches and groups giving food to the homeless. At a Central Community Police Advisory Board meeting, regularly attended by BID personnel, the following report appears under car updates:

> Senior Lead Officer Ken Lew provided an update on the Central Area. Officer advised CPAB Members and community guest that he has had an ongoing problem with the "Queen of Angels" Church. He has received numerous complaints from

community members resulting from the "Queen of Angels" staff feeding the home-less population. The church has established (2) feeding times, which have created problems for many community regarding the homeless. The homeless population often loiters in front of businesses, defecate[s] in the surrounding area, and cause[s] additional disruption. Officer Lew met with Father Estrada (Queen of Angels) and he advised Officer Lew that he would reduce the feeding of homeless to once a day.[115]

A month later it was announced the church would cease serving all meals to the homeless by Thanksgiving. The ironic timing is not noted in the minutes.[116] Religious charity here yields to the power and pressure of property values and untroubled consumption.

Despite all of this, the population of Skid Row continued to resist. And then, in April 2006, almost exactly coincident with the passage of the Residential Hotel Ordinance, *Jones v. The City of Los Angeles* was decided in favor of the plaintiffs, and the city was enjoined from enforcing 41.18(d) until a settlement had been reached. From the ACLU press release:

> "This decision is the most significant judicial opinion involving homelessness in the history of the nation," Rosenbaum said. "The decision means in Los Angeles it is no longer a crime to be homeless. The homeless in our community, twenty percent of whom are veterans and nearly a quarter of whom are children, can no longer be treated as criminals because of involuntary acts like sleeping and sitting where there are not available shelter beds to take them off the mean streets of the city."[117]

This began an extended period of negotiations between the ACLU, advocates, and the city as to how 41.18(d) should be enforced. After the first day of the court-ordered mediation, an unsigned editorial appeared in the *Los Angeles Times* written by someone involved in or close to those negotiating from the city's position. They write:

> AFTER NEARLY 12 MONTHS of platitudes from civic leaders about confronting the homeless crisis, skid row in downtown Los Angeles this summer looks worse, not better. And the people who claim to be helping the downtrodden bear a good portion of the blame.
>
> In the last six months, the number of sidewalk tents has nearly tripled, leaving block after block of chaos and open lawlessness on skid row. The number of rapes and homicides in the area has jumped.[118]

The correlation between allowing people to sit, lie, and sleep on the sidewalk with rape and homicide is not made entirely clear, but echoes the connections between homelessness and crime made by the city, the CCA and the CCEA. LAPD Chief Bratton and City Attorney Delgadillo vowed to fight the ruling, saying, "it would be difficult to clean up skid row otherwise."[119] A later article states:

> Bratton on Monday said the ACLU case has stymied the LAPD's fight against crime and blight on skid row, which the chief said is getting worse. Before April's court decision, he said an LAPD count found 1,345 homeless people living on skid row and 187 tents. A July 25 count found 1,527 homeless and 539 tents; a Sept. 18 count found 1,876 homeless and 518 tents.[120]

Yet compromise was reached in September. It allowed people to sleep on public thoroughfares in a specified area in Skid Row between 9 p.m. and 6 a.m. without harassment from LAPD or, as specified in the *Los Angeles Times* article, business owners. The business community was outraged. Carol Schatz of the CCA was quoted as saying, "Any settlement that leaves people living on the street in filthy conditions and permits chaos from 9 to 6 every night in one critical area of the city is unacceptable."[121] The city council appeared to agree, rejecting the compromise, though Bratton defended it:

> Bratton also said critics need to understand that the injunction limits what the LAPD can do.
>
> "If they can come up with a better idea, I'd like to hear it—other than bulldozing them all out of there. I am sorry, but the court is not going to allow that," Bratton said. "We all would like to see it gone."[122]

But the Safer Cities Initiative was ready to be rolled out, with fifty police concentrated into the few blocks of Skid Row. This was something of a metaphorical bulldozer, judged effective by supporters and activists alike, however much they differed in their opinions of it. A reduced cleanup of encampments continued, along with a new phase in the effort to clear downtown of its traditional residents.

Chapter 8

Beating Back the Onslaught

The Safer Cities Initiative

It is the saga of changing police activity in Skid Row that makes most clear the ways in which exclusionary violence has articulated with the new neoliberal and color-blind discourses to create a new way of excluding a population from both the spatial community and the community of consent. It has done so by substituting the word and idea of criminal for human beings of African American and Latino descent. As Michelle Alexander writes:

> Rather than rely on race, we use our criminal justice system to label people of color "criminals" and then engage in all the practices we supposedly left behind. Today it is perfectly legal to discriminate against criminals in nearly all the ways that it was once legal to discriminate against African Americans. Once you're labeled a felon, the old forms of discrimination—employment discrimination, housing discrimination, denial of the right to vote, denial of educational opportunity, denial of food stamps and other public benefits, and exclusion from jury service—are suddenly legal. As a criminal, you have scarcely more rights, and arguably less respect, than a black man living in Alabama at the height of Jim Crow. We have not ended racial caste in America; we have merely redesigned it.[1]

What follows explores the strategic ways in which exclusion through labeling has been put into effect in the pursuit of displacement and development, cementing partnerships between business and government and expanding the power of both to create privileged spaces from which people of color need to be erased.

Once again we return to 2002, when Mayor Hahn hired Chief William Bratton, former head of the Boston and New York police departments. In a report done for Skid Row's Union Rescue Mission, researchers from the Center for Religion and Civic Culture write that Bratton:

> has a record of ridding downtown New York of homeless street people through his zero tolerance policing and [he] brings that agenda with him to Los Angeles. Police Chief Bratton's implementation of "broken windows theory" has been criticized as contributing to an overly aggressive police force. Given this history, it will be imperative to track Bratton's record in Los Angeles, an important role for agencies like URM.[2]

Chief Bratton and Mayor Giuliani have been popularly credited with the invention of "quality of life" policing based on Wilson and Kelling's theories. While this is perhaps somewhat exaggerated, such policing methods are undoubtedly the basis for Bratton's reputation.[3]

Bratton was brought in because of his track record for implementing exactly the kind of policies that LA was already planning. The LAPD produced an internal strategic document titled "Homeless Reduction Strategies," produced three weeks before Bratton was sworn in. It proposed:

> A minimum of twenty additional officers deployed, in addition to the existing eight officers currently assigned to the enforcement of homeless quality of life type issues ... working with the City Council offices, the Business Improvement Districts, and the City Attorney to "impact the problem of the criminal homeless" ... the addition of at least 20 officers ... adoption of "anti-camping and anti-public urination/defecation ordinances" and "disbursement [sic] of Social Services providers from within Central Area."[4]

In November 2002, the first police sweeps of downtown started. Meanwhile, the mayor had brought in an ambitious man labeled by the *New Yorker* as the "CEO cop," who aimed to be to modern policing what Lee Iacocca was to Chrysler, and whose plan to get to the top rested on the "scientific" new methods promoted by Kelling and Wilson.[5]

There has been a great deal of controversy over the effectiveness of Kelling and Wilson's theories, as well as zero-tolerance policing as advocated by Chief Bratton. One of the principal charges often leveled at the practice has been that it is simply a justification for policies that serve to further criminalize poor communities of color and remove them in aid of gentrification and development. Some of the early discourse from the formation of LA's first BID certainly sustains this argument. In the first newsletter of the new Downtown Property Owners Association from fall 1994, they are quite explicit about what they want in terms of policing:

> *Good News*: LAPD statistics show that Downtown LA is one of the safest parts of the city, with fewer felonies and violent crimes than other areas such as West LA. *Bad News*: Downtown property owners and tenants may get less than their fair share of police protection compared with other parts of the city because of "underreporting" of nuisance crimes in Downtown.

> Nuisance crimes—generally non-violent misdemeanors—include car break-ins, purse-snatchings, shoplifting, pick pocketing, aggressive panhandling, drug dealing, prostitution, public urinating and defecating, drunkeness and sidewalk encampments.

> *Key*: Police allocations are based on LAPD crime statistics in each of the city's police divisions, so *underreporting of crimes in an area means that fewer police will be*

assigned to that area. While many of us who work and/or live Downtown have become accustomed to nuisance crimes, we cannot be apathetic, and *we must report them.*[6]

While using all of the language of "quality of life" and "nuisance crimes" wielded by Wilson and Kelling, it represents a rather ironic reversal of their "broken windows" theory that claims—as do the CCA, CCEA, BIDs, LAPD, politicians, and the city attorney's office—that the police force's concentration on this kind of misdemeanor crime is so important because it reduces violent crime. In a press release from February 16, 1995, the DPOA notes that "BIDs are operating in Philadelphia, Houston, Phoenix, New Orleans, Baltimore, New York, and Denver, where they've dramatically improved property values and the quality of life in their downtowns." The support for property values rather than the control of violent crime levels is clearly key, while this kind of policing is also part of a larger phenomenon of mass incarceration of communities of color, which has soared even as crime rates have fallen.[7] Studies conducted of crime in Los Angeles have continued to show lower rates in the downtown area than elsewhere in the city over a decade later.[8]

Although planning for the initial sweeps in November 2002 was in place prior to Bratton's arrival, he would broaden them strategically and publicly. As a *Los Angeles Times* article headlines, "LAPD Tests New Policing Strategy: Chief picks three areas as proving grounds for his 'broken windows' system to fight crime"; Skid Row was, of course, one of the three areas.[9]

An LAPD presentation to the Downtown Los Angeles Neighborhood Council reports that what we now know as the Safer Cities Initiative actually officially began in July 2003.[10] Their overview states that the SCI "will seek to prevent violent crime, alleviate fear and improve the quality of life in the city's residential neighborhoods and business districts," and that the first stage will consist of collecting crime data to develop strategic plans, after which the initiative "will be working to forge a permanent partnership among government, law enforcement, and the community with the capacity to successfully manage community safety problems."[11] The memo lists those working to form the initiative: George Kelling and Bill Sousa of Rutgers University; the deputy mayor and a representative from the mayor's Office of Criminal Justice Planning; Kathy Godfrey, chief of staff for Council District 9; six members of the LAPD; three representatives from the city attorney's office; three representatives from different missions working in Skid Row; and Tracey Lovejoy, director of the CCEA.

Through these meetings, Kelling played a crucial role in the development of the initiative. Part of Bratton's transition team, he was paid $20,000 by the city on a three-month contract, and would charge the city a total of $556,000 for his work through 2006.[12] The minutes from the September 19, 2003, meeting of the LA Safer City Project–Central City East show how the project developed:

LAPD was estimating that 50 additional officers would be needed to enforce a proposed anti-camping ordinance in Skid Row, and that it would take "a couple of months of enforcement action to change the culture, and then foot beat would be needed to maintain." For his part Kelling was arguing that it would be necessary to "get the high moral ground" and that "the group should have op-ed pieces ready for submission, explaining the strategy and tactics of the group, before enforcement action begins."

In the same meeting they decided to wait until after the holidays to start up the initiative, and to bring an anti-camping ordinance before the city council.

In discussing the November 6, 2003, meeting to develop a coordinated press strategy, Professor Gary Blasi of the UCLA School of Law highlights their proposed PR spin as contrasted to their focus on what they want to achieve through the initiative, and as developing the "message of the effort (i.e., the problem is "lawlessness," not "homelessness")."[13] He writes that:

> there was no discussion at the meeting about lawlessness other than violations that inevitably accompany homelessness in the absence of adequate shelter or other facilities: sleeping or sitting on the sidewalk, conducting biological functions in locations other than bathrooms. Rather, the focus was entirely on discouraging visible homelessness in Skid Row. For example, the second item on the agenda addressed whether the sidewalks in Skid Row could be narrowed to make sidewalk dwelling more difficult.[14]

Although it would figure prominently in the public relations effort that accompanied the SCI in Skid Row, in the meetings of August, September, October, and November 2003, there was in the minutes of these meetings not a single mention of any "crime" that does not necessarily accompany homelessness when there is a lack of shelter or other facilities.

LAPD was also meeting with key people in the Downtown Center BID, as reported in the October 2003 minutes: "cooperative operations and management of local community oriented policing efforts. These meetings have been productive. LAPD and DCBID have agreed to a set of program sharing efforts that will expand the amount of LAPD-BID combined operations." It was not just BID staff working with LAPD on the ground, but its president and head of the CCA who were moving to influence the process at the highest level:

> Carol E. Schatz met with Chief William Bratton on Friday, July 23 to discuss increasing complaints to the DCBID due to aggressive panhandling, open drug use and other quality of life issues in the Downtown area. Chief Bratton at the meeting expressed his concern, and immediately toured the Downtown area to see first hand what the issues were. As a result of his meeting with Carol, Chief Bratton and

his staff are working on an operational plan to address the quality of life issues that are impacting Downtown Los Angeles.[15]

As stated in the 2004 minutes of the DCBID and Toy-Downtown Industrial BIDs, Schatz met Chief Bratton on three occasions over the next few months, and he presented to the CCA board. This seems to contrast with a lack of engagement with the CCEA—the BID worked closely with LAPD, but at a slightly lower level of political influence. However, it seems that the CCEA and CCA did not feel the process was moving fast enough, so the CCEA initiated a new, more activist tactic to pressure the city and to claim space in ways additional to the ubiquitous presence of their red-shirted security guards. A July 5, 2005, press release from the CCEA took on the traditional language of protest (echoing the CCA's report and their own statements to the press from November 2002):

> Taking Back the Streets of Skid Row
> What: Kickoff Neighborhood Watch Walk to demonstrate a united front in support of increased police enforcement in Skid Row.
> The Neighborhood Watch Walk will demonstrate a united front in support of increased police enforcement in Skid Row. It kicks off a concerted effort to clean up the criminal element in this population, according to Captain Andrew Smith, commanding officer of LAPD's Central Area.

In a guest opinion published a few weeks later in the *Los Angeles Downtown News* written by the CCEA's new head, Estela Lopez, director of the Toy and Downtown Industrial BIDs, she states:

> A few weeks ago, for the first time ever, social service providers and formerly homeless individuals took to the streets alongside law enforcement, business and property owners to clean up Skid Row. One hundred strong we marched to show that drug activity and the criminal element that it attracts to the area will no longer be tolerated.

She claims that by joining the effort, downtown residents "will be making history":

> Groups usually perceived as being adversarial are now in agreement that the situation in Skid Row has reached dangerous new levels. Drug use and sales, prostitution and other crimes are taking place on sidewalks day and night. Business owners and their employees walk a gauntlet-type environment to and from work.[16]

In October, the CCEA renewed and maximized press coverage of their continuing walks by creating a premium photo op with their press release title: "Children of Para Los Niños to Cheer On Skid Row Walkers."[17] The CCEA held their annual meeting the same month. Praised by Council Member Jan Perry for "turning the tide in the quality of life in the Central City East Area," Captain Andy Smith also praised Ms. Lopez for the close working relationship between the BIDs and LAPD. The example he gave was the way in which Lopez had "sparked" media coverage of Skid Row issues.[18]

The CCEA continued pushing for increased police action. In November, Council Member Jan Perry succeeded in ensuring the presence of six of the other fourteen members of the city council to join her at the monthly CCEA Neighborhood Watch Walk.[19] To assemble seven council members together for a local neighborhood watch walk represented something of a coup for both Perry and downtown business interests, and signaled citywide political support for the CCEA's claiming of Skid Row. In the Toy-Downtown Industrial BIDs' December meeting, Lopez reported back on a meeting with Council Member Huizar and LAPD Captain Smith around encampments, an upcoming fact-finding trip to New York to learn how officials there had dealt with homelessness, and signs of success in reframing the Skid Row debates in their terms:

> Lopez showed clips from a recent CNN segment that featured Skid Row. The tape was submitted to all councilmembers as well as the mayor's office. Lopez acknowledged the benefits of the media attention and intends on capitalizing on this. Lopez indicated that one of the positive effects of the media attention is raising the awareness that the issue is not about housing but rather eliminating the element of crime.[20]

As this effort progressed, LA CAN members noticed a surge in BID security activities corresponding to these political meetings and increasingly publicized walks. After the 1999 lawsuit and the two years of training and monitoring, BID security guards had become much more respectful of the community, though clearly not without continuing issues. However, as LA CAN writes: "In the summer of 2005, LA CAN members again became concerned, and outraged, about the use of private security to promote gentrification and mass displacement and began to notice an increase in civil and human rights violations by guards."[21]

The *LA Times* continued its cooperative and regular coverage of the "blighted" Skid Row, offering a gloomy headline: "Defeat Plagues Efforts to Clean Up Skid Row; Previous attempts to solve homelessness have been mired in debate, political maneuvering."[22] The sixty-four-member board of the Blue Ribbon committee to solve homelessness continued to grapple with the issues without producing a plan. Their survey, conducted in January 2005, revealed 91,000 homeless in Los Angeles County, 35 percent of them chronically so.[23] Despite the existence of only around 14,000 shelter beds in the county and no available beds in Skid Row itself, the CCA and CCEA continued to frame the issues around criminality rather than lack of housing or employment.[24]

By early 2006, the debate on two proposals to clean up Skid Row became public. Of the two proposals, one is from Assistant Chief Gascon—a plan to completely rid Skid Row of its tent and box cities very similar to the one Bratton had wanted to put into place in 2002. Minutes from his talk as special guest at the Toy and Downtown Industrial BID board meeting are as follows:

> Gascon began with acknowledging the attention currently being focused on the area and with LAPD in the forefront he wanted to give a sense of what they will be embarking on in the effort to clean it up. He outlined the details of a plan that consisted of scrutinizing encampments and putting together a strategy to once a week clean out tents, cardboard boxes, booking people/property as necessary. He acknowledged what he was saying was basically long and slow process of a gradual diminution in number because of constant aggressive pursuits. This would mean moving into a new phase. He recognized that there would be opportunities and challenges that would require having to alter the culture of the area. Issues in Skid Row have been happening for generations. Changes he has planned will cause disagreements and will be met with resistance. The process will include issuance of warnings, photos, and directions to services. Then returning with clean up crews to remove trash/debris until it is understood the conditions are unacceptable. Intention is to create displacement. The enforcement process will target narcotics and weapons with significant sentencing beyond serving in county jail.[25]

Gascon was talking about far more than simply cleaning up encampments here, and the connection between "cleaning" and "sending to jail" is all too clear, as is the way the two efforts slotted together.

George Kelling authored the second plan, as outlined in the minutes:

> Kelling argues that rather than removing homeless people wholesale from the streets, the LAPD should focus on criminals, including drug dealers and prostitutes, who he says create a "culture of lawlessness" in the area . . . If police can reduce the drug dealing, prostitution and petty crimes that plague skid row, "there could be more efficient dealing with the homeless in the area who are in need of social services," he said. Kelling's plan relies on the LAPD's ability to deploy substantially more officers into skid row, he said—a "flood the zone" tactic that Bratton has used effectively to reduce crime in parts of South Los Angeles.[26]

This was the plan that was eventually officially chosen as the least divisive; however, elements of Gascon's plan are clearly visible in the ways that the various law-enforcement efforts unfolded.

The CCEA again took a hand to push the debate in the press; in the words of the *LA Times*: "The push to clean up Los Angeles' skid row reached an unlikely milestone Tuesday morning when downtown business leaders moved in to steam-clean the sidewalks on one of the district's filthiest streets."[27] It mentions the vow of Mayor Villaraigosa and other city leaders to improve Skid Row, and quotes Estela Lopez claiming that the size and scope of the encampments has grown, along with health concerns, while describing how the police moved homeless people along and machines commenced the steam cleaning. Anat Rubin, a new reporter at the *Los Angeles Daily Journal* describes the event from a very different point of view:

> So they decided to hose down this one random block, and they had like 3 cops and I just remember thinking, is this how it works here? The BIDs call the LAPD and the LAPD is like yes, we shall come work this for you? You know, we will protect the reporters and the men in hazmat suits and we will make this strong showing, we will make somehow this event about hosing down the street, we'll make it a criminal justice event, and I remember thinking that was incredible . . . it was SO offensive, and so absurd. But it also was a very big showing of her power I thought. Because she was like I'm going to have a media event to remind people that skid row is a bad place so that they remember what we do, what we're about to do, that anything is better than what it was.[28]

She states that, looking back, it was clear this was part of the effort to use media to build political will to implement the SCI.

The mayor officially launched the Safer Cities Initiative in September of 2006. Fifty new police officers, at a cost of approximately $6 million to the city, were brought into an area of Skid Row of 0.85 square miles. As one Skid Row resident recalls:

> The very first day of the launch they just decided that 50 rookie officers in 50 shiny new uniforms with the hats wearing white rubber gloves and those little white plastic handcuffs tied on they little waistband, they walked out single file right down 6th street right down to San Pedro, they walked from 6th and Wall to San Pedro, I mean a long line, then they turned around and faced the wall and arrested everybody that was sleeping standing or sitting against that wall right there. They arrested about 70 people. From that point on, that day on, I knew that it was going to be hell to pay on skid row.[29]

The impact of the SCI on downtown's poorer residents has been clearly documented by Professor Blasi, working with colleagues and a team of twelve students from the UCLA School of Law Fact Investigation Clinic.[30] In the first year of the SCI, 12,000 citations were issued, averaging 1,000 a month, with a majority being for pedestrian violations. This represents between forty-eight and sixty-nine times the rate at which similar citations were issued in any other comparable area across Los Angeles.[31] Such citations are not simply an annoyance for most of Skid Row's evidence, as the report explains:

Citations issued to indigent and mentally disabled people unable to obtain legal help or represent themselves at a hearing inevitably lead to arrest warrants. With penalties, the "bail/fine" for a pedestrian signal violation is $159 (compared, for example, to the total $221 monthly income of General Relief recipients).[32]

Thousands of low-income residents found themselves with arrest warrants, newly criminalized if they had not been arrested before. The SCI also averaged about 750 arrests per month on other quality-of-life violations. While acknowledging that crime declined significantly over the period, the report notes that few arrests were for serious, violent crimes, and that the most common violent crime—robbery—actually declined 45 percent outside of the initiative's boundaries, as compared to 39 percent within them.[33]

Shortly after the SCI was launched, the ACLU filed a court request to extend a 2003 lawsuit agreement prohibiting the LAPD from stopping and searching Skid Row residents without reasonable suspicion. The cases cited in the press release offer a revealing look at daily life for Skid Row residents under the SCI:

Cecil Bledsoe, who helps the homeless on Skid Row find housing, was walking with a cane early this month when police pulled up and forced him and about five other people against a wall. Only after searching Bledsoe did an officer ask if he had any warrants out for his arrest or was on parole or probation. Bledsoe does not. Paul Johnson, who is not on parole, was handcuffed and searched after he questioned the police practice of randomly asking about residents' parole status. "Everybody down here is on probation or parole," he says officers told him before driving him to a police station. Johnson was released without citation.[34]

In her follow-up op-ed in the *LA Times*, Ramona Ripston of the ACLU writes:

The Los Angeles Police Department has a message for skid row residents: The 4th Amendment doesn't apply here. That's the constitutional protection from arbitrary searches, and LA police officers have been violating it since late last year by detaining, handcuffing and going through people's pockets and possessions on the slimmest pretenses.

These aren't the hard-core criminals police promised to round up when the LAPD assigned 50 more officers to skid row last September. They're ordinary people whose only mistake was being homeless in the wrong part of town.[35]

To Skid Row's inhabitants, the SCI represented more than lines of cops marching down the street—it meant occupation.[36] LA CAN member Deborah Burton testified before the city council on September 29, 2009:

I used to feel safe in my community, but since the safer city initiative was placed in 2006, I don't feel safe anymore. I don't feel safe as I walk to my home or my job.

> Walking in my community is like walking in a minefield. You don't know when five or six police are going to jump out at you, throw you against the wall, put you in handcuffs, search you, and then let you go. I'm angry. I see this too many times. When asked what the individual did to warrant such a treatment I'm told mind your business or just no response at all. I feel like just because we're black and live in the downtown community, I'm a criminal.

General Dogon, another LA CAN member, echoed her words in the same hearing:

> When I walk out of my house I see the pigs got some black man in handcuffs thrown up against the wall and for forty minutes they running his name for a warrant check like he got warrants in 15 different states and two minutes later they let him go. Every day, two or three times a day we go through this.[37]

That this has been the experience of Black and Brown (and a fair number of white) low-income residents on the streets of Skid Row is hardly complex. But the complexities of how the political will and legal support for such human rights violations continue despite research, public outcry, and powerful testimony shows both the power of business interests driving the efforts to cleanse downtown, the power of a newly articulated neoliberal ideology of market and individual responsibility, and the ways in which the Skid Row community is once again understood to lie outside of a public with a commonly shared set of rights. The problem for the business community continues to be the same as stated in 1932:

> that Negroes do now, and for over ten years last past, have been used to congregate, walk, drive, pass and appear at all hours of the day and night, openly, publicly, continuously, notoriously, constantly and extremely noticeable, on the sidewalks, roads, streets, in the houses and all about said lot, tract and locality.[38]

As in 1932, the Skid Row community's class, status, and race sets them outside of social consensus and entirely into the realm of requiring domination and force—the business community has helped reclaim this understanding to argue that those outside of the community of consent have no right to remain a part of the physical community, equating the boundaries of the social and the spatial. Thus, the return of capital to the downtown area and its demand for segregated space has articulated with and deepened a process of establishing a renewed hegemonic white domination over peoples of color, taking advantage of, and facilitating, the consensus around the mass incarceration of people of color as described by Alexander.[39] Gentrification and renewal is one spatial strand constructed by and constructing this new consensus, in which efforts to increase property values force ever more people of color into the prison systems, while prison itself—the stripping of rights from convicted felons as well as the stigma that society attaches to them upon release—is often a principal cause of individuals living in Skid Row or finding themselves homeless.

The dynamics of this process are evident, unlike its effectiveness, in the testimony of those who have run afoul of it. Three years into the SCI, we find people with multiple tickets, weeks in jail, and back in the neighborhood.

> Diamond guesses he's been in the downtown jail known as Twin Towers 25 or 30 times, just for tickets. And he says that's pretty common.
>
> "When I go there . . . I know more people there than I see on a daily basis walking around here, 'cause it's all people from downtown and it's all people there mostly on petty stuff."[40]

While the mass ticketing showed that prisons were being used as one long-term solution to homelessness, the reality was that in spite of California's leading role in the building of prisons and the mass incarceration of its inhabitants, there was simply not enough room for Skid Row's population.[41] Arrests for failure to pay tickets resulted in a few days in an overcrowded jail and then release back to the street. This required new strategies to achieve a more permanent solution—above and beyond cleanups of encampments, sweeps, and broad criminalization of the population. In addition to the SCI, the CCA, CCEA, and LAPD were concurrently working on additional initiatives to help take specific populations—drug addicts and parolees—off the streets.

In analyzing Skid Row, the 2002 LAPD Homeless Reduction Strategy cited "reliable estimates claim[ing] some 60% of this population to be mentally impaired and 80% to be substance abusers."[42] What makes homelessness so visible in Skid Row is both its concentration, and the high percentage of what experts term the "chronically" homeless, with severe mental issues and/or problems with addiction.[43] Thus, targeting drugs and drug dealers has long been a justification for heavy-handed policing in the area. From the CCEA's beginning and its push for LAPD sweeps of encampments in 1987, the elimination of drug dealing was cited as the primary aim. The LAPD again cited drug dealers as one of the primary targets for their strategy testing in February 2003, but Bratton betrayed a telling prejudice in his remarks to the *LA Times*:

> If the small things are left undeterred, they turn into big things. So the homeless take over a portion of the park. Drug dealers follow. Drug dealers beget violence. It then begins to affect the whole business area and businesses begin to die.[44]

According to this logic, by getting rid of the homeless you get rid of the drug dealers, and businesses can thrive again. Those who are homeless are portrayed as both the source and the victims of the drug trade.

It is precisely here, in the war on drugs and the stigmatization of parolees, that Alexander argues the new Jim Crow system has been built. To give a national context to the SCI and the concurrent targeting of addicts, it is worth quoting here:

> black men have been admitted to state prison on drug charges at a rate that is more than thirteen times higher than white men. The racial bias inherent in the drug war is a major reason that 1 in every 14 black men was behind bars in 2006, compared with 1 in 106 white men. For young black men, the statistics are even worse. One in 9 black men between the ages of twenty and thirty-five was behind bars in 2006, and far more were under some form of penal control—such as probation or parole. These gross racial disparities simply cannot be explained by rates of illegal drug activity among African Americans. [45]

In some ways, it is hardly surprising that the CCEA and CCA should focus on the "war on drugs" with the LAPD to "disperse" an entrenched, primarily African American community suffering from high and interrelated rates of mental illness and drug addiction.

The neighborhood watch walks sponsored by the CCEA were very much about raising the public profile of the drug issue; an email on a downtown list-serve in 2005 states that the walk is "our call for public safety—all people who live Downtown, and especially Skid Row residents, deserve a crime-free, gang-free, drug-free and empowered community to call their own." The distance between the BIDs, with their wealthy, professional, and almost entirely white audience, and the low-income residents of color living downtown is that the email expects that the presence of LAPD and BID guards will make its participants feel safer. This is perhaps one of the largest faultlines separating one population from the other.

It was not until June 2005, however, that the full actions of the CCEA and the CCA to push the LAPD into increased enforcement specifically around drug activity were made clear—as was the claim to increase powers for BID security teams. The operations report to the June 28 board meeting states:

Criminal Predator Enforcement
Strong reported that at a meeting last week LAPD Captain Andrew Smith reported he was working to form a team of prosecuting city attorneys and police modeled after the anti-gang "CLEAR" team [Community Law Enforcement And Recovery]. The team would use its expertise against those involved in narcotics sales and use. Smith is working closely with CCEA and the Downtown Center BID on the recent increase in drug related crimes in Central City East and the Historic Core. Such efforts may take several weeks to organize and have impact. In the interim, Strong requested that CCEA security officers be allowed to make supervised drug detention and arrests. The Board gave unanimous approval.

Estela Lopez is scheduling meetings with City Attorney Rocky Delgadillo and with the District Attorney's office to discuss the sidewalk drug crime situation. The meetings would be led by CCEA and would include a coalition that is comprised of the Central City Association and the Midnight Mission (representing several area social service providers), as well as Skid Row residents. All are in agreement that street drug dealing threatens both the business community as well as the positive effect the social service providers are working for.[46]

The same meeting notes that a neighborhood watch walk will be held to "bring attention to the drug culture in the community." In the press release for the walk, Estela Lopez states:

There is such a proliferation of narcotics that it makes it difficult for service providers to help people get cleaned up. "We need to give these folks a fighting chance," said Captain Smith. He added that the drug atmosphere attracts a criminal element to the area as well. "We want them out of the entire Downtown area."[47]

Notices about a "crackdown" on drug-related offences in the Historic Core appeared in the president's report to the DCBID the same month, and the minutes report CEO Schatz continuing to push for such a crackdown on drug and quality of life offences.[48]

The CCA and CCEA were also pushing this issue at a state level. After several meetings with State Assembly Member Gil Cedillo, two bills were put forward as part of a package to "alleviate Downtown homelessness."[49] SB 1318 provided sentence enhancements for drug crime, while SB 1320 prohibited persons on probation for drug crimes from entering Skid Row. These bills would clearly have a huge impact on a community with a large percentage of addicts. As the bills passed in the legislature, SB 1318's penalty for drug dealing was reduced, and SB 1320 was lost entirely.[50] But these bills were not forgotten, nor abandoned—they were simply implemented on a local level. In September, only days after the official launch of the SCI, District Attorney Steve Cooley announced that they would be making a "stay-away" order a condition of probation for all those convicted of drug offences.[51] Such orders would be routinely given to anyone arrested on Skid Row, putting their name in a database to allow the LAPD to arrest them immediately anywhere in Skid Row, even if they had not committed any other crime.[52]

In an *LA Times* editorial published two weeks later and clearly designed to lay the groundwork for more stringent enforcement policies, the anonymous author demanded "DA, Do More Downtown." They write:

the city and the police department are finally starting to wrest back control of skid row. Two weeks ago, officers began arresting transients for sleeping on sidewalks during daylight hours, removed scores of homeless encampments and have made more than 800 arrests.

But if making more arrests is all the city's law enforcement apparatus plans to do, the initiatives will be for naught. Today, far too many downtown criminals who get convicted of serious offenses serve only days of their sentences, then return to the scene of the crime. Even while the Los Angeles Police Department cracks down, the district attorney maintains a damaging revolving-door policy in which those who commit crimes on skid row serve less time than if they sold heroin or committed another felony elsewhere in the city.[53]

Despite the state of emergency declared in California prisons, the author is pushing for longer periods of incarceration. Giving some credit to Cooley's new "stay-away" policy, they write, "Better would be if the DA joined other law enforcement officials to come up with a plan to ensure that the worst skid row offenders stay locked up long enough to make their arrests worth everyone's while." The district attorney was in fact doing just that.

After her first meeting with Pete White and Becky Dennison of LA CAN, reporter Anat Rubin walked away thinking that half of what they had told her could not be true . . . but after digging she found things to be worse than even they thought.[54] In her opinion, the most shocking evidence of how the city was attempting to clear Skid Row was the new effort by the DA to prosecute drug offences to the full. Cases coming out of Skid Row were being physically marked with a red "5th Corridor" stamp and treated specially by prosecutors, who suddenly refused to plea bargain. The cases coming to public defenders suddenly weren't possession cases but sales cases, even though the amount in question might be only $5 dollars' worth of crack.

> I had public defenders tell me on the phone, this is the worst thing, I have never felt more helpless in my life. Imagine telling a client that they're going away for ten years on nothing . . . on nothing. And you know, they had people with stripes [people falling under the "three strikes rule"], and they were going to get . . . they could go away for life. That to me was the craziest . . . it was just so . . . so coordinated, it was like the cops were doing one thing, and the judges and the prosecutors were doing this thing and both of those things together, you know were going to mean they were going to put people away for much longer than they had been able to put people away for before, and that . . . this all came from the BIDs. I mean the enforcement, safer cities initiative, those were people who championed this.[55]

This opinion comes both from Rubin's years writing about Skid Row for her paper's "poverty beat," but also from the many public defenders with whom she spoke. In her article published in the *Daily Journal*, she quotes an anonymous public defender:

> This is a blatant DA policy that they are going to treat these cases differently. It's not abnormal for the DA to have a policy. But this policy is about targeting the homeless in that area because the city is redeveloping that area. It's a policy to get people off the streets and into state prison, jumping right over rehab and jail.[56]

The response from the DA's office was that sentencing had been too lenient before, and that due to dissatisfaction from the public and the police, they were treating the cases more seriously even though there was no direction from superiors not to plea bargain. But the evidence from the public defenders certainly makes this claim seem something of a stretch. Rubin states that to publish the story she "talked to 12 public defenders, because my editor was like there's no way, there's no way this is happening." The quotes she obtained are telling; for example, public defender Rigoberto Arrechiga stated:

> I completed one of these trials in December, where a guy had a miniscule amount, no money on him, no phone or pager, no individually wrapped drugs in multiple bags—just some rock cocaine in his pocket. The guy had no prior record of sales. He got four years in state prison.

Twenty-four police officers were involved in the "sting."

Rubin states that of the 1,400 arrests made by undercover narcotics officers in the approximately three months after the initiative's start, 1,043 were labeled as "possession for sale." Given the testimony of public defenders, that means most likely hundreds of addicts were unduly prosecuted harshly to remove them from Skid Row. The human cost of such arrests lies not only in the experience of arrest, detention, traumatic court process, and years in prison, but also in the consequences a felony conviction has on an addict's life, leading to denial of drug treatment, services and support such as food stamps, and access to public housing.

Along with drug addicts, parolees were also singled out and targeted for special treatment by the CCA and CCEA—the words "parolee" and "criminal" in the organizations' correspondence and minutes appear to be interchangeable. Again, to put this increased enforcement of parole conditions into a national context, Alexander writes:

> To put the matter more starkly: *About as many people were returned to prison for parole violations in 2000 as were admitted to prison in 1980 for all reasons.* Of all parole violators returned to prison in 2000, only one-third were returned for a new conviction; two-thirds were returned for a technical violation such as missing appointments with a parole officer, failing to maintain employment, or failing a drug test.[57]

Parole sweeps became more common, with LA CAN documenting many of their operations:

> On Friday February 1, 2008—which also happened to be the first day of Black History Month—LAPD planned a parole raid on a hotel near 5th and Towne. There were at least 30 LAPD officers and 10 parole agents on-site. A community resident

alarmed by the sheer number of officers descending on the community called the office of LA CAN to report it.[58]

Such documentation and publication is perhaps one of the key reasons that the SCI and the special crackdown on parolees and drug offenders did not accomplish all that its founders desired. LA CAN created Community Watch in November 2005 in response to increasingly oppressive policing (even before the rollout of the SCI) as "an alternative private security presence in the community—one trained to ensure that civil and human rights violations by the Los Angeles Police Department and Business Improvement District (BID) security guards and others are stopped."[59] Community Watch participants' following BID security and cops around with video cameras was effective in stopping, or at the least recording, some of the worst abuses, and LA CAN has been working in conjunction with public defenders to support those arrested. Such work has required incredible bravery, resulting in Community Watch members threatened and arrested on multiple occasions.[60] The regular presence of Community Watch groups on the streets has also served to defend public space in response to the claims staked by the BIDs and the LAPD, a visible presence of community watching the cops and the security guards and laying claim to their rights to exist in their own community.

What has ensued, particularly since the winning of the Residential Hotel Ordinance and the formation of Community Watch, has been an ever fiercer battle—perhaps not changed in quality but certainly changed in degree—over who exactly had a "right to the city."[61] In terms of claiming public space, LA CAN's Community Watch teams are on the streets, hold regular community events and barbecues, and have persisted in building a healthier and safer community with a focus on food justice, community gardens, and women's rights. Their work involves preserving their community, as well as a sense of pride, humanity, and the right to public space in the face of ideological dehumanization and brutal state force.

The SCI was also having an impact. A 2006 LA Times article shows a fairly wide consensus among service providers both on Skid Row and as far away as Venice that SCI seemed to be forcing people to leave Skid Row for other neighborhoods, at least during the day.[62] But an article in the Economist summarized its effects neatly in the title: "On the skids: The police have cleaned up Skid Row. They have not got rid of it."[63] In April 2008, the LA Times published a piece titled "Skid row effort hits a wall: Is the well-publicized cleanup campaign slowing? The area is still safer than two years ago, but many wonder where things are headed."[64] The number of arrests had plateaued, but the LAPD continued their allocation of fifty officers to Skid Row, and Estela Lopez of the CCEA believed it was time to look at where to go next. Her thoughts on the subject are made clear in an email to LAPD officer Sergio Diaz, who was the LAPD representative at the Toy and Industrial BIDs' annual meeting. She wrote to him:

One question in regard to the "where do we go from here" not for public discussion: I have been thinking the past week or so about the so-called anti-camping ordinance that, as I recall, was going to be revisited after the Jones settlement and subsequent vacation of the court's initial decision. My point is, are we now ready to seek legislative support to stabilize the area? I would appreciate your thoughts.[65]

He responded that once the approximately 1,200 units of affordable housing mandated by the settlement were constructed, the police would be able to enforce 41.18(d) once again, and promised to be in touch with Perry's chief of staff, Kathy Godfrey, on the subject of a new ordinance.

While the BIDs contemplated their next steps, the second anniversary of the SCI became a mobilizing date for those opposing it. A march was called and a letter circulated that was signed by at least twenty-four organizations, including multiple legal services, affordable housing developers, Skid Row service organizations, and community groups. It listed the reasons the community felt it vital to oppose the SCI:

- 750 arrests per month or 18,000 arrests in two years in a community that's home to 13,000 people.
- 1,000 misdemeanor citations each month for "crimes" such as crossing the street against a flashing red hand. When a poor or homeless Skid Row resident can't pay the fine, the citation turns to warrant and leads to arrest.
- Among the most appalling human and civil rights violations in the recent history of the United States. Persons who are poor, homeless, living with severe disabilities and African Americans are targeted.
- Thousands shut out of federally funded housing and food programs. When people return from jail, their criminal record forces them to live on the street, where they cost taxpayers $100,000 each year as they circulate through emergency rooms and jails.
- $6 million each year for additional officers to police 50 square blocks—about equal to the amount the city invests annually in homeless services for the entire City of Los Angeles (469 square miles). Over two years, that money could have been used to get 750 people off the streets and into housing with support services. That would have reduced street-dwelling homeless in Skid Row by about 60%.

LA CAN protested by marching, feasting, listening to speeches, and blocking traffic on First and Main streets to make their opposition to the SCI clear:

For the past six months, we targeted our opposition of SCI primarily on the Police Commission because they have both the power and the responsibility to evaluate this initiative and demand changes. As a first step, one of our demands was for the

Police Commission to hold a public hearing to get better informed about the devastation caused by SCI. That finally happened on November 18th.[66]

Another blow to the SCI came in December 2008, when the city and the ACLU reached a final agreement on the LAPD's stop-and-search policies. From the ACLU's press release:

"This settlement will ensure important checks on the LAPD's aggressive tactics on Skid Row. The constitution protects every Angeleno against unlawful stops and searches, from those living in Hollywood Hills to those sleeping on the streets of downtown," said Peter Bibring, an ACLU/SC staff attorney. "But abuses are bound to occur as long as the city tries to address homelessness on Skid Row as a law enforcement problem rather than a social problem."[67]

In April 2009, under advocate and financial pressure, the mayor proposed a budget that cut funding for the SCI. The BIDs immediately responded, sending a flurry of emails among themselves and allies in the city, pressuring council members Perry and Parks to champion the restoration of funding and writing a joint letter to the mayor.[68] In response to their pressure, the SCI continued for a third year at full funding. In April 2010, an additional layer of policing was added, with the announcement of a new injunction from the city attorney's office: a ban on eighty named drug dealers from appearing on Skid Row. Estela Lopez of the CCEA appeared at the news conference to praise the new injunction, saying of the drug trade, "Our ability to bring greater economic ability to this area simply cannot be fulfilled with this kind of activity."[69]

Through this entire period, the CCEA also continued with its monthly Neighborhood Watch walks. Its goals were clearly explained in a press release issued on the three-year anniversary of the walk, while also highlighting support for the SCI and achievements of the BIDs:

"Our objective, born of frustration and rage over the public health and public safety threats to this community, was to take back the streets of Skid Row," said Lopez. "What actually happened was a complete shift from helplessness to hope, for both those sheltered and unsheltered."

The Walk takes place on the first Wednesday of every month. It continues, according to Councilwoman Jan Perry, because the job of restoring dignity to Skid Row is far from over. "The Skid Row Neighborhood Watch Walk is a reminder of the work that still needs to be done," Perry states, "and helps us highlight the incredible needs of the homeless."

There are presently between 500 and 700 people sleeping in tents and cardboard boxes, down from as many as 2,000 when the Walk began in 2005 . . . A dedicated unit of fifty LAPD officers, many of whom volunteered for this assignment, enforce against criminal predators who pose a threat to the vulnerable, unsheltered and mentally ill. Two Business Improvement Districts (BIDs) financed by area property owners pay for the pick-up of between five and seven tons of trash from Skid Row sidewalks daily. Dark streets are now illuminated by dozens of new streetlights installed by the Bureau of Street Lighting and the Department of Water and Power.[70]

The walks, attended by press and politicians and escorted by police and BID security, continued, increasingly becoming a point of contention in the ways they laid claim to space. In a 2011 letter from LA CAN asking the CCEA to desist in their walk, directors Pete White and Becky Dennison state clear objections:

> For the past two months, LA CAN and other community partners have been legally protesting the Skid Row Walk, as we believe it supports and promotes the criminalization of homelessness and poverty and is comprised only of those from outside of our community. LA CAN members, comprised primarily of Skid Row residents, urge you to end this condescending and offensive walk through our community.
>
> The CCEA's monthly walk is instead dominated by police officers and representatives of the business community. These are exactly the same institutions that are promoting the unprecedented levels of police presence, citations and arrests in Skid Row that have made many homeless and poor residents less safe and/or less stable. You do not represent the interests of the low-income community, nor our vision for public safety.[71]

The letter signaled an increasingly personal confrontation between the CCEA and LA CAN. This came to a head in 2011 and 2012, when Estela Lopez claimed that she had been assaulted by the use of a bullhorn too close to her. In her support, the city attorney filed a lawsuit against Deborah Burton, a long-time LA CAN member and one of the leaders of the Community Watch program.[72] Additional help in documenting the case came from the officer in charge of the SCI, Lt. Shannon.[73] The Neighborhood Walks ceased pending the lawsuit, which came before the judge in July 2013.

"CLEANING OUT" SKID ROW REDUX

Perhaps one of the clearest examples of the BIDs' power to network and mobilize multiple government entities toward a single goal is seen in the renewed conflict over the city's ability to confiscate the possessions of those on the street. In April 2011, *Tony Lavan et al. v. City of Los Angeles et al.* was filed—yet another class-action lawsuit against the city for the confiscation and destruction of personal property belonging to those who were homeless. The lawsuit stated that "[t]he only reason for this policy is to destroy the property of individuals . . . who are homeless and who are regarded by the city as nothing more than garbage to be removed from city streets."[74] An injunction against the city's practice was granted by a federal judge in June to replace the temporary restraining order issued in April. While the judge did not discuss the politics of gentrification and displacement in the judgment granting the injunction, he was scathing in his appraisal of the weakness of the city's case and wrongly aggressive application of precedent in violating rights to property:

> The Court is troubled by the City's straight-faced misstatement of the law, especially in light of abundant authority to the contrary . . . The City offers no explanation as to why those abandoned-property cases stand for such a sweeping proposition of law. In order to prevent further reliance on inapplicable cases, the Court explains why those cases do not support the City's legal position despite the City's failure to do the same . . . How the City sincerely believes that Abel, Knight and Wider indicate lack of Fourth Amendment protections for the homeless population's property is beyond comprehension . . . The only explanation for the City's untenable position is that it assumes that all the homeless' property is abandoned. But, as discussed below, such an assumption is unwarranted, especially in light of Plaintiffs' clear showing that the City confiscated and destroyed unabandoned property in this case.[75]

Like the BIDs' slotting this destruction of personal property under city maintenance in the "trash track," the LAPD consistently refer to the injunction as the "Sanitation" Temporary Restraining Order. The city attorney and the BIDs, particularly Estela Lopez from the CCEA, began fighting to overturn it.[76] Lopez notes in an email to SCI officer Lt. Paulson that the two principal concerns for her members are "the growing number of transients on our streets, as compared to years 2006–2009," and "the injunction against LAPD clearing abandoned property off skid row sidewalks."[77] In February 2012, Lopez emailed the mayor, the city attorney, city council members, county officials, other downtown BIDs, and Skid Row organizations, inviting them to an emergency meeting with her board and high figures from the LAPD. The emails were personalized, showing her connections and also her power. To the city attorney's office she writes, for example:

> I am writing to request the participation of City Attorney Trutanich and Chief Deputy Bill Carter at a meeting on Monday, February 27th at 4pm at CCEA's offices to discuss the growing violence and public health hazards on skid row sidewalks.

The main body of the text is essentially the same to everyone:

> It appears that what many of us feared is coming to pass. The downturn in the economy, the release of state prisoners, and the court injunction limiting removal of property is having a cumulative affect on skid row. Many streets are tent villages once again as they were prior to the 2006 implementation of the Safer Cities

Initiative. I had my staff do a quick re-cap of key indicators, comparing January 2011 to January 2012:

Abandoned property Up 158%

Encampments Up 97%

Illegal dumping Up 500%

LAFD Assistance Up 1000% (persons sick, injured or deceased)

LAPD Assistance Up 500%

I am deeply concerned that we might be at a tipping point.[78]

She called the meeting, and everyone turned up (some represented by high-level staff members) except the mayor. In a further email pressuring him to meet with the new group thus formed, Lopez sent a second email, stating that Skid Row once more resembled a Third-World country.[79]

Once all the key politicians, city and county departments, and business community were on board, the CCEA started with the press. The *LA Times* ran an article at the end of March with the headline "Skid row street population surges back in Los Angeles: A city initiative had helped to reduce the numbers and clean up the sidewalks, but the weak economy and other factors have reversed the trend."[80] On April 9, Carol Schatz of the CCA published an op-ed piece also in the *LA Times* stating that advocates were causing more harm than good in their misguided attempts to help people living on the streets keep their belongings:

> Rather than simply establishing and refining rules under which homeless people can continue to live on city sidewalks in squalor, shouldn't activists and the courts focus on how to help homeless people off the streets? Protecting deplorable conditions by court order is tantamount to condemning the unfortunate to a lifetime of slow, deliberate deterioration.
>
> Meanwhile, the rights of a few to leave their possessions on public property have trumped the rights of the many who need to use the sidewalks for their intended purpose without threat to their health and safety.[81]

Once again a discourse of rights is claimed in defense of the "many"—there is no doubt whose rights matter here, despite a veneer of compassion. Even with the presses and other mobilizations of support, the city's request for a rehearing of the injunction before a larger panel at the ninth circuit lost a third time in December 2012. Yet the coalition of local government and business brought together by the CCEA still was not ready to quit.

In February 2013, the *Los Angeles Times* broke the story: "Feds try to curb outbreak of TB on skid row."[82] They cite county officials (who had been key participants in the meetings called by Estela Lopez, and who had themselves called in the federal Centers for Disease Control and Prevention) as calling it the greatest outbreak in a decade. This was in spite of the fact that their figures show seventy-eight cases and eleven deaths since 2007, making it an "outbreak" that took place over six years. As the article goes on to state, "Tuberculosis is easily transmitted by inhaling droplets from infected patients when they sneeze, cough or laugh. When left untreated, TB can be deadly." Though it later states that the Skid Row strain is one that can be treated, the operative words in that paragraph remain "easily transmitted" and "deadly."[83] In arguing why the LAPD and city officials should be able to remove (and destroy) people's personal possessions from the sidewalk, Estela Lopez is quoted:

> "No one's mental illness, tuberculosis or staph infection gets better lying on a public sidewalk," Lopez said. "These are human beings who are often unable to make rational decisions for themselves and they need our help. Instead, we give them options that are self-destructive like you can amass and hoard your belongings on the sidewalk."[84]

An ironic statement, considering the other option is to keep no possessions at all.

On February 25, the *LA Times* blog reported that an internal LAPD memo "warned officers who patrol the skid row area to wear protective masks and minimize face-to-face contact with suspects or the public if there is reason to believe that they are infected with tuberculosis." Pictures show masked LAPD officers patrolling the streets.[85] On February 27, the city attorney's office announced that it was appealing the *Lavan* decision to the Supreme Court, citing the immediate public health threat of the TB "outbreak."

That same day, the health department released a fact sheet on TB, retreating from much of the content of the previous articles. Now found on LA CAN's website, it states:

> Should the public be concerned?
> No, the general public should not be overly concerned. The public needs to know that there is no immediate danger to their health related to the current situation. TB is spread from person to person through the air, and usually requires prolonged, close contact. You cannot get TB from contact with clothes, drinking glasses, eating utensils, handshakes, contact with surfaces, or passing someone on the street.[86]

Within the space of only a few days, a public health crisis had been announced by LA County and so promoted into a panic by local media that it had been picked up by the national and international press. The LAPD and BID security had started wearing face masks in Skid Row. The city attorney had filed an appeal of the *Lavan* case to the Supreme Court based on the immediate health risk. Yet, after some awkward questions from advocates, LA County had retreated and put forward a fact sheet stating that the health crisis was actually nothing the public needed to worry about.

The Supreme Court decided not to hear the case. This hardly detracts from the concerted efforts of city and county agencies to support the confiscation and destruction of homeless people's property, and to support development interests facilitating capital's return to downtown and the creation of privileged social space. It is also remarkable how hard the city attorney pushed the case in the courts, even after a negative decision that contained a fairly damning personal indictment of their office's legal abilities. In part, the decision is a testament to LA CAN and their allies, unmoved in their resolve to fight unapologetically for the Skid Row community, who have claimed their place in society, their human rights to be respected, and housing in central LA.

CONCLUSIONS

In the return of capital to downtown, we can see how deeply entrenched the connection between whiteness and property's value remains, as business interests have felt it necessary to attempt the brutal displacement of an entire community—itself produced by the forces of racism combined with the globalized capital restructuring driving downtown's development—to better sell a social space of privilege and happiness.[87] The CCA and CCEA have worked to articulate various supports to effect and justify the creation of a more marketable and privileged white space in central LA: new strategies of privatizing and privately policing public spaces through BIDs; the initiation of intense geographic concentrations of LAPD officers who make arrests on quality-of-life issues; shifts in district attorney policy around drug prosecutions connected to the ongoing wholesale criminalization of communities of color; the mobilization of neoliberal discourses of individual responsibilities and choice along with the need for the power of the government to secure public health and safety; and work to enlist and coordinate various government agencies and offices in the effort to push downtown's long-term residents of color—whether just poor or homeless—outside of the physical community and outside of the community of consent. The reactive struggle forced onto residents and groups like LA CAN has been the defense not just of existing affordable housing and the legal right to carry out the functions required for life, but of the moral recognition of their place in the community and their very humanity, as it was similarly won during the 1960s.

LA CAN's success in preserving residential hotels and the rights of those who are homeless has provoked ever more extreme efforts to cleanse downtown, proving the power of a belief in segregated social space (required to underpin property values) where there is no place for the poor and people of color in a downtown to which money, resources, and the white middle classes have returned. The struggle to introduce this aspect of Jim Crow into the downtown community exposes a broader spatial aspect to the racial project of criminalization as theorized by Alexander.[88] It highlights the flexibility of downtown interests in navigating between neoliberal ideologies and strategies such as those underpinning the BIDs' privatized control of public space, as well as the coordination and support of government agencies such as the police and public health departments in pursuit of their aims. The efforts of organized business leaders highlight the continuing centrality of a logic that connects race to property value—developed during California's foundation and deepened through struggle, white flight, and suburbanization—to the political economy of property development. This has made race as central to understanding the return of capital to the city centers of the US, and the resulting dynamics of gentrification and displacement, as space has been in understanding current ideas of community, whether of coercion or consent, and the continuing hegemony of white privilege.

Chapter 9

Neoliberalism Found?

City of Segregation emerged from academic reflections carried out at one remove from many years of work as a tenant organizer in central Los Angeles. Coming from the southwest side of Tucson, Arizona, and reasonably familiar with a degree of segregation and quite an ugly amount of racism, I still remember the shock of moving to LA with its greater and more toxic intensity of segregation—not just between white people and everyone else (which I recognized), but between everyone. Organizing and fighting alongside fragmented Latino, African American, and Asian communities to improve our neighborhoods and working on environmental justice campaigns around slum housing, we found we also had to fight for people's rights to remain in their homes and on their streets as they improved. My colleague Tafarai Bayne coined the campaign slogan "Better Neighborhoods, Same Neighbors," because it seemed that as soon as residents succeeded in improving an area they were forced out of it. We fought every eviction we could, but still the complexion of neighborhoods changed as long-term residents left after losing legal battles or being worn down by long campaigns of harassment and intimidation by their landlords.

That race marked this process as deeply as income was highly visible, a truth observed from spending time on city streets, despite academic arguments separating gentrification from racial cleansing, and the fact that census data remained too distant, too faulty to prove these changes over the short term. Working in central LA, nothing could be more obvious than that race and racism were not only key to the displacement that we experienced, but also to understanding why we had to fight to improve a physical and social infrastructure that was failing all of its residents. In turn we needed to understand how those dynamics connected us to the city and county of LA as a whole and our place within it.

Grappling with the spatially experienced fact of a continuing deep and death-dealing segregation—one of the most visible, universal, and heartbreaking aspects of all US cities—is no small task, and this book is just one contribution to the attempt to understand how it emerged through a racist past, how it still exists even after a "victorious" civil rights struggle, and what it means for the present despite being treated as peripheral in so many accounts of the city. Thus, this book has engaged in an "unearthing of silences," a return to the archives and a recovering not just of the retrospective significance of the past, but its bearing on the struggles of the present.[1] In this it joins the recent work of scholars such as Carol Anderson and Keeanga-Yamahtta Tayler, seeking to understand the current resurgence of white anger and violence embodied in reactions to the many converging groups and networks simply fighting to save Black lives.[2]

Its contribution lies in showing how this history reveals the continuing centrality of race in the creation of the use and exchange values of land and how this has cemented white privilege into material place, allowing openly racist praxis to yield to the discourses of a "color-blind" or "post-racial" society without endangering white privilege itself. Thus, white privilege has been preserved through white space, despite the changes that victorious civil rights movements have forced in ideologies, policies, and racial geographies. We continue to see physically segregated white communities that map onto similarly segregated social understandings of community as being made up of whites only. Peoples of color have never been fully accepted into either these physical or social communities despite some gains in the 1960s. Those who are not white have thus always been, and continue to be, subject to violence and a regime more geared toward domination. Segregated space remains one physical, visible monument to this continued exclusion, another the still-rising numbers of our dead, murdered by police and vigilantes.

In bringing the significance of this history, and this narrative itself, into the present, this book argues that despite struggle, white privilege and its spatiality remain central to the construction of our cities, and that the links between race and land's use and exchange values forged during the period of open white supremacy continue through to the present. Struggle against segregation has not yet broken the hegemony of social forces united by race for white domination, in spite of winning enough ground to shift ideologies, practices, and policies. Thus, white supremacy remains as cemented into the economics of real estate as the materiality of the segregated and unequal spaces it produces; however, it may be recast and recoded into more neoliberal discourses and practices of rights and individual responsibilities. This explains the massive resources that have been employed in keeping peoples of color out of newly built privileged neighborhoods as much as it does their attempted erasure from those older, more central neighborhoods chosen for redevelopment as part of capitalist cycles of uneven development and global restructuring.

Race remains as central to the urban form and dominant ideologies as it always has been, even though it has been marginal to so many accounts of the city. Running throughout the Black struggles studied here is the constant, though not always fully articulated, acknowledgment of the centrality of white hegemony as the driving force in the formation of both the physical city and ideological understandings of community. The constant and powerful struggle by African Americans and other communities of color for their place in the city—from Charlotta Bass mobilizing community support to protect families integrating neighborhoods and battling restrictive covenants over the first four decades of the twenty-first century, to CORE's 1960s struggles to integrate the suburbs and make housing discrimination illegal—has forced political and legal changes, and lip service to equality and rights for all. In practice, however, rather than fully recognizing the justice of these struggles, whites have responded through new forms of ideology and practice labeled as neoliberal, and have mobilized in defence of white space and privilege.

This can be seen through changes in development strategies, the growth of organizations like BIDs and CIDs, and other increasingly privatized residential communities able to maintain exclusivity and resources for social reproduction through gates, security, design, regulations, and succession to the extent possible from the larger region. It can be seen in state repression, with ever more methods of criminalizing the poor and peoples of color, increased police brutality, and skyrocketing rates of incarceration. It can be seen in discourse, in the neoliberal rhetoric of market over government, color-blindness, individual responsibility, and property rights. For intellectuals of color as for activists, the centrality of race to the historical development of capitalism and neoliberalism as we find it at the current conjuncture is clear.[3] Yet it remains peripheral to so many theorizations of both neoliberalism and struggle, indicating that the veil described so eloquently by Du Bois is as real as ever. While hope lies in a grassroots, polycultural resistance against all forms of oppression, the problem of the twenty-first century remains the color line.[4]

This spatial understanding also builds on and supports Alexander's theorizations of the new Jim Crow so crucial to understanding the mobilizations in Ferguson, Baltimore, and around the country in support of #blacklivesmatter.[5] While the mass criminalization of African Americans and other peoples of color certainly seems key to the new system of racial control, it seems that the "new" Jim Crow, like the "old," should consist of a series of interlocking laws and practices not only of mass disenfranchisement but also of segregation.[6] This book shows that in support of residential segregation, there is an older logic based in white supremacy that runs beneath the current neoliberal discourses and practices now used to justify it. This same logic underlies the criminalization of both the space of the ghetto and its inhabitants—just as the efforts to racially cleanse Skid Row for development through criminalizing homelessness and poverty have capitalized on these connections while driving them deeper. The current spatial configuration of Los Angeles, like other cities, supports these older logics of "us" and "them" and allows them to grow unchallenged. In the rhetoric of groups like today's Tea Party, it is hard to see that much has changed since this 1944 letter from a Los Angeles resident to California's Governor Warren to ask for his help against the "Negroes":

> I don't believe in intermarriage, of course, I don't believe in residential mixing, believing that the colored folks should live in their respective sections and fraternize among themselves, not feel they have a right to "mix" with the whites.

> I believe in the unalienable rights of every man, whatever his race cred [sic] or color; but only so long as he minds his own business and does not tread on the toes of others.[7]

These sentiments acknowledge the rights of everyone, but that above them all are the rights of white Americans to retain their privilege along with their segregated neighborhoods.

In starting with struggle itself and examining the changes it had won and lost, neoliberalism emerges as something of a distraction, the result of an opportunistic search for what would best preserve white supremacy through segregation, and the spatial power and privileges segregation confers. Destabilizing this racial hegemony along with capitalist relations of exploitation forms the real prize, the battle to be fought and won in transforming both cities and the nation into just and equitable spaces where racism is no longer "a death-dealing displacement of difference within hierarchies."[8]

Thinking about neoliberalism as an "ideology found" recognizes this opportunistic search. The overturning of covenants in 1948 and the mass protests in Torrance's exclusive white suburbs in the 1960s both saw white American homeowners and developers alike searching for ways to better protect white privilege and neighborhoods. Increased privatization and securitization proved to be the answer. The resonances between neoliberalism and existing discourses of individual and property rights over collective social rights, a rejection of government authority in support of "minorities" against discrimination, and practices of privatization made neoliberalism's prescriptions of small government facilitating the free market and rationalizations of inequity very useful. Neoliberalism helped rearticulate a desire and strategy to preserve spatial and racial privilege with an ideology able to justify it in non-racialized terms. In Los Angeles, increasing privatization of space and municipal functions came first, rather than simply being part of a "rollout" of top-down ideology as is sometimes argued in theorizations of neoliberalism, even when allowing for local adaptations.[9] Los Angeles's BIDs started in the 1990s but arguably are based as much on a longer history of privatization and control of public space as they are an "example par excellence of the changes in how urban management is being practiced in the most industrialized economies of the world" as part of the rollout of neoliberalism.[10] When the BIDs and the private market proved ineffective in cleansing downtown of its poor, the business associations running them had little hesitation in once more mobilizing and promoting the power of the state.

I would argue that neoliberalism's importance as an object of struggle does not change the fact that it remains disposable if it ceases to serve white domination and preserve white privileged space. Today's social movements face the relentless privatization of government and the selling off of public assets, the invidious language of the market that has invaded every sphere, and the ever deeper focus on the individual over the community. LA CAN's framing of their work as a struggle for human rights (to housing, jobs, food, etc.) in opposition to neoliberalism can help connect similar efforts in a global framework to provide a basis for wider solidarity. Yet LA CAN builds this solidarity with an awareness of what is really at stake: the oppression that their members survive every day, and the ways in which race is central to this oppression. Neoliberalism is ultimately a tool for those working to support capitalist white privilege and its spatial privileges, and thus it is the battle against racism and capitalism that must be theorized and fought, even if only in small steps looking toward this larger goal.

The first step must surely consist of finally piercing the veil described by Du Bois over 100 years ago, gaining widespread understanding among whites and all races of the structural role that white supremacy continues to play in the US, and gaining their support in its dismantling. This must be in service of a true opening up of understandings of community, and what this book demonstrates above all is that this must not be simply an ideological opening, but also a material, spatial one. This would mark a true victory, not least because it would help bring to an end the vicious regime of coercion that daily results in brutal displacement, tragedy, and death. LA CAN's work, and that of other grassroots groups doing this kind of organizing and politicization around rights to space, points a way forward. The inspirational work across a broad coalition of activists and academics in developing a vision and platform for transformative change undertaken by the Movement for Black Lives is another.[11] Both demand theory in service to movement led by those most marginalized across all intersectional oppressions, who have always been and will be the agents of lasting transformation. This is how we need to work together to cross the color lines, imagine a new future, and theorize how we can get there even as we walk.

Map Credits

Map 1.
Data comes from the Southern California Association of Governments GIS library.

Map 2.
The 1960 and 2010 census data and tract shapefiles are courtesy of NHIS; sources for racial faultlines and 1890–1940 community boundaries can be found in Appendix A, and those for Contested Spaces in Appendix B, of Andrea Gibbons, *Segregation in search of ideology? Hegemony and Contestation in the Spatial and Racial Configuration of Los Angeles* (London, PhD thesis presented to the London School of Economics, 2014). Given the archival record, I have sadly left the smaller communities found in Pasadena and Pacoima for later study.

Map 4.
Information on KKK activity comes from Daniel Cady, "Bringing in the Sheets: Robert Shuler, the Ku Klux Klan, and the Southernization of Southern California," in *Race, Religion, Region: Landscapes of Encounter in the American West*, Fay Botham and Sara M. Patterson (eds.) (Tucson, AZ: University of Arizona Press, 2006): 41–59; Christopher N. Cocoltchos, "The Invisible Empire and the Search for the Orderly Community: The Ku Klux Klan in Anaheim, California," in *The Invisible Empire in the West: Toward a New Historical Appraisal of the Ku Klux Klan of the 1920s*, Shawn Lay (ed.) (Urbana and Chicago: University of Illinois Press, 1992); Kenneth T. Jackson, *The Ku Klux Klan in the City, 1915–1930* (New York: Oxford University Press, 1967); Becky Nicolaides, *My Blue Heaven: Life and Politics in the Working Class Suburbs of Los Angeles, 1920–1965* (Chicago: University of Chicago Press, 2002); Jane Beemer Shults, "The Ku Klux Klan in Downey during the 1920s" (Long Beach: unpublished master's thesis submitted to California State University, 1991); Phyllis Anne Sowers, "'Klanaheim': Suburbia, Civic Identity and the Second Ku Klux Klan" (Long Beach: unpublished master's thesis presented to California State University, 2012); the *Torrance Herald* and the *California Eagle*.

Map 5.
Small clusters of African Americans could also be found in Pacoima in the San Fernando Valley, and in Pasadena from an early period; see Jack Languth, "Housing Integration in the San Fernando Valley," *Valley Times Today*, March 6, 1963, and Paul Robinson, "Race, Space and the Evolution of Black Los Angeles," in *Black Los Angeles: American Dreams and Racial Realities*, Darnell Hunt and Ana-Christina Ramón (eds.) (New York and London: New York University Press, 2010). Little information is available on these areas, as they were not covered in the same way by the *California Eagle*. Where information is available I have recorded incidents across these areas, but I focused my study on the main center of African American organizing in Central and South Central LA. The homeowner association boundaries are as described in the *Eagle*.

Map 7.
HOLC map courtesy of LaDale Winling, downloaded from Urban Oasis, urbanoasis.org (accessed December 14, 2013).

Map 9.
City map from SCAG's GIS library; racial incidents drawn by me.

Map 10.
Gilda Haas and Alan Heskin, "Community Struggles in Los Angeles," *International Journal of Urban and Regional Research* 5(4) (1981): 546–63. BID boundaries as a GIS data file are from the LA Department of City Planning, planning.lacity.org (accessed August 23, 2013).

Notes

INTRODUCTION

1. Melany De la Cruz-Viesca et al., *The Color of Wealth in Los Angeles*, report, Duke University, The New School, the University of California, Los Angeles, Insight Center for Community Economic Development (San Francisco: Federal Reserve of San Francisco, 2016); see also Douglas S. Massey, "Residential Segregation is the Linchpin of Racial Stratification," *City & Community* 15(1) (March 2016): 4–7 for a summary of the latest studies. For a discussion of the difference between simple income and "wealth" as the sum total of assets saved over a lifetime as well as inherited wealth, and the ways in which the indicator of wealth shows much deeper inequality along racial lines in America, see M. Oliver and T. Shapiro, *Black Wealth, White Wealth* (New York: Routledge, 1995).
2. Douglas S. Massey, "Residential Segregation is the Linchpin of Racial Stratification," *City & Community* 15(1) (March 2016): 4–7.
3. Philip J. Ethington, W.H. Frey, and D. Myers, "The Racial Resegregation of Los Angeles County, 1940–2000." Public Research Report No. 2001-04 (2001).
4. Philip Ethington, "Segregated Diversity: Race-Ethnicity, Space, and Political Fragmentation in Los Angeles County, 1940–1994." Report prepared for the John Randolph Haynes and Dora Haynes Foundation (2000).
5. See Kenneth B. Clark, *Dark Ghetto: Dilemmas of Social Power* (Middletown, CT: Weslyan University Press, 1965) and Daniel J.B. Mitchell, *Violence in the City: An End or a Beginning?* (McCone Commission on the Los Angeles Riots, 1965).
6. Karl Taeuber and Alma Taeuber, *Negroes In Cities: Residential Segregation and Neighborhood Change* (Chicago: Aldine Publishing Company, 1965).
7. Douglas S. Massey and Nancy A. Denton, *American Apartheid: Segregation and the Making of the Underclass* (Cambridge, MA: Harvard University Press, 1993). Scott J. South and Kyle D. Crowder, "Residential Mobility Between Cities and Suburbs: Race, Suburbanization, and Back-to-the-City Moves," *Demography* 34(4) (1997): 525–38. Statistical analyses of residential segregation of middle class African Americans consistently have found that "race powerfully shapes their residential options." Richard D. Alba, John R. Logan, and Brian J. Stults, "How Segregated Are Middle-Class African Americans?" *Social Problems* 47(4) (2000): 543–58. See also Camille Zubrinsky Charles, "The Dynamics of Racial Residential Segregation," *Annual Review of Sociology* 29 (2003): 167–207; John R. Logan, Richard D. Alba, and Shu-Yin Leung, "Minority Access to White Suburbs: A Multiregional Comparison," *Social Forces* 74(3) (1996): 851–81; John Yinger, *Closed Doors, Opportunities Lost: The Continuing Costs of Housing Discrimination* (New York: Russell Sage Foundation, 1995); Steven Grant Meyer, *As Long As They Don't Move Next Door: Segregation and Racial Conflict in American Neighborhoods* (Oxford: Rowman & Littlefield Publishers Inc., 2000); Scott J. South and Kyle D. Crowder, "Residential Mobility Between Cities and Suburbs: Race, Suburbanization, and Back-to-the-City Moves," *Demography* 34(4) (1997): 525–38, among others.
8. Scott J. South and Kyle D. Crowder, "Residential Mobility Between Cities and Suburbs: Race, Suburbanization, and Back-to-the-City Moves," *Demography* 34(4) (1997): 525–38.

9. Patrick Sharkey, "The Intergenerational Transmission of Context," *American Journal of Sociology* 113(4) (2008): 931–69, page 933.

10. Ibid. See also Patrick Sharkey, *Stuck in Place: Urban Neighborhoods and the End of Progress Toward Racial Equality* (Chicago: University of Chicago Press, 2013) for updated figures and an extended discussion of neighborhood effects on equality.

11. Philip Ethington, W.H. Frey, and D. Myers, "The Racial Resegregation of Los Angeles County, 1940–2000." Public Research Report No. 2001-04 (2001).

12. Joel Garreau, *Edge City: Life on the New Frontier* (New York: Doubleday, 1991), page 3.

13. Stuart Elden, *Understanding Henri Lefebvre: Theory and the Possible* (London: Continuum, 2004).

14. Mike Davis, *City of Quartz* (London & New York: Verso, 2006); Edward Soja, *Postmetropolis: Critical Studies of Cities and Regions* (Malden, MA: Blackwell Publishers, 2000).

15. Michael Dear and Steven Flusty first claimed the existence of the LA School in "Postmodern Urbanism," *Annals of the Association of American Geographers* 88 (1998): 50–72, supported by Soja in numerous works such as *Postmetropolis: Critical Studies of Cities and Regions* (Malden, MA: Blackwell Publishers, 2000), and through the more recent work of Michael Dear and Nicholas Dahmann, "Urban Politics and the Los Angeles School of Urbanism," *Urban Affairs Review* 44(2) (2008): 266–79. This body of work emerged primarily from UCLA and challenged more conventional and empirical traditions. That such a school exists has been quite controversial; for a collection of arguments both for and against the school, see the issue devoted to it in *Urban Geography*, 1999, 20(5), and for one of the best summaries of the claims of the LA School in relation to other literatures on globalization, see Steven Erie's *Globalizing LA: Trade, Infrastructure, and Regional Development* (Stanford: Stanford University Press, 2004).

16. Janet Abu-Lughod, *New York, Chicago, Los Angeles: America's Global Cities* (Minneapolis: University of Minnesota Press, 1999).

17. Cedric Robinson, *Black Marxism: The Making of the Black Radical Tradition* (London: Zed Books, 1983). In David Harvey's study of US cities, the focus is post–World War II and tends to examine racial segregation as a means of fragmenting class consciousness; this shapes his detailed studies of Baltimore on the redlining of the ghetto in *Social Justice and the City* (Bath: The Pitman Press, 1973) and residential differention by ethnicity, class, and race in *The Urbanization of Capital* (Baltimore, MD: Johns Hopkins University Press, 1985). Likewise, Neil Smith's detailed studies also focus on more current processes of capital flow and gentri- fication, beginning in the 1970s, and only begin to unravel the way that race intersects with investment capital. See *The New Urban Frontier: Gentrification and the Revanchist City* (London: Routledge, 1996) among other writing, particularly around the struggles on New York's Lower East Side.

18. Ruth Wilson Gilmore, "Fatal Couplings of Power and Difference: Notes on Racism and Geography," *The Professional Geographer* 54(1) (2002): 15–24, page 16.

19. Ibid.; see also Ruth Wilson Gilmore, *Golden Gulag: Prisons, Surplus, Crisis, and Opposition in Globalizing California* (Berkeley: University of California Press, 2007) and Kimberlé Crenshaw, Neil Gotanda, Gary Peller, and Wendell Thomas (eds.), *Critical Race Theory* (New York: New Press, 1995) among others for more on constructions of race and critical race theory.

20. Albert Memmi, *Racism* (Minneapolis: University of Minnesota Press, 1999).

21. See Noel Ignatiev, *How the Irish Became White* (New York; London: Routledge, 1995) and David R. Roediger, *The Wages of Whiteness* (New York: Verso, 1991), among others for detailed studies of this.

22. Barbara Fields, "Ideology and Race in American History," in *Region, Race, and Reconstruction: Essays in Honor of C. Vann Woodward*, ed. Morgan J. Koussar and James McPherson, 143–77 (New York: Oxford University Press, 1982).

23. Leland T. Saito, *Race and Politics: Asian Americans, Latinos, and Whites in a Los Angeles Suburb* (Chicago: University of Illinois Press, 1998).

24. Scott Kurashige, *The Shifting Grounds of Race: Black and Japanese Americans in the Making of Multiethnic Los Angeles* (Princeton: Princeton University Press, 2008). This is a fascinating

historical work of critical race theory charting the period beginning before World War II through the rebellions of the 1960s, trying to answer how African Americans became linked to ideas of the "urban crisis" while the Japanese came to be seen as a model minority and signifier of the multicultural city.

25. Tomas Almaguer, *Racial Faultines: The Historical Origins of White Supremacy in California* (Berkeley & Los Angeles: University of California Press, 1994). For more on racial hierarchies, see David Gutierrez, *Walls and Mirrors: Mexican Americans, Mexican Immigrants, and the Politics of Ethnicity* (Berkeley: University of California Press, 1995); Laura Pulido, *Black, Brown, Yellow, and Left: Radical Activism in Los Angeles* (Berkeley: University of California Press, 2006); Laura Pulido, "Rethinking Environmental Racism: White Privilege and Urban Development in Southern California," *Annals of the Association of American Geographers* 90(1) (2000): 12–40; Lisa Y. Ramos, "Not Similar Enough: Mexican American and African American Civil Rights Struggles in the 1940s," in *The Struggle in Black and Brown: African American and Mexican American Relations During the Civil Rights Era* (Lincoln: University of Nebraska Press, 2012); George Sanchez, *Becoming Mexican American: Ethnicity, Culture, and Identity in Chicano Los Angeles, 1900-1945* (New York: Oxford University Press, 1993); and Henry Yu, *Thinking Orientals: Migration, Contact, and Exoticism in Modern America* (New York: Oxford University Press, 2001). LA has also contained the largest number of Native Americans outside of Arizona's Navajo reservation since 1970. While low in concrete numbers given North America's genocidal policies, Nicholas G. Rosenthal, *Reimagining Indian Country: Native American Migration & Identity in Twentieth-Century Los Angeles* (Chapel Hill: University of North Carolina Press, 2012) examines the ways in which Native Americans in LA have moved between whiteness and romanticized "Other," and how they struggle to survive in the city.

26. See Camille Zubrinsky Charles, "The Dynamics of Racial Residential Segregation," *Annual Review of Sociology* 29 (2003): 167–207; and Philip Ethington, W.H. Frey and D. Myers, "The Racial Resegregation of Los Angeles County, 1940–2000." Public Research Report No. 2001-04 (2001).

27. Camille Zubrinsky Charles, *Won't You Be My Neighbor: Race, Class, and Residence in Los Angeles*. (New York: Russell Sage Foundation, 2006), page 159.

28. Ibid.

29. John Logan and Harvey Molotch, *Urban Fortunes: The Political Economy of Place* (Berkeley: University of California Press, 1987).

30. Tomas Almaguer, *Racial Faultines: The Historical Origins of White Supremacy in California* (Berkeley and Los Angeles: University of California Press, 1994); David R. Roediger, *The Wages of Whiteness* (New York: Verso, 1991) and *How Race Survived US History: From Settlement and Slavery to the Obama Phenomenon* (London and New York: Verso, 2008).

31. For critiques, see Gillian Hart, "The Provocations of Neoliberalism: Contesting the Nation and Liberation after Apartheid," *Antipode* 40(4) (2008): 678–705; Daniel Martinez HoSang, Oneka LaBennett, and Laura Pulido (eds.), *Racial Formation in the Twenty-First Century* (Berkeley: University of California Press, 2013); Michael Omi and Howard Winant, *Racial Formation in the United States: From the 1960s to the 1990s* (New York: Routledge, 1994); David Roberts and Minelle Mahtani, "Neoliberalizing Race, Racing Neoliberalism: Placing "Race" in Neoliberal Discourses," *Antipode* 42(2) (2010): 248–57; and Tony Samara, "Order and Security in the City: Producing Race and Policing Neoliberal Spaces in South Africa," *Ethnic & Racial Studies* 33(4) (2010): 637–55.

32. For a brilliant discussion of positionality and the different kinds of questions this raises for communities of color and poor communities, as well as its transformational effect on stakes and strategies of struggle, see Laura Pulido, *Environmentalism and Economic Justice: Two Chicano Struggles in the Southwest* (Tucson: University of Arizona Press, 1996).

33. See the Los Angeles Alliance for a New Economy (LAANE), "Poverty, Jobs and the Los Angeles Economy" (Los Angeles, 2008); Michelle Alexander, *The New Jim Crow: Mass Incarceration in an Age of Colorblindness* (New York: The New Press, 2012); Michael A. Stoll,

"Search, Discrimination, and the Travel to Work," in *Prismatic Metropolis: Inequality in Los Angeles*, Lawrence D. Bobo, Melvin L. Oliver, James H. Johnson Jr., and Abel Valenzuela Jr. (eds.) (New York: Russell Sage Foundation, 2000): 417–52; and William Julius Wilson, *The Truly Disadvantaged: The Inner City, the Underclass, and Public Policy* (Chicago: University of Chicago Press, 1987).

34. See, for example, Julie E. Press, "Spatial Mismatch or More of a Mishmash? Multiple Jeopardy and the Journey to Work," in *Prismatic Metropolis: Inequality in Los Angeles*, Lawrence D. Bobo, Melvin L. Oliver, James H. Johnson Jr., and Abel Valenzuela Jr. (eds.) (New York: Russel Sage Foundation, 2000): 453–88, who found race to be a more important factor than gender for Black women seeking work.

35. Allen J. Scott, "High-Technology Industrial Development in the San Fernando Valley and Ventura County: Observations on Economic Growth and the Evolution of Urban Form," in *The City: Los Angeles and Urban Theory at the End of the Twentieth Century*, Allen J. Scott and Edward W. Soja (eds.) (Berkeley: University of California Press, 1996): 276–310; and Allen J. Scott, *Metropolis: From the Division of Labor to Urban Form* (Berkeley: University of California Press, 1988). See also Manning Marable, *How Capitalism Underdeveloped America* (Boston: South End Press, 1983), and for LA specifically: Raymond A. Rocco, "Latino Los Angeles: Reframing Boundaries/Borders," in *The City: Los Angeles and Urban Theory at the End of the Twentieth Century*, Allen J. Scott and Edward W. Soja (eds.) (Berkeley: University of California Press, 1996): 365–89; Edward Soja, "Los Angeles, 1965–1992: From Crisis-Generated Restructuring to Restructuring-Generated Crisis," in *The City: Los Angeles and Urban Theory at the End of the Twentieth Century*, Allen J. Scott and Edward W. Soja (eds.) (Berkeley: University of California Press, 1996): 426–62; and Jennifer Wolch, "From Global to Local: The Rise of Homelessness in Los Angeles during the 1980s," in *The City: Los Angeles and Urban Theory at the End of the Twentieth Century*, Allen J. Scott and Edward W. Soja (eds.) (Berkeley: University of California Press, 1996): 390–425 among others. For studies on actual employment patterns in LA, see Stoll, who found that "low-skilled blacks, particularly those living in minority areas, search significantly greater distances for work than comparable Latinos and whites," hypothesized as a combination of spatial mismatch, perceptions of hostility, and racial discrimination in suburban areas—Michael A. Stoll, "Search, Discrimination, and the Travel to Work," in *Prismatic Metropolis: Inequality in Los Angeles*, Lawrence D. Bobo, Melvin L. Oliver, James H. Johnson Jr., and Abel Valenzuela Jr. (eds.) (New York: Russell Sage Foundation, 2000): 417–52.

36. See Karen Brodkin, *Power Politics: Environmental Activism in South Los Angeles* (Rutgers University Press, 2009); Laura Pulido, *Black, Brown, Yellow, and Left: Radical Activism in Los Angeles* (Berkeley: University of California Press, 2006); and "Rethinking Environmental Racism: White Privilege and Urban Development in Southern California," *Annals of the Association of American Geographers* 90(1) (2000): 12–40; Sonya Winton, "Concerned Citizens: Environmental (In)Justice in Black Los Angeles," in *Black Los Angeles: American Dreams and Racial Realities*, Darnell Hunt and Ana-Christina Ramón (eds.) (New York: New York University Press, 2010): 343–59.

37. See Paul M. Ong, *The State of South LA* (Los Angeles: UCLA School of Public Affairs, 2008), and Jordan Rickles, Paul M. Ong, and Douglas Houston, *School Integration and Residential Segregation in California: Challenges for Racial Equity*. UC/ACCORD Public Policy Series (Los Angeles: University of California All-Campus Consortium on Research for Diversity, 2004).

38. See Angela Bowden and Joanna Lee, *The Role of Race and Class in Determining Access to Healthcare in LA County* (Community Institute for Policy Heuristics, Education and Research, 2005); *LA's Hidden Health Crisis* (Los Angeles: Strategic Actions for a Just Economy (SAJE), 2010); and *Shame of the City* (Los Angeles: Strategic Actions for a Just Economy (SAJE), 2007).

39. See, for example, Alison Hope Alkon and Julian Agyeman, *Cultivating Food Justice: Race, Class, and Sustainability* (Cambridge, MA: MIT Press, 2011). A report by Linda Ashman, Jaime de la Vega, Marc Dohan, Andy Fisher, Rosa Hippler, and Billi Romain, *Seeds of Change: Strategies for Food Security in the Inner City*, Department of Urban Planning, UCLA (Los

Angeles: The Community Food Security Coalition, 1993), revealed the lack of fresh quality produce, that 27 percent of residents in one South Central neighborhood went hungry an average of five days a month and that due to higher food prices they spent an average of $275 more a year than residents in the suburban group.

40. See *Making Change* (Los Angeles: Strategic Actions for a Just Economy [SAJE], 2002) and Neal Richman and Bill Pitkin, *The Case of Los Angeles, USA. Understanding Sums: Case Studies for the Global Report* (United Nations, 2003).

41. See Alex Alonso, "Out of the Void: Street Gangs in Black Los Angeles," in *Black Los Angeles: American Dreams and Racial Realities*, Darnell Hunt and Ana-Christina Ramón (eds.) (2010), page 140; Dionne Bennett, "Looking for the 'Hood and Finding Community," in *Black Los Angeles: American Dreams and Racial Realities*, Darnell Hunt and Ana-Christina Ramón (eds.) (New York: New York University Press, 2010): 215–31; and Josh Sides, "Straight into Compton: American Dreams, Urban Nightmares, and the Metamorphosis of a Black Suburb," *American Quarterly* 56(3) (2004): 583–605.

42. Jennifer Wolch, "From Global to Local: The Rise of Homelessness in Los Angeles during the 1980s," in *The City: Los Angeles and Urban Theory at the End of the Twentieth Century*, Allen J. Scott and Edward W. Soja (eds.) (Berkeley: University of California Press, 1996): 390–425.

43. Daniel Flaming and Paul Tepper, *10-Year Strategy to End Homelessness* (Los Angeles: Bring LA Home! The Partnership to End Homelessness, 2004).

44. Mike Davis, *City of Quartz* (London & New York: Verso, 2006).

45. See Gerald Horne, *Fire This Time: The Watts Uprising and the 1960s* (Charlottesville: University of Virginia Press, 1995) and Robert Gooding-Williams (ed.), *Reading Rodney King / Reading Urban Uprising*, (New York: Routledge, 1993), among many of the excellent works on this subject.

46. Laura Pulido, "Rethinking Environmental Racism: White Privilege and Urban Development in Southern California," *Annals of the Association of American Geographers* 90(1) (2000): 12–40, page 15.

47. George Fredrickson, *White Supremacy: A Comparative Study of Race in American and South African History* (New York: Oxford University Press, 1981); Michael Omi and Howard Winant, *Racial Formation in the United States: From the 1960s to the 1990s* (New York: Routledge, 1994); Laura Pulido, "Rethinking Environmental Racism: White Privilege and Urban Development in Southern California," *Annals of the Association of American Geographers* 90(1) (2000): 12–40. See also Thomas Byrne Edsall and Mary D. Edsall, *Chain Reaction: the Impact of Race, Rights, and Taxes on American Politics* (New York: Norton, 1991); George Lipsitz, *The Possessive Investment in Whiteness* (Philadelphia: Temple University Press, 1998); and Jill Quadagno, *The Color of Welfare: How Racism Undermined the War on Poverty* (New York: Oxford University Press, 1994).

48. W.E.B. Du Bois, *The Souls of Black Folk* (New York: Library of America, 1990), page 3.

49. Vijay Prashad, *Everybody was Kung Fu Fighting: Afro-Asian connections and the myth of cultural purity* (Boston: Beacon Press, 2002).

50. These addresses are drawn from multiple sources, the principal being news stories from the *California Eagle* and the *Sentinel*. They range from cases over restrictive covenants to bombings, with a range of burning crosses, mob actions, harassment, and vandalism in between the two. They represent a fairly exhaustive representation of what was reported in these two Black-owned papers from 1914 through the mid-1960s, based on a review of all the *California Eagle* issues available and exhaustive word searches of the *Sentinel* archive. Undoubtedly I have missed some stories—and I believe far more went unreported, given how many stories here represent the culmination of months, if not longer, of harassment incidents—but these 132 incidents give a clear sense of the shape this struggle took. Although the *Eagle* reports on a handful cases against other ethnic groups, much more work remains in studying their stories through their own papers. The racial faultlines are mapped as described from newspapers, memoirs, oral histories, and testimony to the Governor's Commission on the Watts Riots as further explored in Chapter 2.

51. Michel-Rolphe Trouillot, in *Silencing the Past: Power and the Production of History* (Boston: Beacon Press, 1997), gives the classic example of this silencing as the disappearance of the

Haitian Revolution from world history, while the connections between Detroit and the Amazon through Ford's factory ownership as described by Greg Gandin, "Empire's Ruins: Detroit to the Amazon," in *Imperial Debris: On Ruins and Ruination*, Laura Ann Stoler (ed.) (Durham and London: Duke University Press, 2013) is one example of many from Stoler's collection.

52. See Michelle Alexander, *The New Jim Crow: Mass Incarceration in an Age of Colorblindness* (New York: The New Press, 2012) and Cornel West, *Race Matters* (New York: Vintage Books, 2001).

53. Carey McWilliams, *Southern California: An Island on the Land* (Salt Lake City: Peregrine Smith Books, 1946).

54. Clement Vose, *Caucasians Only: The Supreme Court, the NAACP, and the Restrictive Covenant Cases* (Berkeley: University of California Press, 1959).

1. AS WORTHY AS YOU: THE STRUGGLES OF BLACK HOMEOWNERS THROUGH THE 1920S

1. Carey McWilliams, *Southern California: An Island on the Land* (Salt Lake City: Peregrine Smith Books, 1946).

2. Ibid.

3. Tomas Almaguer, *Racial Faultines: The Historical Origins of White Supremacy in California* (Berkeley & Los Angeles: University of California Press, 1994); Carey McWilliams, *Southern California: An Island on the Land* (Salt Lake City: Peregrine Smith Books, 1946).

4. See David M.P. Freund, *Colored Property: State Policy and White Racial Politics in Suburban America* (Chicago and London: University of Chicago Press, 2007); Thomas Sugrue, *The Origins of the Urban Crisis* (Princeton: Princeton University Press, 1996); George Lipsitz, *The Possessive Investment in Whiteness* (Philadelphia: Temple University Press, 1998), among others.

5. This is a widely used historical term usually attributed to the Chicago School and prevalent in many works published from the 1930s onwards—see Horace R. Cayton and St. Clair Drake, *Black Metropolis* (London: Jonathan Cape, 1946); Loren Miller and Bernard J. Sheil, *Racial Restrictive Covenants*, pamphlet (Quincey Press, 1946); or Loren Miller's *The Petitioners: The Story of the Supreme Court of the United States and the Negro* (New York: Pantheon Books, 1966).

6. Loren Miller, *The Petitioners: The Story of the Supreme Court of the United States and the Negro* (New York: Pantheon Books, 1966).

7. See Regina Freer, "LA Race Woman: Charlotta Bass and the Complexities of Black Political Development in Los Angeles," *American Quarterly* 56(3) (2004): 607–32; and "Charlotta Bass: A Community Activist for Racial and Economic Justice," in *The Next Los Angeles: The Struggle for a Livable City*, Robert Gottlieb, Regina Freer, Mark Vallianatos, and Peter Dreier (eds.) (Berkeley: University of California Press, 2005).

8. Charlotta Bass, "Early History of the Negro Press in California," undated manuscript, Southern California Research Library.

9. See Regina Freer, "Charlotta Bass: A Community Activist for Racial and Economic Justice," in *The Next Los Angeles: The Struggle for a Livable City*, Robert Gottlieb, Regina Freer, Mark Vallianatos, and Peter Dreier (eds.) (Berkeley: University of California Press, 2005); and Charlotta Spears Bass, *Forty Years: Memoirs from the Pages of a Newspaper* (Los Angeles: unpublished manuscript available at Southern California Research Library, 1960).

10. For a good article on what we do know of Charlotta Bass, see Regina Freer, whose work has helped ensure Charlotta Bass's centrality in the history of Black struggle in LA and more broadly, particularly Bass as an inspiration for today's and tomorrow's freedom fighters. See "Charlotta Bass: A Community Activist for Racial and Economic Justice," in *The Next Los Angeles: The Struggle for a Livable City*, Robert Gottlieb, Regina Freer, Mark Vallianatos, and Peter Dreier (eds.) (Berkeley: University of California Press, 2005).

11. See Douglas Flamming, *Bound for Freedom: Black Los Angeles in Jim Crow America* (Berkeley: University of California Press, 2005).

12. Melina Abdullah and Regina Freer, "Bass to Bass: Relative Freedom and Womanist Leadership in Black Los Angeles," in *Black Los Angeles: American Dreams and Racial Realities* (New York and London: New York University Press, 2010): 323–42, page 325.

13. Charlotta Spears Bass, *Forty Years: Memoirs from the Pages of a Newspaper* (Los Angeles: unpublished manuscript available at Southern California Research Library, 1960), page i, italics in the original.

14. Ibid., page 3.

15. See Michel-Rolphe Trouillot's powerful *Silencing the Past: Power and the Production of History* (Boston: Beacon Press, 1997) on history and the power of silences.

16. Charlotta Spears Bass, *Forty Years: Memoirs from the Pages of a Newspaper* (Los Angeles: unpublished manuscript available at Southern California Research Library, 1960).

17. Regina Freer, "LA Race Woman: Charlotta Bass and the Complexities of Black Political Development in Los Angeles," *American Quarterly* 56(3) (2004): 607–32.

18. Charlotta Spears Bass, *Forty Years: Memoirs from the Pages of a Newspaper* (Los Angeles: unpublished manuscript available at Southern California Research Library, 1960), page 13.

19. Ibid., page 12.

20. Regina Freer, "LA Race Woman: Charlotta Bass and the Complexities of Black Political Development in Los Angeles," *American Quarterly* 56(3) (2004): 607–32.

21. C. Van Woodward, *The Strange Career of Jim Crow: A Commemorative Edition* (Oxford: Oxford University Press, 2002).

22. Michael Jones-Correa, "The Origins and Diffusion of Racial Restrictive Covenants," *Political Science Quarterly* 115(4) (2000–2001): 541–68; Loren Miller and Bernard J. Sheil, *Racial Restrictive Covenants*, pamphlet (Quincey Press, 1946).

23. Willis O. Tyler, "Defense Attorney Analyzes Historic 'Sugar Hill' Decision," *California Eagle*, 13, December 1945.

24. Michael Jones-Correa, "The Origins and Diffusion of Racial Restrictive Covenants," *Political Science Quarterly* 115(4) (2000–2001): 541–68.

25. Charlotta Spears Bass, *Forty Years: Memoirs from the Pages of a Newspaper* (Los Angeles: unpublished manuscript available at Southern California Research Library, 1960), page 14.

26. Ibid.

27. See Douglas Flamming, *Bound for Freedom: Black Los Angeles in Jim Crow America* (Berkeley: University of California Press, 2005) on an evaluation of the idea of a "Golden Age" in LA, and for more about early Watts or "mudtown," an area generally left out of the pages of the *California Eagle*, see Arna Bontemps and Jack Conroy, *Anyplace But Here* (New York: Hill and Wang, 1966).

28. W.E.B. Du Bois, *The Souls of Black Folk* (New York: Library of America, 1990); Marilyn Lake and Henry Reynolds, *Drawing the Global Colour Line: White Men's Countries and the International Challenge of Racial Equality* (Cambridge: Cambridge University Press, 2008).

29. Carey McWilliams, *Southern California: An Island on the Land* (Salt Lake City: Peregrine Smith Books, 1946), page 23. Martin Luther King writes in *Why We Can't Wait* (New York: Signet Books, 1964): "Our nation was born in genocide when it embraced the doctrine that the original American, the Indian, was an inferior race. Even before there were large numbers of Negroes on our shores, the scar of racial hatred had already disfigured colonial society . . . It was upon this massive base of racism that the prejudice toward the nonwhite was readily built, and found rapid growth."

30. Clark Davis, *Company Men: White-Collar Life and Corporate Cultures in Los Angeles, 1892–1941* (Baltimore: Johns Hopkins University Press, 2000), pages 73–74.

31. Loren Miller and Bernard J. Sheil, *Racial Restrictive Covenants*, pamphlet (The Quincey Press, 1946), page 6. *The Cross and Flag* was a newspaper founded by white supremacist and Nazi sympathizer Gerald L.K. Smith, published from 1942 to 1976; see Glen Jeansonne, "Arkansas's Minister of Hate: A Research Odyssey," *The Arkansas Historical Quarterly* 59(4) (2000): 429–35. His speaking appearances in LA were accompanied by widespread protest,

such as a mass rally against fascism held in the Olympic Auditorium (*California Eagle,* July 19, 1945).

32. Some idea of their widespread use comes from lawsuits to protect restrictive covenants brought by both the Los Angeles Investment Co. (developer of several hundred acres by 1913) and the Janss Investment Co. (responsible for subdivision of 100,000 acres by 1925), to prevent African American occupancy on land they had developed in order to protect its value (*Los Angeles Times,* April 25, 1925).

33. *California Eagle,* May 16, 1914.

34. Janet Abu-Lughod, *New York, Chicago, Los Angeles: America's Global Cities* (Minneapolis: University of Minnesota Press, 1999); Marc A. Weiss, *The Rise of the Community Builders: The American Real Estate Industry and Urban Land Planning* (New York: Columbia University Press, 1987).

35. Marc A. Weiss, *The Rise of the Community Builders: The American Real Estate Industry and Urban Land Planning* (New York: Columbia University Press, 1987).

36. David M.P. Freund, *Colored Property: State Policy and White Racial Politics in Suburban America* (Chicago: University of Chicago Press, 2007).

37. Quoted in Rose Helper, *Racial Policies and Practices of Real Estate Brokers* (Minneapolis: University of Minnesota Press, 1969), page 191.

38. Quoted in Rose Helper, *Racial Policies and Practices of Real Estate Brokers* (Minneapolis: University of Minnesota Press, 1969), page 21.

39. Laurenti found that even after the official change in 1950, most realtors "appear to under-stand the article in the same sense as before, and to continue to act accordingly," while local real estate boards continued to use this language in their own codes of ethics; see Luigi Laurenti, *Property values and race; studies in seven cities. Special research report to the Commission on Race and Housing* (Berkeley: University of California Press, 1960).

40. David M.P. Freund, *Colored Property: State Policy and White Racial Politics in Suburban America* (Chicago and London: University of Chicago Press, 2007). Quote is from Rose Helper, *Racial Policies and Practices of Real Estate Brokers* (Minneapolis: University of Minnesota Press, 1969), page 21, footnote 25.

41. Constance C. Jensen, John Lindberg, and George L. Smith, "The Minority Group Housing Market in San Francisco, with Special reference to Real Estate Broker and Mortgage Financing Practices" (Berkeley: unpublished master's research project, School of Social Welfare, University of California, 1955) found that brokers in the San Francisco area believed that nonwhites depreciated property values and that they would be at risk for introducing a non-white into a white neighborhood. All had encountered whites' unwillingness to sell to non-whites, neighborhood opposition and difficulties in obtaining financing as being the princi-pal barriers. Their interviews with banks and mortgage lenders revealed similar beliefs about property values, and reluctance to lend to people of color in white areas, believing it depressed the values of the surrounding areas.

42. David M.P. Freund, *Colored Property: State Policy and White Racial Politics in Suburban America* (Chicago and London: University of Chicago Press, 2007).

43. Marc A. Weiss, *The Rise of the Community Builders: The American Real Estate Industry and Urban Land Planning* (New York: Columbia University Press, 1987).

44. California Real Estate Association, *News Bulletin* 1(1) (1920), page 1. I was unable to access a full archive of the California Real Estate Association magazine. Apart from a few photocop-ied articles or full issues found in other archive searches, all quotes are drawn from two sources that reviewed all issues up through the mid-1960s to collect any passages having to do with race in preparation for the campaign against CREA's attempt to overturn the Rumford Fair Housing Act through Proposition 14. Both were found in the Max Mumford Archive, Box 2, Folder 16. The first set are inserted in a longer document compiled by Leonard D. Cain, Jr., *Absolute Discretion: Selected Documents on "Property Rights" and "Equal Protection of the Laws,"* (Sacramento: Sacramento Committee for Fair Housing, 1964). My guess is that the second document is the full list of quotations as prepared for Cain by Dr. Paul F.C. Mueller as noted in Cain's acknowledgments; however, without an author or date listed, I have simply cited it under its title "The CREA: A History of Opposition to Open Occupancy."

45. California Real Estate Association July 25, 1927, page 35.
46. Ibid.
47. Ibid.
48. Charlotta Spears Bass, *Forty Years: Memoirs from the Pages of a Newspaper* (Los Angeles: unpublished manuscript available at Southern California Research Library, 1960), page 95.
49. Ibid.
50. *Letteau v. Ellis*, 122 Cal. App 524 (1932).
51. *Title Guarantee and Trust Co v. Garrott*, 42 Cal. App. 152, 183 Pac. 470 (1919); Willis O. Tyler, "Defense Attorney Analyzes Historic 'Sugar Hill' Decision," *California Eagle*, December 13, 1945.
52. *Los Angeles Investment Co v. Gary*, 181 Cal. 680, 186 Pac. 596, 9 A.L.R. 115 (1919).
53. *Janss Investment Co v. Walden*, 196 Cal. 753, 239 Pac. 34 (1922).
54. *Los Angeles Times*, April 24, 1925.
55. A judge ruled against the defendant in *Wayt v. Patee*, for example, despite acknowledging the technical fault with the covenant. Wendell Green, "Progress Seen in Long Fight Against Racial Restrictions," *Sentinel*, February 28, 1946.
56. Stuart Hall, "Race, Articulation and Societies Structured in Dominance," in *Sociological Theories: Race and Colonialism* (Paris: UNESCO, 1980): 305–45.
57. Ibid.
58. D.O. McGovney, "Racial Residential Segregation by State Court Enforcement of Restrictive Agreements, Covenants or Conditions in Deeds is Unconstitutional," *California Law Review* 33(1) (1945): 5–39.
59. Loren Miller, *The Petitioners: The Story of the Supreme Court of the United States and the Negro* (New York: Pantheon Books, 1966).
60. The groundbreaking silent film *Birth of a Nation*, directed by D.W. Griffiths, 1915, regularly shown and regularly protested for decades, celebrated the KKK's initial formation and served as inspiration for its reinstitution. Kenneth T. Jackson, *The Ku Klux Klan in the City, 1915–1930* (New York: Oxford University Press, 1967). Charles C. Alexander's *The Ku Klux Klan in the Southwest* (University of Kentucky Press, 1965) describes the rise of the Klan both in terms of the simmering racism brought to life by a series of articles in the liberal New York *World* that sought to destroy an early and localized Klan through its coverage and instead helped it grow through the publicity, and through the amount of money being generated through membership fees divvied up through various promoters and local and regional Klan officials pocketing the money.
61. Kenneth T. Jackson, *The Ku Klux Klan in the City, 1915–1930* (New York: Oxford University Press, 1967), page 22. This was in spite of the fact that the military continued to be completely segregated and most African Americans were only allowed to serve as drivers or stevedores until steps were taken to begin desegregation during World War II; see Carol Anderson, *Eyes Off the Prize: The United Nations and the African American Struggle for Human Rights, 1944–1955* (Cambridge: Cambridge University Press, 2003).
62. Ida B. Wells, *Southern Horrors: Lynch Law in All Its Phases* (New York: New York Age Print, 1892); Carol Anderson, *Eyes Off the Prize: The United Nations and the African American Struggle for Human Rights, 1944–1955* (Cambridge: Cambridge University Press, 2003).
63. Christopher N. Cocoltchos, "The Invisible Empire and the Search for the Orderly Community: The Ku Klux Klan in Anaheim, California," in *The Invisible Empire in the West: Toward a New Hsitorical Appraisal of the Ku Klux Klan of the 1920s*, Shawn Lay (ed.) (Urbana and Chicago: University of Illinois Press, 1992); Kenneth T. Jackson, *The Ku Klux Klan in the City, 1915–1930* (New York: Oxford University Press, 1967); Becky Nicolaides, *My Blue Heaven: Life and Politics in the Working Class Suburbs of Los Angeles, 1920–1965* (Chicago: University of Chicago Press, 2002).
64. See Becky Nicolaides, *My Blue Heaven: Life and Politics in the Working Class Suburbs of Los Angeles, 1920–1965* (Chicago: University of Chicago Press, 2002).
65. Christopher N. Cocoltchos, "The Invisible Empire and the Search for the Orderly Community: The Ku Klux Klan in Anaheim, California," in *The Invisible Empire in the West: Toward a New*

Hsitorical Appraisal of the Ku Klux Klan of the 1920s, Shawn Lay (ed.) (Urbana and Chicago: University of Illinois Press, 1992), page 105.

66. Ibid.
67. Ibid.; Phyllis Anne Sowers, "'Klanaheim': Suburbia, Civic Identity and the Second Ku Klux Klan" (Long Beach: unpublished master's thesis presented to California State University, 2012).
68. Augustus Hawkins, interview by Carlos Vásquez, *Oral History Interview with Augustus F. Hawkins* (1988), page 20.
69. David M.P. Freund, *Colored Property: State Policy and White Racial Politics in Suburban America* (Chicago and London: University of Chicago Press, 2007), *California Eagle,* April 15, 1922.
70. *California Eagle,* March 7, 1924.
71. *California Eagle,* December 26, 1924.
72. Ibid.
73. *California Eagle,* March 24, 1923.
74. Booker T. Washington, *Up From Slavery* (New York: Signet Classics, 2010 [1901]), page 163.
75. *California Eagle,* November 20, 1925.
76. *California Eagle,* February 12, 1926.
77. *California Eagle,* February 19, 1926. For other names and women in higher leadership positions, see the improvement association notes, generally found on page 6 of the *Eagle* in 1926. The president of the Hollenbeck Association was a Mrs. J. Scott, for example, and Mrs. Slaughter was "chairman" of the Home Beautification and Improvement Committee.
78. *California Eagle,* February 19, 1926.
79. *California Eagle,* April 23, 1926.
80. *California Eagle,* June 4, 1926.
81. Douglas Flamming, *Bound for Freedom: Black Los Angeles in Jim Crow America* (Berkeley: University of California Press, 2005).
82. US Department of the Interior, "National Register of Historic Places: Historic Resources Associated with African Americans in Los Angeles" (2009); J. Max Bond, *The Negro in Los Angeles* (Los Angeles: R and E Research Associates, 1972).
83. *California Eagle,* April 30, 1926.
84. Melina Abdullah and Regina Freer, "Bass to Bass: Relative Freedom and Womanist Leadership in Black Los Angeles," in *Black Los Angeles: American Dreams and Racial Realities* (New York and London: New York University Press, 2010): 323–42; and Regina Free, LA Race Woman: Charlotta Bass and the Complexities of Black Political Development in Los Angeles," *American Quarterly* 56(3) (2004): 607–32.
85. *California Eagle,* April 30, 1926.
86. *California Eagle,* June 25, 1926.
87. *California Eagle,* December 10, 1926.
88. Ibid.
89. Ibid.
90. Ibid.
91. Charlotta Spears Bass, *Forty Years: Memoirs from the Pages of a Newspaper* (Los Angeles: unpublished manuscript available at Southern California Research Library, 1960), page 58.
92. Ibid., page 59.
93. Ibid. See also Charles E. Cobb, Jr., *This Nonviolent Stuff'll Get You Killed: How Guns Made the Civil Rights Movement Possible* (Durham: Duke University Press Books, 2015) and, for a similar sense of pragmatism from Ella Baker in her biography by Barbara Ransby, *Ella Baker and the Black Freedom Movement: A Radical Democratic Vision* (Chapel Hill: University of North Carolina Press).
94. *California Eagle,* October 15, 1925 and May 7, 1926.
95. *California Eagle,* June 18, 1926.
96. The legal battles taking place in the Crestmore district (alternatively described as the Crestmoor district), would continue until *Shelley v. Kraemer* was decided by the Supreme Court in 1948, with multiple lawsuits being filed and defended, and a renewed effort from

white homeowners in 1941 to ensure that all properties were covered by restrictive covenants; see Wendell Green, "Progress Seen in Long Fight Against Racial Restrictions," *Sentinel*, February 28, 1946.

97. *California Eagle*, December 10, 1926.

98. *California Eagle*, September 2, 1927.

99. Occasional notices in the *Eagle* show the continued existence in some form of at least the East Adams Association in 1930 and the Westside Improvement Association (led by another leader among African American women, Betty Hill), which won open access to a local swimming pool for African Americans in 1931 (E.F. Anderson 1980; *California Eagle*, June 13, 1930; *California Eagle*, June 2, 1931).

100. Charlotta Spears Bass, *Forty Years: Memoirs from the Pages of a Newspaper* (Los Angeles: unpublished manuscript available at Southern California Research Library, 1960), page 100.

101. Ibid., page 101.

102. Douglas Flamming, *Bound for Freedom: Black Los Angeles in Jim Crow America* (Berkeley: University of California Press, 2005).

2. VICTORY ABROAD AND AT HOME: THE SECOND CAMPAIGN AGAINST RACE-RESTRICTIVE COVENANTS

1. See Marc A. Weiss, *The Rise of the Community Builders: The American Real Estate Industry and Urban Land Planning* (New York: Columbia University Press, 1987) and David M.P. Freund, *Colored Property: State Policy and White Racial Politics in Suburban America* (Chicago: University of Chicago Press, 2007).

2. Charles Abrams, *Forbidden Neighbors: A Study of Prejudice in Housing* (New York: Harper & Brothers, 1955), page 258.

3. See Loren Miller and Bernard J. Sheil, *Racial Restrictive Covenants*, pamphlet (Quincey Press, 1946), as well as testimony to the Governor's Commission on the LA Riots, and multiple addresses such as to the Urban League in 1955 and the ACLU in 1960, among many others (see *Loren Miller Papers*, Huntington Library, Box 5, Folder 6).

4. Stuart Hall, "Race, Articulation and Societies Structured in Dominance," in *Sociological Theories: Race and Colonialism* (Paris: UNESCO, 1980): 305–45, page 332, quoting Antonio Gramsci, *Prison Notebooks* (New York: International Publishers, 1971).

5. Henri Lefebvre, *The Production of Space* (Oxford: Blackwell, 1991), page 142.

6. David M.P. Freund, *Colored Property: State Policy and White Racial Politics in Suburban America* (Chicago: University of Chicago Press, 2007).

7. Ibid., page 113.

8. Ibid.

9. *Testbed for the Redlining Archives of California's Exclusionary Spaces*, salt.unc.edu/T-RACES/colormap.html (accessed September 10, 2013).

10. Ibid.

11. *California Eagle*, January 31, 1946.

12. David M.P. Freund, *Colored Property: State Policy and White Racial Politics in Suburban America* (Chicago: University of Chicago Press, 2007), page 115.

13. Ibid., page 115.

14. David M.P. Freund, *Colored Property: State Policy and White Racial Politics in Suburban America* (Chicago: University of Chicago Press, 2007), page 20.

15. Marc A. Weiss, *The Rise of the Community Builders: The American Real Estate Industry and Urban Land Planning* (New York: Columbia University Press, 1987).

16. United States Federal Housing Administration, *Underwriting Manual: Underwriting Analysis Under Title II, Section 203 of the National Housing Act* (Washington, April 1936), page 233.

17. David M.P. Freund, *Colored Property: State Policy and White Racial Politics in Suburban America* (Chicago: University of Chicago Press, 2007).

18. Ibid., page 130.

19. *California Eagle,* October 19, 1939.
20. Ibid.
21. *California Eagle,* April 4, 1940.
22. Charlotta Spears Bass, *Forty Years: Memoirs from the Pages of a Newspaper* (Los Angeles: unpublished manuscript available at Southern California Research Library, 1960).
23. Johnny Otis, *Upside Your Head! Rhythm and Blues on Central Avenue* (Middleton, CT: Wesleyan University Press, 1993), pages 20–21.
24. There were recognizable gangs forming from the 1920s onwards, often around activities such as theft and prostitution, but they had none of the prominence that gangs now play in the community or the media; see Alex Alonso, "Out of the Void: Street Gangs in Black Los Angeles," in *Black Los Angeles: American Dreams and Racial Realities,* Darnell Hunt and Ana-Christina Ramón (eds.) (2010), page 140; and Mike Davis, *City of Quartz* (London and New York: Verso, 2006) for further discussion, though very little has been written about African Americans apart from work by Alex Alonso, *Territoriality Among African-American Street Gangs* (unpublished master's thesis, University of Southern California, 1999); Gregory C. Brown, James D. Vigil, and Eric R. Taylor, "The Ghettoization of Blacks in Los Angeles: The Emergence of Street Gangs," *Journal of African American Studies* 16 (2012): 209–25; Karen Umemoto, *The Truce: Lessons From an LA Gang War* (Ithaca, NY: Cornell University Press, 2006), and the autobiography of CRIP founder Stanley Tookie Williams, *Blue Rage, Black Redemption: A Memoir* (New York: Touchstone, 2007). This is in contrast to a spate of literature on Latin American gangs; see, for example, Luis Rodriguez, *Always Running: La Vida Loca: Gang Days in LA* (New York: Touchstone, 2005); James Vigil, *Barrio Gangs: Street Life and Identity in Southern California* (Austin: Texas University Press, 1988); Thomas J. Ward, *Gangsters Without Borders: An Ethnography of a Salvadoran Street Gang* (New York, Oxford: Oxford University Press, 2013); and Elana Zilberg, *Space of Detention: The Making of a Transnational Gang Crisis Between Los Angeles and San Salvador* (Durham, NC: Duke University Press, 2011).
25. Alex Alonso, *Territoriality Among African-American Street Gangs* (unpublished master's thesis, University of Southern California, 1999); Gregory C. Brown, James D. Vigil, and Eric R. Taylor, "The Ghettoization of Blacks in Los Angeles: The Emergence of Street Gangs," *Journal of African American Studies* 16 (2012): 209–25.
26. Gregory C. Brown, James D. Vigil, and Eric R. Taylor, "The Ghettoization of Blacks in Los Angeles: The Emergence of Street Gangs," *Journal of African American Studies* 16 (2012): 209–25.
27. Alex Alonso, *Territoriality Among African-American Street Gangs* (unpublished master's thesis, University of Southern California, 1999).
28. HOLC, *Area Description—Central District: Testbed for the Redlining Archives of California's Exclusionary Spaces,* 1939, salt.unc.edu/T-RACES/data/la/ad/ad0416.pdf (accessed September 10, 2013).
29. Charles Abrams, *Forbidden Neighbors: A Study of Prejudice in Housing* (New York: Harper & Brothers, 1955), page 147, quoting Nelson L. North, *Real Estate Selling and Leasing* (New York: Prentice Hall, 1938), page 139.
30. Henri Lefebvre, *The Urban Revolution* (Minneapolis: University of Minnesota Press, 2003), page 84.
31. Charles Abrams, *Forbidden Neighbors: A Study of Prejudice in Housing* (New York: Harper & Brothers, 1955), page 147, quoting the National Association of Home Builders, "Homes Associations for the Small Operator—Their Value in Building Sound Neighborhoods," *Land Planning Service* Bulletin no. 3 (November 1947).
32. See Beth Tompkins Bates, "A New Crowd Challenges the Agenda of the Old Guard in the NAACP, 1933–1941," *American Historical Review,* April 1997: 340–77, page 360; Douglas Flamming, *Bound for Freedom: Black Los Angeles in Jim Crow America* (Berkeley: University of California Press, 2005); Eric S. Gellman, *Death Blow to Jim Crow: the National Negro Congress and the Rise of Militant Civil Rights* (Chapel Hill: University of North Carolina Press, 2012).
33. As quoted in Beth Tompkins Bates, "A New Crowd Challenges the Agenda of the Old Guard in the NAACP, 1933–1941," *American Historical Review,* April 1997: 340–77, page 360.

34. Lawrence S. Wittner, in the "The National Negro Congress: A Reassessment," *American Quarterly* 22(4) (1970): 883–901, describes various Cold War studies on communism that make this claim. His research, however, showed that in reality the CP played a minor role, and in fact the NNC enjoyed a broad base of support from the left wing. He writes: "Among the prominent non-Communists who spoke at or sent messages of greeting to its meetings were Franklin Roosevelt, Eleanor Roosevelt, Fiorello LaGuardia, John L. Lewis, Norman Thomas, Walter Reuther, Philip Murray, Walter White, Ralph Bunche and A. Philip Randolph." Beth Tompkins Bates, in "A New Crowd Challenges the Agenda of the Old Guard in the NAACP, 1933–1941," *American Historical Review*, April 1997: 340–77, notes the pivotal nature of this early study in transforming our historical understanding of the NNC's relationship to the CP, as well as the nature of its work. Carol Anderson's *Eyes Off the Prize: The United Nations and the African American Struggle for Human Rights, 1944–1955* (Cambridge: Cambridge University Press, 2003) gives more details of the relationship between the two.

35. Charlotta Spears Bass, *Forty Years: Memoirs from the Pages of a Newspaper* (Los Angeles: unpublished manuscript available at Southern California Research Library, 1960); Douglas Flamming, *Bound for Freedom: Black Los Angeles in Jim Crow America* (Berkeley: University of California Press, 2005).

36. *California Eagle*, May 2, 1940.

37. Regina Freer, "Charlotta Bass: A Community Activist for Racial and Economic Justice," in *The Next Los Angeles: The Struggle for a Livable City*, Robert Gottlieb, Regina Freer, Mark Vallianatos, and Peter Dreier (eds.) (Berkeley: University of California Press, 2005).

38. Scott Kurashige, *The Shifting Grounds of Race: Black and Japanese Americans in the Making of Multiethnic Los Angeles* (Princeton: Princeton University Press, 2008).

39. Charlotta Spears Bass, *Forty Years: Memoirs from the Pages of a Newspaper* (Los Angeles: unpublished manuscript available at Southern California Research Library, 1960); Regina Freer, "Charlotta Bass: A Community Activist for Racial and Economic Justice," in *The Next Los Angeles: The Struggle for a Livable City*, Robert Gottlieb, Regina Freer, Mark Vallianatos, and Peter Dreier (eds.) (Berkeley: University of California Press, 2005); Scott Kurashige, *The Shifting Grounds of Race: Black and Japanese Americans in the Making of Multiethnic Los Angeles* (Princeton: Princeton University Press, 2008).

40. Howard L. Holtzendorff, "Los Angeles Faces Its First Real Crisis of WWII," in *Conference on Housing and Racial Discrimination* (Los Angeles, 1945), page 13.

41. Charlotta Spears Bass, *Forty Years: Memoirs from the Pages of a Newspaper* (Los Angeles: unpublished manuscript available at Southern California Research Library, 1960).

42. LA was extremely reluctant to build social housing, and the housing authority continually faced charges of communism for its activities; see George Lynell, "Countdown to Chaos? 30 Years After the Watts Riots, Two Angelenos Look Back and Ask: Why Did it Happen and Will it Happen Again?" *Los Angeles Times*, August 11, 1995. Struggles over public housing never took on the scale or resonance that they did in East Coast cities as in the end, only 21 projects consisting of 8,000 apartments were built; see Research Group on the Los Angeles Economy, *The Widening Divide: Income Inequality and Poverty in Los Angeles* (Los Angeles: University of California Los Angeles, 1989).

43. *California Eagle*, July 22, 1943.

44. *California Eagle*, December 11, 1942.

45. Interview with Welford Wilson by E. Frederick Anderson, *The Development of Leadership and Organization Building in the Black Community of Los Angeles from 1900 Through WWII* (Saratoga, CA: Century Twenty One Publishing, 1980), page 114.

46. Charlotta Spears Bass, *Forty Years: Memoirs from the Pages of a Newspaper* (Los Angeles: unpublished manuscript available at Southern California Research Library, 1960), page 108.

47. *California Eagle*, November 4, 1943.

48. Police brutality was an ongoing problem as seen in the pages of the *Eagle*, and it exploded against the Mexican-American community when a group of youths were railroaded into a conviction of murder in the infamous Sleepy Lagoon case, and again when white sailors rioted in the Mexican-American community, beating up any youth found in a zoot suit—best

known as the "zoot-suit riots" in the white press. For more on these incidents, see Rodolfo Acuña, *Occupied America: the Chicano's Struggle Toward Liberation* (San Francisco: Canfield Press, 1972); Beatrice Griffith, *American Me* (Portsmouth, NH: Greenwood Publishing Group, 1960); and George Sanchez, *Becoming Mexican American: Ethnicity, Culture, and Identity in Chicano Los Angeles, 1900–1945* (New York: Oxford University Press, 1993). Charlotta Bass worked with the Mexican-American community to hold several public forums and protests around these events. Charlotta Spears Bass, *Forty Years: Memoirs from the Pages of a Newspaper* (Los Angeles: unpublished manuscript available at Southern California Research Library, 1960).

49. *California Eagle,* July 29, 1943.
50. *California Eagle,* November 11, 1943.
51. Kevern Verney, *The Debate on Black Civil Rights in America* (Manchester: Manchester University Press, 2006).
52. *California Eagle,* October 28, 1943.
53. Wendell Green, "Progress Seen in Long Fight Against Racial Restrictions," *Sentinel,* February 28, 1946.
54. Charlotta Spears Bass, *Forty Years: Memoirs from the Pages of a Newspaper* (Los Angeles: unpublished manuscript available at Southern California Research Library, 1960), page 108.
55. *California Eagle,* July 29, 1943.
56. *California Eagle,* November 18, 1943.
57. *California Eagle,* November 24, 1943.
58. WWII-era letter from Adams to Washington Association members, Loren Miller Papers, Huntington Library, Box 5, Folder 6.
59. Memo on pending restrictive covenant cases, undated, Loren Miller Papers, Huntington Library, Box 42, Folder 3.
60. *Gone With the Wind,* 1939; *California Eagle,* March 24, 1943.
61. *California Eagle,* December 9, 1943.
62. *California Eagle,* August 24, 1944.
63. *California Eagle,* August 2, 1944.
64. The Home Protective Association is also at times referred to as the HOPA by the *California Eagle*; see also Charlotta Spears Bass, *Forty Years: Memoirs from the Pages of a Newspaper* (Los Angeles: unpublished manuscript available at Southern California Research Library, 1960).
65. Ibid.
66. Ibid.
67. Ibid., page 109.
68. Ibid., page 105.
69. *California Eagle,* September 14, 1944.
70. *California Eagle,* September 21 1944.
71. Charlotta Spears Bass, *Forty Years: Memoirs from the Pages of a Newspaper* (Los Angeles: unpublished manuscript available at Southern California Research Library, 1960), page 110.
72. Ibid.
73. *California Eagle,* November 16, 1944.
74. *California Eagle,* November 23, 1944.
75. *California Eagle,* December 7, 1944.
76. Ibid.
77. "Proceedings of the Conference on Housing and Racial Discrimination," Saturday, February 24, 1945, 1st Congregational Church of Los Angeles. Loren Miller Papers, Huntington Library, Box 5 Folder 6. While a number of interracial councils were formed, a representative of the American Council on Race Relations found them to be "of white inspiration," of white middle- and upper-class composition, and consistently made up of the same elite members. See Scott Kurashige, *The Shifting Grounds of Race: Black and Japanese Americans in the Making of Multiethnic Los Angeles* (Princeton: Princeton University Press, 2008, page 224).

78. "Proceedings of the Conference on Housing and Racial Discrimination," Saturday, February 24, 1945, 1st Congregational Church of Los Angeles. Loren Miller Papers, Huntington Library, Box 5 Folder 6.
79. Ibid.
80. See Regina Freer, "LA Race Woman: Charlotta Bass and the Complexities of Black Political Development in Los Angeles," *American Quarterly* 56(3) (2004): 607–32.
81. Ibid., page 623, and Charlotta Spears Bass, *Forty Years: Memoirs from the Pages of a Newspaper* (Los Angeles: unpublished manuscript available at Southern California Research Library, 1960). For more on these two incidents, see Rodolfo Acuña, *Occupied America: the Chicano's Struggle Toward Liberation* (San Francisco: Canfield Press, 1972).
82. *California Eagle,* January 1, 1945.
83. See, for example, *California Eagle,* August 28, 1947.
84. *California Eagle,* January 8, March 1, 1945.
85. Charlotta Spears Bass, *Forty Years: Memoirs from the Pages of a Newspaper* (Los Angeles: unpublished manuscript available at Southern California Research Library, 1960), page 132.
86. Ibid.
87. *California Eagle,* August 9, 1945.
88. See *California Eagle,* January 1, 1945; Civic Unity pamphlet, 1947 from the SCL—human relations commission collection.
89. Tom Sifton, *Los Angeles Transformed: Fletcher Bowron's Urban Reform Revival, 1938–1953* (University of new Mexico Press, 2005).
90. *California Eagle,* August 9 and August 30, 1945. The Mobilization For Democracy would merge with the National Negro Congress to become the Civil Rights Congress in 1946. Lasting until 1956, it was a multiracial organization that refused to disavow ties to communists despite the onset of the Cold War. It focused on police brutality and fought the death penalty; Charlotta Bass sat on its board. See Gerald Horne, *Communist Front? The Civil Rights Congress, 1946–1956* (Rutherford, New Jersey: Associated University Presses, 1988).
91. *California Eagle,* August 30, 1945; *California Eagle,* November 8, 1945.
92. *California Eagle,* November 15, 1945 and Scott Kurashige, *The Shifting Grounds of Race: Black and Japanese Americans in the Making of Multiethnic Los Angeles* (Princeton: Princeton University Press, 2008).
93. *California Eagle,* November 29, 1945.
94. *California Eagle,* December 20, 1945.
95. Charlotta Spears Bass, *Forty Years: Memoirs from the Pages of a Newspaper* (Los Angeles: unpublished manuscript available at Southern California Research Library, 1960).
96. Jill Watts, *Hattie McDaniel: Black Ambition, White Hollywood* (Amistad Press, 2007); *Time,* "California: Victory on Sugar Hill," December 17, 1945.
97. New York Times, October 3, 1946.
98. *California Eagle,* June 12, 1946.
99. *California Eagle,* August 5, September 19, 1946
100. *Southwest Wave,* February 22, 1945. Loren Miller Papers, Huntington Library, Box 43, Folder 3.
101. Charlotta Spears Bass, *Forty Years: Memoirs from the Pages of a Newspaper* (Los Angeles: unpublished manuscript available at Southern California Research Library, 1960); Mike Davis, *City of Quartz* (London and New York: Verso, 2006); *California Eagle,* April 11, May 16 and 23, August 15, December 12, 1946.
102. *EWP,* Negroes, dated August 31, 1943; November 9, 1943; December 9, 1944; February 27, 1946.
103. See Carol Anderson, *Eyes Off the Prize: The United Nations and the African American Struggle for Human Rights, 1944–1955* (Cambridge: Cambridge University Press, 2003) for discussion of the complicated internal politics of the National Negro Congress and its relationship to the Communist Party and to other civil rights organizations like the NAACP. In November 1946, a group of men organized to stay with the Williams family, a mother and daughter who had been terrorized since their move into a white neighborhood, as documented in the *California Eagle,* November 28, 1946.

104. *California Eagle,* November 28, 1946.
105. Ibid.
106. *California Eagle,* July 10, 1947.
107. *California Eagle,* October 16, 1947.
108. *California Eagle,* September 25, 1947.
109. *California Eagle,* September 25, 1947.
110. Clement Vose, *Caucasians Only: The Supreme Court, the NAACP, and the Restrictive Covenant Cases* (Berkeley: University of California Press, 1959), page 73.
111. Ibid.
112. *California Eagle,* October 30, November 6, 1947.
113. *California Eagle,* November 13, 1947.
114. Carol Anderson, *Eyes Off the Prize: The United Nations and the African American Struggle for Human Rights, 1944–1955* (Cambridge: Cambridge University Press, 2003); Gerald Horne, *Fire This Time: The Watts Uprising and the 1960s* (Charlottesville: University Press of Virginia, 1995).
115. *California Eagle,* December 4, 1947.
116. *California Eagle,* February 19, 1948.
117. Clement Vose, *Caucasians Only: The Supreme Court, the NAACP, and the Restrictive Covenant Cases* (Berkeley: University of California Press, 1959).

3. WHITE REACTION: OLD WALLS TORN DOWN AND NEW ONES RAISED

1. *California Eagle,* June 10, 1948.
2. *California Eagle,* August 5, 1948.
3. *California Eagle,* January 18, 1950.
4. Petition for rehearing *Barrows v. Jackson* 9346 US 249 (1953), as quoted in Clement Vose, *Caucasians Only: The Supreme Court, the NAACP, and the Restrictive Covenant Cases* (Berkeley: University of California Press, 1959), page 246.
5. *California Eagle,* September 9, 1949, March 16, 1950.
6. *California Eagle,* September 16, October 21, November 18, 1948.
7. *California Eagle,* February 10, August 18, September 9, 1949.
8. *California Eagle,* September 8, 1949.
9. *California Eagle,* September 8, 1950.
10. *California Eagle,* March 20, 1952.
11. *California Eagle,* December 7, 1950.
12. Paul Weeks, "Migration Causes Big Jump in LA's Negro Population," *Mirror-News,* April 30, 1956.
13. *UCLA ACLU* Box 30, Folder 3.
14. Rose Helper, *Racial Policies and Practices of Real Estate Brokers* (Minneapolis: University of Minnesota Press, 1969), page 35.
15. Gregory Hise, *Magnetic Los Angeles: Planning the Twentieth-Century Metropolis* (Baltimore and London: Johns Hopkins University Press, 1997).
16. Bruce Hartford, "Oral History" (February 2002).
17. Rose Helper, *Racial Policies and Practices of Real Estate Brokers* (Minneapolis: University of Minnesota Press, 1969).
18. John Anson Ford Papers, Huntington Library, Box 76.
19. This dynamic is described by multiple studies of whiteness, such as Noel Ignatiev's *How the Irish Became White* (New York; London: Routledge, 1995) and George Lipsitz, *The Possessive Investment in Whiteness* (Philadelphia: Temple University Press, 1998). See also Eric Avila, *Popular Culture in the Age of White Flight: Fear and Fantasy in Suburban Los Angeles* (Berkeley: University of California Press, 2004) for cultural constructions of whiteness in the suburbs.
20. *California Eagle,* December 7, 1950.
21. *California Eagle,* June 5, 1950.
22. *California Eagle,* June 30, 1950.

23. California Real Estate Association, August 10, 1948.
24. California Real Estate Association, August 1948.
25. California Real Estate Association 1950, quoted in Leonard D. Cain, Jr., *Absolute Discretion: Selected Documents on "Property Rights" and "Equal Protection of the Laws,"* (Sacramento: Sacramento Committee for Fair Housing, 1964).
26. California Real Estate Association 1948, page 10, quoted in Leonard D. Cain, Jr., *Absolute Discretion: Selected Documents on "Property Rights" and "Equal Protection of the Laws,"* (Sacramento: Sacramento Committee for Fair Housing, 1964).
27. Charlotta Spears Bass, *Forty Years: Memoirs from the Pages of a Newspaper* (Los Angeles: unpublished manuscript available at Southern California Research Library, 1960), page 113.
28. Michelle Alexander, *The New Jim Crow: Mass Incarceration in an Age of Colorblindness* (New York: The New Press, 2012); C. Van Woodward, *The Strange Career of Jim Crow: A Commemorative Edition* (Oxford: Oxford University Press, 2002).
29. Henri Lefebvre, *Writings on Cities* (Cambridge, MA: Blackwell, 1996), page 84.

4. CORE AND THE TESTING OF THE WHITE SUBURBS

1. Scott Kurashige, *The Shifting Grounds of Race: Black and Japanese Americans in the Making of Multiethnic Los Angeles* (Princeton: Princeton University Press, 2008).
2. Ibid.
3. Public Broadcasting System, Biography of Publisher Charlotta Bass, pbs.org/blackpress/news_bios/ca_eagle.html (accessed May 2, 2017).
4. Douglas Flamming, *Bound for Freedom: Black Los Angeles in Jim Crow America* (Berkeley: University of California Press, 2005).
5. David Harvey, *The Limits of Capital* (London: Verso, [1982] 2007).
6. August Meier and Elliott Rudwick, *CORE: A Study in the Civil Rights Movement, 1942–1968* (Urbana: University of Illinois Press, 1973).
7. James Farmer, *Lay Bare the Heart: An Autobiography of the Civil Rights Movement* (New York: Penguin-Plume, 1986), page 89.
8. August Meier and Elliott Rudwick, *CORE: A Study in the Civil Rights Movement, 1942–1968* (Urbana: University of Illinois Press, 1973), page 10.
9. Ibid; Peter Ralph Bartling, *The Unfinished Revolution: The Civil Rights Movement From 1955 to 1965* (Los Angeles: self-published dissertation, 2010).
10. See Peter Ralph Bartling, *The Unfinished Revolution: The Civil Rights Movement From 1955 to 1965* (Los Angeles: self-published dissertation, 2010) and James Farmer, *Lay Bare the Heart: An Autobiography of the Civil Rights Movement* (New York: Penguin-Plume, 1986).
11. James Farmer, *Lay Bare the Heart: An Autobiography of the Civil Rights Movement* (New York: Penguin-Plume, 1986).
12. CORE pamphlet, "All About CORE" (no date).
13. Peter Ralph Bartling, *The Unfinished Revolution: The Civil Rights Movement From 1955 to 1965* (Los Angeles: self-published dissertation, 2010); James Farmer, *Lay Bare the Heart: An Autobiography of the Civil Rights Movement* (New York: Penguin-Plume, 1986).
14. For those interested in the everyday travails of organizing, there is a fascinating internal report dated September 7, 1961, that states: "LA CORE meets 2 [times] monthly, 30–50 people attend 3/4 regularly, they are keeping no membership records and have no formal process of training, indoctrination, or trial period . . . but they are planning on setting up an orientation. About 30 reg members, committees—publicity, action, membership, finance (to be set up). No conscious effort made to integrate potential new members, though in the month he was there, 20 expressed interest. Many came to meetings not to return." Wisconsin MSS 14, 1961.
15. CORE, "All About CORE" (no date).
16. CORE, "Cracking the Color Line" (1961).
17. James Farmer, *Lay Bare the Heart: An Autobiography of the Civil Rights Movement* (New York: Penguin-Plume, 1986); August Meier and Elliott Rudwick, *CORE: A Study in the Civil Rights Movement, 1942–1968* (Urbana: University of Illinois Press, 1973).

18. James Farmer, *Lay Bare the Heart: An Autobiography of the Civil Rights Movement* (New York: Penguin-Plume, 1986).
19. See Richard Iton, *Solidarity Blues: Race, Culture and the American Left.* (Chapel Hill and London: University of North Carolina Press, 2000) and Mark Solomon, *The Cry Was Unity: Communists and African Americans, 1917–36* (Jackson: University Press of Mississippi, 1998). For a different kind of retelling that focuses on organizing tactics and strategy, see Robert Fisher, *Let the People Decide: Neighborhood Organizing in America* (New York: Twayne Publishers, 1994).
20. August Meier and Elliott Rudwick, *CORE: A Study in the Civil Rights Movement, 1942–1968* (Urbana: University of Illinois Press, 1973), page 64.
21. CORE, "All About CORE" (no date).
22. Paul Weeks, "Housing Equality Major Negro Aim: Leader Says LA Segregation is Cutting Off Understanding," *Los Angeles Times*, June 24, 1963.
23. CORE, "Cracking the Color Line" (1961).
24. Centinela Bay Human Relations Commission, "Progress Report" (May 1962).
25. Ibid.
26. CORE, "All About CORE" (no date).
27. Debbie Louis Papers, University of California, Los Angeles, Box 12, Folder 14.
28. CORE April 1962; Centinela Bay Human Relations Commission, "Progress Report" (May 1962).
29. Field Report of Genevieve Hughes November 1–12, 1961, January 8, 1962. *WISC* MSS14, Box 51, Folder 2.
30. *California Eagle*, January 11, 1962.
31. *California Eagle*, February 22, 1962.
32. *Los Angeles Times*, February 23, 1962.
33. *Los Angeles Times*, March 7, 1962.
34. *California Eagle*, March 8, 1962. For a history of the ways in which Monterey Park continued to become a majority Chinese suburb, see John Horton, *The Politics of Diversity: Immigration, Resistance and Change in Monterey Park, California* (Philadelphia: Temple University Press, 1995). Saito's work demonstrates how racism and racial violence continued through the 1990s, as anti-Asian feeling led to numerous hate incidents—see Leland T. Saito, *Race and Politics: Asian Americans, Latinos, and Whites in a Los Angeles Suburb* (Chicago: University of Illinois Press, 1998).
35. Saito's study of Monterey Park politics in the 1990s revealed a large Asian population with strong memories of discrimination in the city throughout the 1950s, where they or their parents had been unable to buy new tract homes except through white intermediaries—see Leland T. Saito, *Race and Politics: Asian Americans, Latinos, and Whites in a Los Angeles Suburb* (Chicago: University of Illinois Press, 1998).
36. *Sentinel*, March 8, 1962.
37. *California Eagle*, March 8, 1962. Kennedy would sign the order, to be effective immediately, on November 20, 1962 (*California Eagle*, November 22, 1962).
38. Robert Farrell, "Sit-Inners Ignore Hint, Hold Fort," *California Eagle*, March 15, 1962, page 1.
39. *Los Angeles Times*, March 13, 1962.
40. *Los Angeles Times*, April 6, 1924.
41. *Los Angeles Times*, April 7, 1962.
42. *Sentinel*, April 12, 1962.
43. Undated letter, Debbie Louis Papers, University of California, Los Angeles, Box 12, Folder 14.
44. *California Eagle*, April 19, 1962.
45. Centinela Bay Human Relations Commission Progress Report, May 1962.
46. Undated CORE manual, Debbie Louis Papers, University of California, Los Angeles, Box 12, Folder 14. The manual itself was put together for a national housing workshop by an Ohio CORE branch, drawing on chapter experiences around the country. LA CORE was undoubtedly the lead on the issue of housing in Southern California; see the report on California's CORE conference proceedings, dated July 20, 1963 (*WISC* MSS14 Series 6, Box 66, Folder 1).
47. *California Eagle*, June 21, 1962.

48. Debbie Louis Papers, University of California, Los Angeles,, Box 12, Folder 14.
49. "CORE-alator" (February 1963).
50. *California Eagle*, November 1, 1962.
51. *Los Angeles Times*, November 4, 1962.
52. *California Eagle*, November 8, 1962.
53. *California Eagle*, November 15 and 22, 1962.
54. *Los Angeles Times*, December 4, 1962.
55. *Sentinel*, August 15, 1963.
56. *California Eagle*, July 26, 1962; CORE leaflet, Debbie Louis Papers, University of California, Los Angeles, Box 12, Folder 14.
57. Dale Ann Sato, *Japanese Americans of the South Bay* (Charleston, SC: Arcadia Publishing, 2009).
58. Ibid.
59. Florante Ibañez and Rosleyn Ibañez, *Filipinos in Carson and the South Bay* (Charleston, SC: Arcadia Publishing, 2009).
60. Emily Straus, *The Making of the American School Crisis: Compton, California and the American Dream* (unpublished dissertation, Brandeis University, 2006).
61. Josh Sides, "Straight into Compton: American Dreams, Urban Nightmares, and the Metamorphosis of a Black Suburb," *American Quarterly* 56(3) (2004): 583–605; Emily Straus, *The Making of the American School Crisis: Compton, California and the American Dream* (unpublished dissertation, Brandeis University, 2006).
62. *California Eagle*, April 10, 1947.
63. *California Eagle*, July 10, 1947; *Sentinel*, April 27, 1947; Emily Straus, *The Making of the American School Crisis: Compton, California and the American Dream* (unpublished dissertation, Brandeis University, 2006).
64. United States Department of Commerce, Bureau of the Census, 1955.
65. Josh Sides, "Straight into Compton: American Dreams, Urban Nightmares, and the Metamorphosis of a Black Suburb," *American Quarterly* 56(3) (2004): 583–605.
66. Edward Warren, "Testimony found in California Governor's Commission on the Los Angeles Riots," "Transcripts, depositions, consultants' reports, and selected documents" (1960); *CE* July 10, 1947.
67. *California Eagle*, May 7, 1953.
68. Loren Miller, "Testimony," in *McCone Commission on the Watts Riots* (1965).
69. United States Department of Commerce, Bureau of the Census, 1955. Sides also makes note of these shifting lines of exclusion—see Josh Sides, *LA City Limits: African American Los Angeles From the Great Depression to the Present* (Berkeley: University of California Press, 2003).
70. *Sentinel*, October 7 and 28, 1948.
71. *California Eagle*, May 14, 1953.
72. *Sentinel*, October 4, 1956.
73. Alex Alonso, *Territoriality Among African–American Street Gangs.* (Los Angeles: unpublished master's thesis, University of Southern California, 1999); Gregory C. Brown, James D. Vigil, and Eric R. Taylor, "The Ghettoization of Blacks in Los Angeles: The Emergence of Street Gangs," *Journal of African American Studies* 16 (2012): 209–25; Edward Warren, "Testimony found in California Governor's Commission on the Los Angeles Riots," "Transcripts, depositions, consultants' reports, and selected documents," (1960).
74. Albert Camarillo, "Cities of Color: The New Racial Frontier in California's Minority–Majority Cities," *Pacific Historical Review* 76(1) (2007): 1–28.
75. Emily Straus, *The Making of the American School Crisis: Compton, California and the American Dream* (unpublished dissertation, Brandeis University, 2006).
76. Becky Nicolaides, *My Blue Heaven: Life and Politics in the Working Class Suburbs of Los Angeles, 1920–1965* (Chicago: University of Chicago Press, 2002).
77. Josh Sides, "Straight into Compton: American Dreams, Urban Nightmares, and the Metamorphosis of a Black Suburb," *American Quarterly* 56(3) (2004): 583-605; Emily Straus, *The Making of the American School Crisis: Compton, California and the American Dream* (unpublished dissertation, Brandeis University, 2006).

78. *Sentinel,* December 14, 1961.
79. *Sentinel,* March 8, 1962.
80. *Los Angeles Times,* September 29, 1962.
81. *Sentinel,* February 14, 1963.
82. *Sentinel,* January 10, 1963.
83. The term *redlining* grew directly from the use of HOLC maps to deny loans to those living in areas designated as red, and came to refer to widespread banking practices of refusing to lend to people living in poor areas with high concentrations of people of color through to the present—long after the HOLC maps have ceased to be of relevance. See Laura Pulido, "Rethinking Environmental Racism: White Privilege and Urban Development in Southern California," *Annals of the Association of American Geographers* 90(1) (2000): 12–40. This corresponded to widespread withdrawals of all banking services from ghettos areas across the country; see Strategic Actions for a Just Economy (SAJE), *Making Change,* 2002, saje.net (accessed June 2012).
84. Derrick Bell, "Racial Realism," *Connecticut Law Review* 24(2) (1992): 363–79, page 83.
85. Albert Camarillo, "Cities of Color: The New Racial Frontier in California's Minority–Majority Cities," *Pacific Historical Review* 76(1) (2007): 1–28; Josh Sides, "Straight into Compton: American Dreams, Urban Nightmares, and the Metamorphosis of a Black Suburb," *American Quarterly* 56(3) (2004): 583–605.
86. See Chapter 2 for Shattuck's own role in organizing a protective association.
87. Testimony of Charles Shattuck before the Assembly Interim Committee on Governmental Efficiency and Economy at its public hearings in Los Angeles on September 28–9, 1961, *SCL* LA Subject Files, Pamphlets, Fair Housing III.
88. Stuart Hall, "Race, Articulation and Societies Structured in Dominance," in *Sociological Theories: Race and Colonialism* (UNESCO), 1980: 305–45, page 338.
89. Margaret Crawford, *Building the Workingman's Paradise: The Design of American Company Towns* (London: Verso, 1995).
90. Ibid., page 18.
91. Ibid., Becky Nicolaides, *My Blue Heaven: Life and Politics in the Working Class Suburbs of Los Angeles, 1920–1965* (Chicago: University of Chicago Press, 2002).
92. Dana Bartlett, "An Industrial Garden City: Torrance," *American City* 10 (1913), page 314.
93. Margaret Crawford, *Building the Workingman's Paradise: The Design of American Company Towns* (London: Verso, 1995).
94. Ibid., page 91.
95. George W. Neill, November 5, 1920, *Torrance Enterprise,* page 1.
96. *Torrance Enterprise* November 5, 1920.
97. These can be seen in copies of early deed transfers, such as those found in *CSDH,* Box 14, Folder 2.
98. United States Department of Commerce, Bureau of the Census, 1955.
99. Ibid.
100. *Press,* October 1, 1951.
101. *Press,* July 7, 1963.
102. Marc A. Weiss, *The Rise of the Community Builders: The American Real Estate Industry and Urban Land Planning* (New York: Columbia University Press, 1987).
103. Gregory Hise, *Magnetic Los Angeles: Planning the Twentieth-Century Metropolis* (Baltimore and London: Johns Hopkins University Press, 1997).
104. *Sentinel,* June 20, 1963.

5. THE SECOND SALVO: DON WILSON AND THE
BATTLE FOR THE SOUTH BAY

1. *Sentinel,* August 2, 1962.
2. *California Eagle,* September 27, 1962.
3. *California Eagle,* October 4 and November 1, 1962.

4. CORE statement on Housing Discrimination, 1962, Debbie Louis Papers, University of California, Los Angeles, Box 12, Folder 14.
5. Undated CORE leaflet C, 1962–63, Debbie Louis Papers, University of California, Los Angeles,, Box 12, Folder 14.
6. CORE letter dated January 28, 1963, Debbie Louis Papers, University of California, Los Angeles, Box 12, Folder 14.
7. *Sentinel,* February 7, 1962.
8. American Friends Service Committee Newsletter, May 1963—*ACLU* Box 30, Folder 1.
9. *California Eagle,* June 14, 1962
10. *California Eagle,* June 28, 1962.
11. *California Eagle,* December 13, 1962.
12. Friends Committee on Legislation, 1963.
13. Daniel Martinez HoSang, *Racial Propositions: Ballot Initiatives and the Making of Postwar California* (Berkeley: University of California Press, 2012).
14. *Los Angeles Times,* May 30, 1963.
15. *Los Angeles Times,* June 1, 1963.
16. *Sentinel,* June 13, 1963.
17. *Los Angeles Times,* June 14, 1963.
18. American Friends Service Committee Newsletter, May 1963—*ACLU* Box 30, Folder 1; *Sentinel,* June 27, 1963.
19. *LAT* June 20, 1963.
20. *Sentinel,* June 27, 1963.
21. American Friends Committee, "The Fight for Fair Housing" (1963).
22. *Sentinel,* March 7, 1963.
23. *Sentinel,* May 2, 1963.
24. *Sentinel,* June 29, 1963.
25. *Los Angeles Times,* June 17, 1963.
26. *Press,* June 19, 1963.
27. *Los Angeles Times,* June 23, 1963.
28. Ibid.
29. *Sentinel,* June 27, 1963.
30. *Los Angeles Times,* June 24, 1963.
31. *Los Angeles Times,* June 5, 1963.
32. John Thurber, "Paul Weeks, 86; reporter covered LA's blacks," *Los Angeles Times,* July 22, 2007.
33. Paul Weeks, "LA Integration Test Approaches," *Los Angeles Times,* June 23, 1963.
34. Paul Weeks, "Housing Equality Major Negro Aim: Leader Says LA Segregation is Cutting Off Understanding," *Los Angeles Times,* June 24, 1963.
35. Ibid.
36. *Sentinel,* June 29, 1963.
37. *Sentinel,* July 14, 1963.
38. *Sentinel,* June 27, 1963.
39. CORE press release April 7, 1963, Debbie Louis Papers, University of California, Los Angeles, Box 12, Folder 14.
40. Bruce Hartford, "Oral History" (February 2002).
41. *Press,* June 26, 1963.
42. Ibid.
43. *Press,* June 26, 1963; *Sentinel,* June 28, 1963.
44. *Press,* June 26, 1963, my italics.
45. June 27, 1963.
46. Paul Weeks, "Owner Agrees to Integrate Torrance Tract," *Los Angeles Times,* July 13, 1963.
47. *Sentinel,* June 28, 1963.
48. *Torrance Herald,* June 30, 1963.
49. *Sentinel,* June 29, 1963.
50. *Torrance Herald,* June 30, 1963.

51. *Sentinel,* June 30, 1963.
52. *Press,* July 3, 1963; *Sentinel,* July 4, 1963.
53. Barbara Dimmick, "CORE's Corner," *Sentinel,* July 4, 1963.
54. *Sentinel,* July 4, 1963.
55. *Sentinel,* June 30, 1963.
56. Barbara Dimmick, "CORE's Corner," *Sentinel,* July 4, 1963.
57. *Sentinel,* July 1, 1963.
58. Barbara Dimmick, "CORE's Corner," *Sentinel,* July 11, 1963.
59. *Los Angeles Times,* July 11, 1963.
60. *Los Angeles Times,* July 11, 1963.
61. *Sentinel,* July 12, 1963.
62. *Torrance Herald,* July 11, 1963; Paul Weeks, "Negro Leader Hopes For Peace At Tract," *Los Angeles Times*, July 12, 1963.
63. Barbara Dimmick, "CORE's Corner," *Sentinel,* July 11, 1963.
64. *Torrance Herald,* July 11, 1963.
65. Paul Weeks, "Negro Leader Hopes For Peace At Tract," *Los Angeles Times*, July 12, 1963.
66. *Press,* July 14, 1963.
67. *Torrance Herald,* July 14, 1963.
68. *Los Angeles Times,* July 14, 1963.
69. Paul Weeks, "Negro Leader Hopes For Peace At Tract," *Los Angeles Times*, July 12, 1963.
70. Paul Weeks, "LA Negro Views of Campaign Vary," *Los Angeles Times*, July 14, 1963.
71. *Press,* July 26, 1963.
72. Paul Weeks, "New Torrance Picketing Seen by CORE Aide," *Los Angeles Times*, July 26, 1963.
73. *Press,* July 26, 1963.
74. Paul Weeks, "New Torrance Picketing Seen by CORE Aide," *Los Angeles Times*, July 26, 1963.
75. *Press,* July 31, 1963.
76. *Torrance Herald,* August 1, 1963.
77. *Press,* July 31, 1963.
78. Don Neff, "Torrance Home Owners Assail Mass Picketing," *Los Angeles Times*, August 4, 1963.
79. Don Neff, "Belief in 'Just Cause' Prompts Tract Pickets," *Los Angeles Times*, August 5, 1963.
80. Paul Weeks, "New Torrance Picketing Seen by CORE Aide," *Los Angeles Times*, July 26, 1963.
81. Paul Weeks, "Brando to Join CORE March on Tract Today," *Los Angeles Times*, July 27, 1963.
82. *Sentinel,* August 10, 1963.
83. *Sentinel,* August 4, 1963.
84. *Sentinel,* August 8, 1963.
85. *Torrance Herald,* August 8, 1963.
86. Barbara Dimmick, "CORE's Corner," *Sentinel,* August 8, 1963.
87. Ibid.
88. *Sentinel,* August 11, 1963.
89. *Torrance Herald,* August 15, 1963.
90. *Sentinel,* August 12, 1963.
91. *Torrance Herald,* August 15, 1963.
92. *Torrance Herald,* August 18, 1963.
93. *Sentinel,* August 15, 1963.
94. *Torrance Herald,* August 22, 1963.
95. *Press,* August 28, 1963.
96. *Torrance Herald,* August 29, 1963.
97. *Sentinel,* August 29, 1963 and *Press,* August 28, 1963.
98. *Sentinel,* September 8, 1963.
99. The John Birch Society was founded in 1958; it was named after a missionary killed by communists in China in 1945 and maintained a virulent anti-communism that believed that President Eisenhower, the federal government, unions, most of the education system, and others were part of a communist conspiracy. See Leonard J. Moore, "John Birch Society," *The Oxford Companion to United States History*, Oxford University Press, 2001.

100. *Torrance Herald,* August 22, 1963.
101. Mrs Donald Salk, *Torrance Herald,* August 29, 1963.
102. *Torrance Herald,* August 22, 1963.
103. *Torrance Herald,* August 29, 1963.
104. *Sentinel,* August 29, 1963.
105. *Sentinel,* September 24 and 25, 1963.
106. *Sentinel,* December 6, 1963.
107. Paul Weeks, "Negro Family Acquires Home in Disputed Tract," *Los Angeles Times,* July 16, 1964.

6. WHITE REACTION: OLD WALLS TORN DOWN AND NEW ONES RAISED

1. Julius Lester, *Look Out Whitey! Black Power's Gon' Get Your Mama!* (New York: Random House, 1969), page 4.
2. James Farmer, *Lay Bare the Heart: An Autobiography of the Civil Rights Movement* (New York: Penguin-Plume, 1986), page 266.
3. Debbie Louis Papers, University of California, Los Angeles, Box 12, Folder 7.
4. *Sentinel,* November 21, 1963.
5. For an impressive in-depth look at this campaign and what it meant for progressive forces in California, see Daniel Martinez HoSang, *Racial Propositions: Ballot Initiatives and the Making of Postwar California* (Berkeley: University of California Press, 2012).
6. August Meier and Elliott Rudwick, *CORE: A Study in the Civil Rights Movement, 1942–1968* (Urbana: University of Illinois Press, 1973), page 401.
7. Charles E. Cobb, *This Nonviolent Stuff'll Get You Killed: How Guns Made the Civil Rights Movement Possible* (Durham: Duke University Press, 2015).
8. See Gerald Horne, *Fire This Time: The Watts Uprising and the 1960s* (Charlottesville: University Press of Virginia, 1995); David Sears and John McConahay, *The Politics of Violence: The New Urban Blacks and the Watts Riot* (Boston: Houghton Mifflin Company, 1973).
9. David O. Sears and John B. McConahay, *The Politics of Violence: The New Urban Blacks and the Watts Riot* (Boston: Houghton Mifflin Company, 1973), page 159.
10. Ibid., page 161.
11. Ibid., page 164. The Curfew Zone was a 46.5-mile area in South Los Angeles instituted as a strategy to quell the Watts uprising; within its boundaries people could be arrested for a crime if found on the streets after 8 p.m.
12. Robert F. Williams, *Negroes with Guns* (Detroit: Wayne State University Press, [1962] 1988).
13. Ibid.
14. Elaine Brown, *A Taste of Power: A Black Woman's Story* (New York: Anchor Books, Doubleday, 1992), pages 126–27.
15. For a sense of how close those in this movement believed they were to achieving radical change, see Gregory C. Brown, James D. Vigil, and Eric R. Taylor, "The Ghettoization of Blacks in Los Angeles: The Emergence of Street Gangs," *Journal of African American Studies* 16 (2012): 209–25; Stanley Tookie Williams, *Blue Rage, Black Redemption: A Memoir* (New York: Touchstone, 2007); and the autobiographies of Angela Davis, *Angela Davis: an Autobiography* (London: Arrow Books, 1976); Huey P. Newton, *Revolutionary Suicide* (London: Wildwood House, 1974); and Bobby Seale, *Seize the Time: the Story of the Black Panther Party and Huey P. Newton* (London: Hutchinson, 1970).
16. See, among others, Ward Churchill and Jim Vander Wall, *Agents of Repression: The FBI's Secret Wars Against the Black Panther Party and the American Indian Movement* (Boston: South End Press, 1988).
17. Gerald Horne, *Fire This Time: The Watts Uprising and the 1960s* (Charlottesville: University Press of Virginia, 1995), page 132.
18. This is, of course, the Nation of Islam, but after the period during which Malcolm X and Muhammad Ali had propelled it into mainstream view. Malcolm X left the NOI in 1964; see Manning Marable's *Malcolm X: A Life of Reinvention* (New York: Viking Press, 2011) for a

particularly rich history of Malcolm X and his changing thinking on the intertwining of race, class, and oppression that went against narrowly defined Black nationalist and entrepreneurial lines.

19. Gerald Horne, *Fire This Time: The Watts Uprising and the 1960s* (Charlottesville: University Press of Virginia, 1995), pages 132–33.
20. Sonya Winton, "Concerned Citizens: Environmental (In)Justice in Black Los Angeles," in *Black Los Angeles: American Dreams and Racial Realities*, Darnell Hunt and Ana-Christina Ramón (eds.) (New York: New York University Press, 2010): 343–59, page 354.
21. Julius Lester, *Look Out Whitey! Black Power's Gon' Get Your Mama!* (New York: Random House, 1969), page 16.
22. Paul Weeks, "Housing Equality Major Negro Aim: Leader Says LA Segregation is Cutting Off Understanding," *Los Angeles Times*, June 24, 1963.
23. Eric John Abrahamson, *Building Home: Howard F. Ahmanson and the Politics of the American Dream* (Berkeley: University of California Press, 2013).
24. Manning Marable, *How Capitalism Underdeveloped America* (Boston: South End Press, 1983).
25. Derrick Bell, "Racial Realism," *Connecticut Law Review* 24(2) (1992): 363–79.
26. Edward W. Soja, *Postmetropolis: Critical Studies of Cities and Regions* (Malden, MA: Blackwell Publishers, 2000).
27. Evan McKenzie, *Privatopia: Homeowner Associations and the Rise of Residential Private Government* (New Haven, CT: Yale University Press, 1994), and Evan McKenzie, "Planning Through Residential Clubs: Homeowners' Associations," *Economic Affairs* 25(4) (2005): 28–31.
28. United States Advisory Commission on Intergovernmental Regulations (ACIR), *Residential Community Associations: Private Governments in the Intergovernmental System?* (Washington DC: ACIR, 1989), page 18.
29. Evan McKenzie, *Privatopia: Homeowner Associations and the Rise of Residential Private Government* (New Haven, CT: Yale University Press, 1994).
30. See David Harvey, *The Limits of Capital.* (London: Verso, [1982] 2007); Neil Smith, "Gentrification and Uneven Development," *Economic Geography* 58(2) (1982): 139–55; Neil Smith, *The New Urban Frontier: Gentrification and the Revanchist City* (London: Routledge, 1996).
31. Sheryll Cashin, "Privatized Communities and the 'Secession of the Successful': Democracy and Fairness Beyond the Gate," *Fordham Urban Law Journal* 28 (2001): 1675–92, page 1681.
32. For those who more explicitly tie the rise of CIDs to the preservation of white neighborhoods, see Edward James and Mary Gail Snyder Blakely, *Fortress America, Gated Communities in the United States* (Washington, DC: Brookings Institution Press & Lincoln Institute of Land Policy, 1997); Evan McKenzie, *Privatopia: Homeowner Associations and the Rise of Residential Private Government* (New Haven, CT: Yale University Press, 1994); Evan McKenzie, "Planning Through Residential Clubs: Homeowners' Associations," *Economic Affairs* 25(4) (2005): 28–31; Steven Grant Meyer, *As Long As They Don't Move Next Door: Segregation and Racial Conflict in American Neighborhoods* (Oxford: Rowman & Littlefield Publishers, Inc., 2000).
33. Derrick Bell, "Racism is Here to Stay: Now What?" *Howard Law Journal* 35 (1991–1992): 79–93; Chester Hartman and Gregory Squires, *The Integration Debate: Competing Futures For American Cities*, Chester Hartman and Gregory Squires (eds.) (Abingdon: Routledge, 2010).
34. Gary Miller, *Cities by Contract: The Politics of Municipal Incorporation* (Cambridge, MA: MIT Press, 1981).
35. Michael Woo, interview by Andrea Gibbons (August 10, 2012).
36. Robert Reich, "The Succession of the Successful," *New York Times*, January 20, 1991.
37. David Harvey, *The Limits of Capital* (London: Verso, [1982] 2007); Henri Lefebvre, *The Production of Space* (Oxford: Blackwell, 1991); Neil Smith, *The New Urban Frontier: Gentrification and the Revanchist City* (London: Routledge, 1996).

7. BATTLE ON SKID ROW

1. County of Los Angeles, *About LA County*, lacounty.gov/government/about-la-county (accessed June 13, 2017).
2. Philip Ethington, W.H. Frey, and D. Myers, "The Racial Resegregation of Los Angeles County, 1940–2000." Public Research Report No. 2001-04 (2001).
3. David Harvey, *The Urbanization of Capital* (Baltimore, MD: Johns Hopkins University Press, 1985); Neil Smith, "Gentrification and Uneven Development," *Economic Geography* 58(2) (1982): 139–55. Without being able to provide empirical evidence covering a wide area, both the detailed case history of the Morrison Hotel discussed further in the chapter, as well as the transformation of Skid Row from a neighborhood where nonprofit development corporations were able to purchase and rehabilitate large hotels as SROs and halfway houses, which then became luxury loft buildings where property values have risen 200 percent since 1999 bears out the rent gap theory (Downtown Central Business Improvement District, 2013).
4. Henri Lefebvre, *The Production of Space* (Oxford: Blackwell, 1991); Henri Lefebvre, *The Urban Revolution* (Minneapolis: University of Minnesota Press, 2003).
5. Edward Goetz, "Land Use and Homeless Policy in Los Angeles," *International Journal of Urban and Regional Research* 16(4) (1992): 540–54; David Harvey, *The Urbanization of Capital* (Baltimore, MD: Johns Hopkins University Press, 1985).
6. Gilda Haas, interview by Andrea Gibbons (August 29, 2012).
7. David Wagner and Pete White, "Why the Silence? Homelessness and Race," in *Freedom Now! Struggles for the Human Right to Housing in LA and Beyond*, Jordan T. Camp and Christina Heatherton (eds.) (Los Angeles: Freedom Now Books, 2012): 42–8.
8. Pete White, General Dogon and Chuck D., "Chuck D's Tour of Skid Row," in *Freedom Now! Struggles for the Human Right to Housing in LA and Beyond*, Jordan T. Camp and Christina Heatherton (eds.) (Los Angeles: Freedom Now Books, 2012): 49–61.
9. See Michael Dear and Jennifer Wolch, *Landscapes of Despair: From Deinstitutionalization to Homelessness* (Oxford: Polity Press, 1987), page i, specifically around deinstitutionalization and a move to "'community care' for the mentally ill, physically handicapped, addicts and parolees that began in the 60s but accelerated through the 70s and early 80s, resulting in what they called at the time 'service-dependant population ghettos.'" They build on this work to include a larger view of other factors creating the growing upsurge of homelessness through the 1980s; see Jennifer Wolch and Michael Dear, *Malign Neglect: Homelessness in an American City* (San Francisco: Jossey–Bass Publishers, 1993). A distillation of the main findings can be found in Jennifer Wolch, "From Global to Local: The Rise of Homelessness in Los Angeles during the 1980s," in *The City: Los Angeles and Urban Theory at the End of the Twentieth Century*, Allen J. Scott and Edward W. Soja (eds.) (Berkeley: University of California Press, 1996): 390–425 for an updated look specifically at race and homelessness in LA, see David Wagner and Pete White, "Why the Silence? Homelessness and Race," in *Freedom Now! Struggles for the Human Right to Housing in LA and Beyond*, Jordan T. Camp and Christina Heatherton (eds.) (Los Angeles: Freedom Now Books, 2012): 42–8.
10. Allen J. Scott, "High-Technology Industrial Development in the San Fernando Valley and Ventura County: Observations on Economic Growth and the Evolution of Urban Form," in *The City: Los Angeles and Urban Theory at the End of the Twentieth Century*, Allen J. Scott and Edward W. Soja (eds.) (Berkeley: University of California Press, 1996): 276–310. Jennifer Wolch, "From Global to Local: The Rise of Homelessness in Los Angeles during the 1980s," in *The City: Los Angeles and Urban Theory at the End of the Twentieth Century*, Allen J. Scott and Edward W. Soja (eds.) (Berkeley: University of California Press, 1996): 390–425.
11. For more on the 1992 uprisings, see Nancy Abelmann and John Lie, *Blue Dreams: Korean Americans and the Los Angeles Riots* (Cambridge, MA: Harvard University Press, 1995); Robert Gooding–Williams, *Reading Rodney King / Reading Urban Uprising* (New York: Routledge, 1993); Darnell Hunt, *Screening the Los Angeles "Riots": Race, Seeing, and Resistance* (Cambridge: Cambridge University Press, 1997); and Victor M. Valle and Rodolfo D. Torres, *Latino Metropolis* (Minneapolis: University of Minnesota Press, 2000).
12. *Jones v. City of Los Angeles*, 04-55324 (9th Circuit, 2006).

13. Los Angeles Housing Department, "Report Back on Motion Regarding Preservation of Single Room Occupancy Housing," Council File: 04-2087 (2005).

14. Downtown Women's Action Coalition, "Many Struggles, Few Options: Findings and Recommendations from the 2004 Downtown Women's Needs Assessment" (Los Angeles, 2004); Downtown Women's Action Coalition, "Downtown Women's Needs Assessment: Findings and Recommendations" (Los Angeles, 2001).

15. Los Angeles Homeless Services Authority, "Greater Los Angeles Homeless Count: Executive Summary" (2011).

16. Raphael Sonenshein, *Politics in Black and White: Race and Power in Los Angeles* (Princeton: Princeton University Press, 1993).

17. Don Spivack, 1988, skidrowjournal.org/history-of-skid-row.html (accessed March 22, 2013).

18. See, for example, the Los Angeles Community Design Center, "Skid Row: Recommendations to Citizens Advisory Committee on the Central Business District Plan for the City of Los Angeles, Part 4: Physical Containment" (Los Angeles, 1976).

19. Harold L. Katz, "Skid Row Housing," *Los Angeles Times*, August 30, 1987; *Los Angeles Times*, "Harold L. Katz Obituary," November 26–8, 2010.

20. Community Redevelopment Agency, "Redevelopment Plan for Central Business District Redevelopment Area" (Los Angeles, 1975), page 18.

21. Ibid., page 14.

22. Edward Goetz, "Land Use and Homeless Policy in Los Angeles," *International Journal of Urban and Regional Research* 16(4) (1992): 540–54; Gilda Haas and Alan Heskin, "Community Struggles in Los Angeles," *International Journal of Urban and Regional Research* 5(4) (1981): 546–63; Barbara Schultz, "Frontline Focus," *Legal Aid Foundation of Los Angeles*, November 2011, www.lafla.org/newsletter_FF.php (accessed May 30, 2012).

23. Gilda Haas and Alan Heskin, "Community Struggles in Los Angeles," *International Journal of Urban and Regional Research* 5(4) (1981): 546–63.

24. Ibid, page 556.

25. Downtown Center Business Improvement District, "Downtown Los Angeles Demographic Study 2011" (2011).

26. Hal Bastian, interview by Andrea Gibbons (September 12, 2012).

27. *DTLA Life* 2014.

28. *The Planning Report*, "CCA's Carol Schatz On LA's Downtown Development Boom," October 12, 2012.

29. Mike Davis, *City of Quartz* (London and New York: Verso, 2006).

30. Gilda Haas and Alan Heskin, "Community Struggles in Los Angeles," *International Journal of Urban and Regional Research* 5(4) (1981): 546–63.

31. Edward Goetz, "Land Use and Homeless Policy in Los Angeles," *International Journal of Urban and Regional Research* 16(4) (1992): 540–54.

32. Susan M. Ruddick, *Young and Homeless in Hollywood: Mapping Social Identities* (New York and London: Routledge, 1996).

33. Edward Goetz, "Land Use and Homeless Policy in Los Angeles," *International Journal of Urban and Regional Research* 16(4) (1992): 540–54.

34. Ibid.

35. Frank Clifford and Penelope McMillan, "LA Officials Say Raids Designed to Rid Skid Row of Encampments of Homeless," *Los Angeles Times*, February 19, 1987.

36. John Regardie, "At the Center of It All," *Los Angeles Downtown News*, July 2, 2010.

37. Formation of the BID in 1996 led to the branding of an official "Fashion District."

38. Mike Davis, *City of Quartz* (London and New York: Verso, 2006); Daniel Martinez HoSang, *Racial Propositions: Ballot Initiatives and the Making of Postwar California* (Berkeley: University of California Press, 2012).

39. Downtown Property Owners Association, "Newsletter" (February 1995).

40. Downtown Industrial BID minutes, December 21, 2004; Toy/Downtown Industrial BID minutes, December 20, 2005; DCBID minutes, September 7, 2005.

41. Kent Smith bio, dated February 2012: fashiondistrict.org/la-fashion-district-bid/us/bid-staff (accessed June 2012). This more independent and professional role has made a better

working relationship with homeless organizations and LA CAN possible as described by Kent Smith, interview by Andrea Gibbons (August 22, 2012), and by Becky Dennison, interview by Andrea Gibbons (August 2, 2011), demonstrating the positive role some individuals can play in mitigating (though ultimately not preventing) some of the harsher results of the practices, discourses, and larger structural forces described in this book.

42. Marla Dickerson, "Activists Claim Skid Row BIDs Are Rousting Homeless," *Los Angeles Times*, May 6, 1999.

43. Ibid.

44. Marla Dickerson, "California; Fashion District Group Agrees to Settle Homeless Lawsuit; Dispute: The deal makes permanent an interim agreement reached last year," *Los Angeles Times*, August 14, 2001; National Law Center on Homelessness and Poverty & National Coalition for the Homeless, "Homes Not Handcuffs: The Criminalization of Homelessness in US Cities" (2009).

45. Los Angeles Community Action Network, n.d.

46. Paulo Freire, *Pedagogy of the Oppressed* (New York and London: Continuum International Publishing Group Ltd., 2001).

47. Los Angeles Community Action Network, n.d.

48. Ibid.

49. See Bruce Hartford, "Oral History," February 10, 2002, crmvet.org/nars/bruce1.htm (accessed 2013); August Meier and Elliott Rudwick, *CORE: A Study in the Civil Rights Movement, 1942–1968* (Urbana: University of Illinois Press, 1973).

50. Anat Rubin, interview by Andrea Gibbons (August 28, 2012).

51. See Michelle Alexander, *The New Jim Crow: Mass Incarceration in an Age of Colorblindness* (New York: The New Press, 2012) among others. The distinction between the "deserving" and "undeserving" poor stretches back at least to Victorian England, in which discourse was eerily similar to today's political debates around crime, homelessness, addiction, and mental health.

52. LA CAN Focus Group, interview by Andrea Gibbons (August 16, 2012).

53. Ibid.

54. Pete White, *Business Improvement Districts: Protecting or Provoking?* (Report prepared by the Los Angeles Community Action Network and the Los Angeles Coalition to End Hunger and Homelessness, 2000).

55. Ibid., page 96.

56. William Wan and Erin Ailworth, "Flak Over Downtown Security Guards; Business owners say the patrols have helped clean up and revitalize the area. But some homeless have sued, alleging harassment," *Los Angeles Times*, August 6, 2004.

57. Marla Dickerson, "California; Fashion District Group Agrees to Settle Homeless Lawsuit; Dispute: The deal makes permanent an interim agreement reached last year," *Los Angeles Times*, August 14, 2001.

58. National Law Center on Homelessness and Poverty & National Coalition for the Homeless, "Homes Not Handcuffs: The Criminalization of Homelessness in US Cities" (2009).

59. Becky Dennison, interview by Andrea Gibbons (August 2, 2011).

60. Ibid.

61. Central City Association, "Downtown's Human Tragedy: It's Not Acceptable Anymore—A Public Health and Safety Plan" (Los Angeles, 2002).

62. Seema Mehta, "Los Angeles; County Files Suit to Block Redevelopment Plan for Downtown," *Los Angeles Times*, June 27, 2002.

63. BIDlines, 2002; LA Fashion District Business Improvement Distict, "BIDlines," (2002); Jocelyn Stewart, "Homeless Advocates Sue LA Over Downtown Plan; Skid row: Coalition says the poorest residents are ignored and asks for details on how they will find housing and jobs," *Los Angeles Times*, August 21, 2002.

64. Jocelyn Stewart, "Homeless Advocates Sue LA Over Downtown Plan; Skid row: Coalition says the poorest residents are ignored and asks for details on how they will find housing and jobs," *Los Angeles Times*, August 21, 2002.

65. Alice Callaghan, "Commentary; Skid Rowers Don't Deserve the Boot; LA plan would oust thousands from hotels," *Los Angeles Times*, May 31, 2002.

66. Figueroa Corridor Coalition for Economic Justice and Los Angeles Coalition to End Hunger & Homelessness, "Share the Wealth: A Policy Strategy for Fair Redevelopment in LA's City Center," (Los Angeles, 2002).

67. Barbara Schultz, "Frontline Focus," *Legal Aid Foundation of Los Angeles*, November 2011, www.lafla.org/newsletter_FF.php (accessed May 30, 2012).

68. Los Angeles Housing Department, "Report Back on Motion Regarding Preservation of Single Room Occupancy Housing," Council File: 04-2087 (2005).

69. Nick Dahmann, "Cartographic Editorial—For Maps! Working Through Cartographic Anxiety in Downtown LA," *Urban Geography* 31(6) (2010): 717–23.

70. Research was carried out by the author while an employee of SAJE between 2004 and 2006. Strategic Actions for a Just Economy (SAJE) is a popular education and community organizing center working on issues of development and environmental justice in South Central Los Angeles (see www.saje.net). I worked there between 2000 and 2006 as both a lead community organizer and researcher. All information on holdings given in this section comes from recorded property deeds and transfers obtained through searches of LexisNexis and Dataquick databases. Records of violations are from www.lacity.gov.

71. *Ramirez et al. v. Hope Pico LLC.*

72. Central City Association, "CCA Delivers" (July 17, 2009).

73. Jocelyn Stewart, "Hotel's Past Is Clouding Its Future; Some worry a plan to turn Bristol from low-cost housing to boutique inn comes at expense of the poor," June 30, 2004.

74. Community Connection, "Historic Protections for LA's Housing of Last Resort Will Help Prevent Gentrification City-Wide," July–August 2008.

75. Cara Mia DiMassa, "1-Year Ban OKd on Loft Conversions; LA City Council acts to preserve low-cost housing as developers eye residential hotels for new projects. Effect on the market is unclear," *Los Angeles Times*, May 11, 2006.

76. Anat Rubin, "Law Firms 'Adopt' Skid Row Residency Hotels: Unique Pro Bono Approach Underscores Debate Over How to Help Los Angeles' Poor," *Daily Journal*, June 5, 2008.

77. Barbara Schultz, "Frontline Focus," *Legal Aid Foundation of Los Angeles*, November 2011, www.lafla.org/newsletter_FF.php (accessed May 30, 2012).

78. Initially this was an Interim Control Ordinance, a temporary ordinance to halt conversions while the full ordinance was being further studied. The full ordinance was passed by the council on May 6, 2008.

79. Los Angeles Housing Department, "Report Back on Motion Regarding Preservation of Single Room Occupancy Housing," Council File: 04-2087 (2005).

80. Community Connection, "Reflections on 2008: LA CAN's Work," December 2008.

81. Ari Bloomekatz, "Suit Alleges Illegal Eviction at Hotel; LA Agencies Failed to Stop a Developer From Forcing Out Longtime Residents of the Alexandria, complaint says. Tenants Cite Lack of Services," *Los Angeles Times*, December 21, 2007.

82. Carol Williams, "1 million for hotel tenants; Developers and LA, accused of harassing residents, settle suit," *Los Angeles Times*, February 13, 2009.

83. Testimony of Becky Dennison and Louis Raftee in front of the LA City Council, September 14, 2007, lacity.granicus.com/MediaPlayer.php?view_id=&clip_id=2086&caption_id=3605120 (accessed March 15, 2013).

84. LA CAN Focus Group, interview by Andrea Gibbons (August 16, 2012).

85. Barbara Schultz, "Frontline Focus," *Legal Aid Foundation of Los Angeles*, November 2011, www.lafla.org/newsletter_FF.php (accessed May 30, 2012).

86. Central City Association, "Downtown's Human Tragedy: It's Not Acceptable Anymore—A Public Health and Safety Plan" (Los Angeles, 2002).

87. Michelle Alexander, *The New Jim Crow: Mass Incarceration in an Age of Colorblindness* (New York: The New Press, 2012).

88. Henri Lefebvre, *Writings on Cities* (Cambridge, MA: Blackwell, 1996), page 84.

89. Central City Association, "Downtown's Human Tragedy: It's Not Acceptable Anymore—A Public Health and Safety Plan" (Los Angeles, 2002), page 2.

90. Ibid., page 5.
91. This clearly forms part of the trend discussed by Del Casino, Jr. and Jocoy on the increasingly prevalent literature on the "chronic" homeless and the need for improved "consumer-services" with greater accountability. They describe how this new neoliberal rhetoric pushes those labelled as "chronic" homeless outside of norms of family and productive citizenship: "Specifying chronic as not just a length of time on the streets, but as a deficiency of ability and family . . . The chronically homeless subject is viewed, in the end, as hopeless. Therefore, the best policy is to target them and clear them from the streets." See Vincent J. Del Casino, Jr. and Christine L. Jocoy, "Neoliberal Subjectivities, the "New" Homelessness, and Struggles over Spaces of/in the City," *Antipode* 40 (2008): 192–9.
92. Central City Association, "Downtown's Human Tragedy: It's Not Acceptable Anymore—A Public Health and Safety Plan" (Los Angeles, 2002), page 7.
93. Ibid., page 7–8.
94. Ibid., page 10.
95. Mike Davis, *City of Quartz* (London and New York: Verso, 2006); Carla Rivera, "Homeless Often Take a One-Way Street to Skid Row; LA's dumping ground for the down and out nears breaking point as people keep pouring in," *Los Angeles Times*, November 30, 2002; Jocelyn Stewart, "Homeless May Be Sleepless if Law Passes; With what could be the nation's biggest population without homes, LA may ban lying or sitting in doorways at night," *Los Angeles Times*, December 26, 2002.
96. On criminalization, see Eugene McCann, "Race, Protest, and Public Space: Contextualizing Lefebvre in the US City," *Antipode* 31(2) (1999): 163–84; Don Mitchell, "The End of Public Space? Peoples Park, Definitions of the Public, and Democracy," *Annals of the Association of American Geographers* 85 (1995): 108–33; Don Mitchell, *The Right to the City: Social Justice and the Fight for Public Space* (New York: The Guilford Press, 2003); Don Mitchell and Lynn Staeheli, *The People's Property?: Power, Politics, and the Public* (New York and London: Routledge, 2008); on LA CAN, see Becky Dennison, interview by Andrea Gibbons (August 2, 2011).
97. Jocelyn Stewart, "ACLU Sues to Block Enforcement of LA Ordinance Against Homeless," *Los Angeles Times*, February 20, 2003.
98. Richard Winton and Kristina Sauerwein, "LAPD Tests New Policing Strategy; Chief picks three areas as proving grounds for his 'broken windows' system to fight crime," *Los Angeles Times*, Febraury 2, 2003.
99. Beth Barrett, "Taking Back the Streets: Tide Turning for Skid Row," *Daily News*, January 19, 2003.
100. Ibid.
101. Ibid.
102. Ibid.
103. Jocelyn Stewart, "ACLU Sues to Block Enforcement of LA Ordinance Against Homeless," *Los Angeles Times*, February 20, 2003.
104. Eric Malnic, "Los Angeles; Police Continue Homeless Sweeps on Skid Row Despite ACLU Suit," *Los Angeles Times*, February 21, 2003.
105. *Jones v. City of Los Angeles*, 04-55324 (9th Circuit, 2006).
106. Philippe Bourgois and Jeff Schonberg, *Righteous Dopefiend* (University of California Press: Berkeley, 2009); Teresa Gowan, *Hobos, Hustlers, and Backsliders: Homeless in San Francisco* (Minneapolis: University of Minnesota Press, 2010).
107. DCBID Board minutes, July 9, 2003.
108. DCBID minutes, June 2, 2004.
109. DCBID minutes, September 4, 2004.
110. This is echoed fairly eerily from the point of view of those living in such encampments in the accounts of Philippe Bourgois and Jeff Schonberg, *Righteous Dopefiend* (University of California Press: Berkeley, 2009).
111. DCBID president's report, April 2005.
112. A specially formed and trained team of LAPD officers, further discussed below in reference to the Safer Cities Initiative.

113. Alice Callaghan, "Battered and Bruised—By the City," *Los Angeles Times*, August 21, 2005.
114. Toy-DIDBID minutes, December 20, 2005.
115. CPAB minutes, October 5, 2005.
116. CPAB minutes, November 11, 2005.
117. ACLU Press Release, April 14, 2006.
118. Unsigned editorial, *Los Angeles Times*, August 16, 2006.
119. Richard Winton and Cara Mia DiMassa, "No Skid Row Accord for City, ACLU." *Los Angeles Times*, August 22, 2006.
120. Richard Winton, "Plan Would End Homeless 'Tent Cities,'" *Los Angeles Times*, September 19, 2006.
121. Ibid.
122. Ashraf Khalil and Richard Winton, "No Celebration on Skid Row; Business owners and others say a city proposal to outlaw daytime tent cities will do little and may make matters worse," *Los Angeles*, September 20, 2006.

8. BEATING BACK THE ONSLAUGHT

1. Michelle Alexander, *The New Jim Crow: Mass Incarceration in an Age of Colorblindness* (New York: The New Press, 2012), page 25.
2. Grace Dyrness, Peter Spoto and Mia Thompson, *Crisis on the Streets: Homeless Women and Children in Los Angeles* (Feasibility Study for the Union Rescue Mission, 2003).
3. Alex S. Vitale, "Innovation and institutionalization: Factors in the development of 'quality of life' policing in New York City," *Policing and Society: An International Journal of Research and Policy* 15(2) (2005): 99–124.
4. Gary Blasi and the UCLA School of Law Fact Investigation Clinic, "Policing Our Way Out of Homelessness? The First Year of the Safer Cities Initiative on Skid Row" (Los Angeles, 2007).
5. William Bratton and Peter Knobler, *Turnaround: How America's Top Cop Reversed the Crime Epidemic* (New York: Random House, 1998).
6. DPOA newsletter, fall 1994—italics in original.
7. Michelle Alexander, *The New Jim Crow: Mass Incarceration in an Age of Colorblindness* (New York: The New Press, 2012).
8. Gary Blasi and the UCLA School of Law Fact Investigation Clinic, "Policing Our Way Out of Homelessness? The First Year of the Safer Cities Initiative on Skid Row" (Los Angeles, 2007).
9. Richard Winton, "Plan Would End Homeless 'Tent Cities,'" *Los Angeles Times*, September 19, 2006.
10. Los Angeles Police Department, "Los Angeles Safer City Initiative: An Overview for the Downtown Los Angeles Neighborhood Committee" (2003).
11. Ibid.
12. Gary Blasi and the UCLA School of Law Fact Investigation Clinic, "Policing Our Way Out of Homelessness? The First Year of the Safer Cities Initiative on Skid Row" (Los Angeles, 2007).
13. Ibid., page 88.
14. Ibid.
15. DCBID minutes, August 2004.
16. Estela Lopez, "Walk With Us: Taking Back the Streets of Skid Row Requires a Community Effort," *Los Angeles Downtown News*, August 1, 2005.
17. CCEA press release, October 3, 2005. Para Los Niños, or For the Children, provides services and after-school activities to low-income children in the Pico-Union area just to the west of downtown.
18. CCEA Newsletter, Winter 2005–2006.
19. CCEA Newsletter, Winter 2005–2006. In LA, only fifteen council members represented almost 3.8 million people in 2010; see the United States Census Bureau, *American Fact Finder*, 2010, factfinder2.census.gov/faces/tableservices/jsf/pages/productview.xhtml ?src=bkmk (accessed June 10, 2014). The level of elected officials' responsiveness to constituents is low and tends to depend on a council member's individual priorities and re-election strategy. Throughout this time period, Council District 9 (Jan Perry's district) covered most

of South Central and a large part of downtown Los Angeles, ensuring that its candidates needed the support and funding of downtown's most powerful developers, while obtaining a considerable majority of their votes from the high-turnout population of Black homeowners in South Central, primarily middle-aged and elderly women; see Gilda Haas, interview by Andrea Gibbons (August 29, 2012).

20. Toy-DIDBID minutes, 2005.
21. Los Angeles Community Action Network, "Community Watch Manual" (2008).
22. Cara Mia DiMassa, "Defeat Plagues Efforts to Clean Up Skid Row; Previous attempts to solve homelessness have been mired in debate, political maneuvering," *Los Angeles Times*, March 12, 2005.
23. Ibid.
24. Grace Dyrness, Peter Spoto, and Mia Thompson, *Crisis on the Streets: Homeless Women and Children in Los Angeles* (Feasibility Study for the Union Rescue Mission, 2003); Gary Blasi, "Shelter Availability in Los Angeles' Skid Row and the Enforcement of LAM.C. §41.18(d)" (Los Angeles, 2006).
25. Toy-DIDBID minutes, February 28, 2006.
26. Cara Mia DiMassa and Richard Winton, "LAPD's Skid Row Divide; The More Radical of Two Proposals Under Debate Would Rid Area of 'Box Cities.' The Other Would Target Crime. Bratton is Expected to Decide Soon," *Los Angeles Times*, March 10, 2006: page 10.
27. Cara Mia DiMassa, "In a Shinier Skid Row, Hard Questions Linger; As Revitalization Efforts for Downtown Move Forward, Advocacy Groups Say the Homeless are Being Swept Away," *Los Angeles Times*, July 12, 2006.
28. Anat Rubin, interview by Andrea Gibbons (August 28, 2012).
29. LA CAN Focus Group, interview by Andrea Gibbons (August 16, 2012).
30. Gary Blasi and the UCLA School of Law Fact Investigation Clinic, "Policing Our Way Out of Homelessness? The First Year of the Safer Cities Initiative on Skid Row" (Los Angeles, 2007).
31. Ibid.
32. Ibid., page 6.
33. Ibid.
34. ACLU Press Release, December 18, 2006.
35. Ramona Ripston, "A Police State on Skid Row: The LAPD is Again Rousting and Searching Homeless People Without Cause," *Los Angeles Times*, March 12, 2007.
36. Among many such references, see Community Connection, December 2008.
37. Video can be found online at: lacity.granicus.com/MediaPlayer.php?view_id=&clip_id=6784&caption_id=9554960 (accessed March 16, 2013).
38. *Letteau v. Ellis* (1932).
39. Michelle Alexander, *The New Jim Crow: Mass Incarceration in an Age of Colorblindness* (New York: The New Press, 2012).
40. Ina Jaffe, "Can Los Angeles Make Skid Row Safer?" *National Public Radio: Morning Edition*, April 21, 2009.
41. In 2006, an emergency proclamation from the California Department of Corrections and Rehabilitation acknowledged that California was the largest state correctional system in the US, with an all-time high of over 170,000 prisoners. It goes on to state that "due to the record number of inmates currently housed in prison in California, all 33 CDCR prisons are now at or above maximum operational capacity, and 29 of the prisons are so overcrowded that the CDCR is required to house more than 15,000 inmates in conditions that pose substantial safety risks, namely, prison areas never designed or intended for inmate housing, including, but not limited to, common areas such as prison gymnasiums, dayrooms, and program rooms, with approximately 1,500 inmates sleeping in triple-bunks"; see Arnold Schwarzengger, "Prison Overcrowding State of Emergency Proclamation," October 4, 2006, gov.ca.gov/news.php?id=4278 (accessed June 16, 2014). For additional discussion of this issue, see Ruth Wilson Gilmore, *Golden Gulag: Prisons, Surplus, Crisis, and Opposition in Globalizing California* (Berkeley: University of California Press, 2007) and Michelle Alexander, *The New Jim Crow: Mass Incarceration in an Age of Colorblindness* (New York: The New Press, 2012).

42. Gary Blasi and the UCLA School of Law Fact Investigation Clinic, "Policing Our Way Out of Homelessness? The First Year of the Safer Cities Initiative on Skid Row" (Los Angeles, 2007).
43. For a moving account of homelessness and addiction, see the ethnographic work of Philippe Bourgois and Jeff Schonberg, *Righteous Dopefiend* (University of California Press: Berkeley, 2009), whose public health focus gives insight into the wide range of interventions and support, particularly housing, needed to help people overcome addiction when they are ready. This is echoed by the findings of Teresa Gowan, *Hobos, Hustlers, and Backsliders: Homeless in San Francisco* (Minneapolis: University of Minnesota Press, 2010).
44. Richard Winton, "Plan Would End Homeless 'Tent Cities,'" *Los Angeles Times*, September 19, 2006.
45. Michelle Alexander, *The New Jim Crow: Mass Incarceration in an Age of Colorblindness* (New York: The New Press, 2012), page 100.
46. Toy-DIDBID minutes, June 28, 2005.
47. CCEA press release, July 5, 2005.
48. President's Report, July 2005; DCBID minutes, July 7, 2005.
49. CCA Delivers, June 16, 2006.
50. Jordan Rau and Cara Mia DiMassa, "Legislation to Help the Homeless Advances," *Los Angeles Times*, August 18, 2006.
51. Richard Winton, "Drug Offenders to Be Banned From Skid Row," *Los Angeles Times*, September 27, 2006.
52. Ibid.
53. *Los Angeles Times*, "'DA, Do More Downtown,'" October 9, 2006.
54. Anat Rubin, interview by Andrea Gibbons (August 28, 2012).
55. Ibid.
56. Anat Rubin, "Prosecutors Target Drugs on Skid Row: Public Defenders Say Plea Deals No Longer Avaliable," *Daily Journal*, January 29, 2007.
57. Michelle Alexander, *The New Jim Crow: Mass Incarceration in an Age of Colorblindness* (New York: The New Press, 2012), page 95. Italics in the original.
58. Community Connection, "Central Division Racial Profiling Nets Wrong Fish," March–April 2008.
59. Los Angeles Community Action Network, "Community Watch Manual" (2008).
60. LA CAN Focus Group, interview by Andrea Gibbons (August 16, 2012).
61. Steve Diaz, interview by Andrea Gibbons (August 15, 2012).
62. Richard Winton, "Skid Row Life Is Like Night and Day," *Los Angeles Times,* October 21, 2006.
63. *The Economist*, "On the Skids: The Police Have Cleaned up Skid Row. They Have Not Got Rid of it," February 8, 2007.
64. Cara Mia DiMassa and Richard Winton, "Skid row effort hits a wall; Is the well-publicized cleanup campaign slowing? The area is still safer than two years ago, but many wonder where things are headed," *Los Angeles Times*, April 12, 2008.
65. Email, September 3, 2008.
66. Community Connection, "Community Stops Traffic on 1st and Main to Protest the Occupation of Skid Row," December 2008.
67. ACLU Press Release, December 18, 2008.
68. Email, April 21, 2009. Bernard Parks was a council member for District 8, and former chief of the LAPD.
69. Kate Linthicum, "Crackdown to target Skid Row drug dealers; An injunction would zero in on specific people and could extend to John Does," *Los Angeles Times*, April 8, 2010.
70. CCEA press release, June 20, 2008.
71. Letter to Estela Lopez, April 28, 2011.
72. Ryan Vaillancourt, "City Attorney Files Battery Charges Against Skid Row Protestor," *Downtown News*, August 9, 2012.
73. Emails from November 7 and 18, 2011.
74. Chris Vogel, "Is LAPD Taking Homeless People's Shopping Carts?" *LA Weekly* blog, April 6, 2011.
75. *Lavan v. City of Los Angeles* (2012).

76. SCI 2012 1st quarter report; email from Estela Lopez to CCEA board, April 30, 2012.
77. Email from Estela Lopez to Shannon Paulson, August 8, 2011.
78. Email, February 16, 2012.
79. Estela Lopez to mayor's staff member, Paul Hernandez, March 7, 2012.
80. Alexandra Zavis, "Skid row hits skids again; A city effort had helped cut the street population, but the economy and other factors have reversed the trend," *Los Angeles Times*, March 31, 2012.
81. Carol Schatz, "Enabling homelessness; A ruling that allows people to pile their belongings on sidewalks hurts everyone," *Los Angeles Times*, April 9, 2012.
82. Anna Gorman and Andrew Blankstein, "Feds try to curb outbreak of TB on skid row," *Los Angeles Times*, February 22, 2013.
83. Ibid.
84. Andrew Blankstein and Alexandra Zavis, "LA seeks to toss ruling on skid row; It will ask high court to overturn ban on destroying homeless people's belongings left on sidewalks," *Los Angeles Times*, Febraury 28, 2013.
85. *LAT* February 25, 2013.
86. Los Angeles County Department of Health, February 12, 2012.
87. Henri Lefebvre, *Writings on Cities* (Cambridge, MA: Blackwell, 1996).
88. Michelle Alexander, *The New Jim Crow: Mass Incarceration in an Age of Colorblindness* (New York: The New Press, 2012).

9. NEOLIBERALISM FOUND?

1. Michel-Rolphe Trouillot, *Silencing the Past: Power and the Production of History* (Boston: Beacon Press, 1997), page 58
2. Carol Anderson, *White Rage: The Unspoken Truth of our Racial Divide* (London: Bloomsbury, 2017); Keeanga-Yamahtta Tayler, *From #BlackLivesMatter to Black Liberation* (Chicago: Haymarket, 2016).
3. See, among others, Daniel Martinez HoSang, *Racial Propositions: Ballot Initiatives and the Making of Postwar California* (Berkeley: University of California Press, 2012); Michelle Alexander, *The New Jim Crow: Mass Incarceration in an Age of Colorblindness* (New York: The New Press, 2012); Manning Marable, *Race, Reform, and Rebellion The Second Reconstruction and Beyond in Black America, 1945–2006* (Jackson: University Press of Mississippi, 2007); Laura Pulido, "Rethinking Environmental Racism: White Privilege and Urban Development in Southern California," *Annals of the Association of American Geographers* 90(1) (2000): 12–40; Cedric Robinson, *Black Marxism: The Making of the Black Radical Tradition* (London: Zed Books, 1983).
4. See Vijay Prashad, *Everybody was Kung Fu Fighting: Afro-Asian connections and the myth of cultural purity* (Boston: Beacon Press, 2002), as well as Paul Gilroy, *After Empire: Melancholia or Convivial Culture?* (London: Routledge, 2004) and Rinku Sen, *Stir It Up: Lessons in Community Organizing and Advocacy* (San Francisco: Chardon Press, 2003).
5. Michelle Alexander, *The New Jim Crow: Mass Incarceration in an Age of Colorblindness* (New York: The New Press, 2012).
6. C. Van Woodward, *The Strange Career of Jim Crow: A Commemorative Edition* (Oxford: Oxford University Press, 2002).
7. Letter to Governor Earl Warren, December 9, 1944. *EWP*: "Negroes" folder.
8. Ruth Wilson Gilmore, "Fatal Couplings of Power and Difference: Notes on Racism and Geography," *The Professional Geographer* 54(1) (2002): 16.
9. Jamie Peck and Adam Tickell, "Neoliberalizing Space," *Antipode* 34(3) (2002): 380–404; Neil Brenner and Nik Theodore, "Cities and the Geographies of 'Actually Existing Neoliberalism'" *Antipode* 34(3) (2002): 349–79. My arguments on neoliberalization are limited to the United States only here, as I believe there is a much better argument for the importance of neoliberalism as a top-down ideology imposed by lenders and powerful governments upon countries of the Global South, beginning with Chile in the 1970s; see David Harvey, *Brief History of Neoliberalism* (Oxford: Oxford University Press, 2005). This also opens the potential for

exploring parallels between white power and privilege as it is maintained in the US and post-colonial studies examining this on a global scale.

10. Kevin Ward "'Policies in Motion,' Urban Management and State Restructuring: The Trans-Local Expansion of Business Improvement Districts" *International Journal of Urban and Regional Research* 30(1) (2006): 54–75; Ellen Reese, Geoffrey Deverteuil, and Leanne Thach, "Weak-Center Gentrification and the Contradictions of Containment Deconcentrating Poverty in Downtown Los Angeles." *International Journal of Urban and Regional Research* 34(2) (2010) 310–27.

11. M4BL (The Movement for Black Lives) website, available at: policy.m4bl.org (no date, accessed September 27, 2017).

Index